White Gold

The Extraordinary Story of Thomas Pellow and North Africa's One Million European Slaves

Giles Milton

Hodder & Stoughton

First published in Great Britain in 2004 by Hodder & Stoughton
A division of Hodder Headline

This paperback edition published in 2005

A Sceptre paperback

3

A CIP catalogue record for this title is available from the British Library

ISBN 0 340 79470 4

Typeset in Bembo by
Palimpsest Book Production Limited,
Polmont, Stirlingshire

Printed and bound by Clays Ltd, St Ives plc

Hodder Headline policy is to use papers that are natural, renewable and recyclable products and made from wood grown in sustainable forests. The logging and manufacturing processes are expected to conform to the environmental regulations of the country of origin.

Hodder & Stoughton
A division of Hodder Headline
338 Euston Road
London NW1 3BH

For Barbara and Wolfram

Rule, Britannia, rule the waves.
Britons never will be slaves.

James Thomson, *Rule, Britannia!*
(early eighteenth century)

We have been forced to draw carts of lead with ropes about our shoulders . . . [and] have carried great barrs of iron upon our shoulders. I believe all Christian people have forgotten us in England, because they have not sent us any releife . . . since we have been in slavery.

John Willdon, British slave (early eighteenth century)

Contents

List of Illustrations

Section 1

Section 2

Acknowledgements

My fascination with the story of white slavery began more than a decade ago while staying in Morocco with the late (and splendidly eccentric) Clive Chandler. Clive's country retreat, Dar Zitoun, law at the heart of the medina in the medieval village of Azzemour. A crumbling Portuguese mansion – lovingly restored – it was perched high above the great Oum er Rbia river. It had once been the residence of a local pasha: there were some who joshed that a pasha lived there still.

I'd telephoned Clive to ask how to find the place. 'Follow the tarmac,' was his cryptic reply. It all made sense when I arrived. The local mayor had ordered a layer of tarmac to be sluiced along the dust-choked alleys that led to Clive's iron-studded front door. He had done so to honour a quintessential Englishman – the first to have settled in this backwater.

Clive's collection of antiquarian books opened my eyes to an extraordinarily colourful period in Moroccan history, while his enthusiasm for his adopted country quickly became infectious. 'Look,' he said one evening as he whisked open some curtains in the tiled atrium. 'Not many people have a Moorish holy man buried inside their house.'

Clive's generosity and hospitality extended over five memorable trips to Morocco. Gin and tonic at sundown, Churchill's speeches playing on the gramophone and the distant sound of Bou'chaib, *cuisinier extraordinaire*, chopping fresh mint in the kitchen. Dar Zitoun was another world.

Not all the research for *White Gold* was undertaken in such congenial surroundings. Each trip to Morocco was followed by many months in public libraries, where I slowly unearthed a wealth of original letters, journals and documents.

I am most grateful to the staff of The National Archives at Kew – home to much original correspondence – and to the helpful librarians in the Rare Books Reading Room of the British Library. I must also thank the staff at the Institute of Historical Research, the Middle East Library, St Anthony's College, Oxford, and the Cornish Studies Library.

Thanks are equally due to Christopher Phipps and the superb team at the London Library, where much of this book was written.

Thank you, also, to Jessica Francis Kane in America for tracking down a copy of Joshua Gee's *Narrative*.

I am immensely grateful to all at Hodder & Stoughton, especially to my editor, Roland Philipps, and to Lizzie Dipple; to Juliet Brightmore, Karen Geary, Celia Levett and Briar Silich.

Many thanks, also, to my agent Maggie Noach and to Jill Hughes and Camilla Adeane.

Special thanks are due to Paul Whyles for reading the manuscript at short notice and suggesting much-needed changes. My thanks, as well, to Frank Barrett and Wendy Driver.

Last of all, a huge thank-you to the four women in my life – to Alexandra for all her encouragement and support, including many evenings spent translating eighteenth-century French documents; and to the chirpy trio – Madeleine, Heloïse and Aurélia.

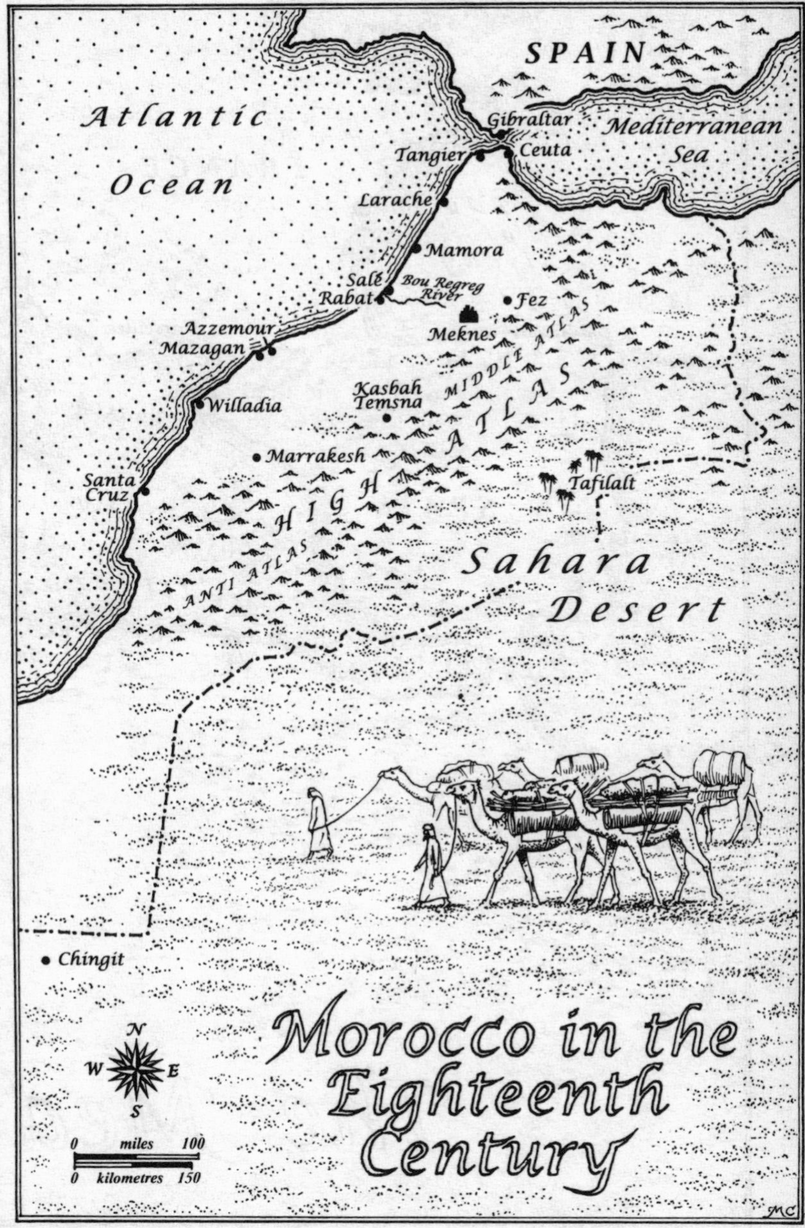
SPAIN
Atlantic Ocean
Gibraltar
Mediterranean Sea
Tangier
Ceuta
Larache
Mamora
Salé
Bou Regreg River
Rabat
Fez
Meknes
Azzemour
Mazagan
MIDDLE ATLAS
Kasbah Temsna
Willadia
HIGH ATLAS
Marrakesh
Tafilalt
Santa Cruz
ANTI ATLAS
Sahara Desert
Chingit
N
W
E
S
0 miles 100
0 kilometres 150
Morocco in the Eighteenth Century
MC

FRANCE
Bay of Biscay
Mila
Genoa
Marseilles
Cape Finisterre
CORSICA
PORTUGAL
Madrid
SPAIN
SARDINIA
Lisbon
BALEARIC ISLANDS
Mediterrane
Cape St Vincent
Cadiz
The Straits of Gibraltar
Gibraltar
Algiers
Tunis
Tangier
Salé
Meknes
MOROCCO
The Medi
MC

0 miles 500
0 kilometres 800
N
W
E
S
Trieste
Adriatic Sea
ITALY
SICILY
MALTA
Sea
Salonika
GREECE
Aegean Sea
Athens
CRETE
RHODES
Istanbul
Black Sea
TURKEY
CYPRUS
Alexandria
Cairo
EGYPT
River Nile
Red Sea
rranean

Prologue

THE CLATTER OF A CHARIOT broke the silence. It was hidden from view by the towering battlements, but could be heard squeaking and rattling through the palace gardens. As it passed through the Gate of the Winds, there was a muffled rumble of footsteps and wheels.

In the ceremonial parade ground no one stirred. The imperial guard stood rigidly to attention, their damascene scimitars flashing in the sunlight. The courtiers lay prostrate beside them, their robes splayed theatrically across the marble. Only the vizier, sweltering in his leopardskin pelt, dared to wipe the beads of sweat from his brow.

The stillness intensified as the chariot drew near. From beyond the courtyard there was a furious cry, followed by the crack of a whip. The hullabaloo grew suddenly louder, echoing through the palace courts and corridors. Seconds later, Sultan Moulay Ismail of Morocco entered the parade ground in his gilded chariot, drawn not by horses but by a harnessed band of wives and eunuchs.

This unfortunate team staggered up to the assembled courtiers before allowing their reins to slacken. As the sultan leaped down from his chariot, two statuesque blacks sprang into action. One whisked flies from Moulay Ismail's sacred body, muttering obsequies all the while. The other, a young lad of fourteen or fifteen, shaded the sultan with a twirling chintz parasol.

Such was the ritual that habitually attended an audience with the great Moulay Ismail, who demanded absolute deference from his subjects and was punctilious in his observance of protocol. But on a sweltering summer's morning in 1716 the sultan scarcely noticed the courtiers grovelling in the dust. His eyes were drawn instead to a band of wretched Europeans herded together in the far corner of the square. Fifty-two Englishmen, bruised and barefoot, stood in mute bewilderment. Seized at sea by the corsairs of Barbary and marched inland to Morocco's imperial capital, they were about to be sold as slaves.

Their story was to cause outrage and horror in their home country; it would also expose the utter impotence of both the British government and its navy. Yet the seizure of these men was neither unique nor unusual; for more than a century, the trade in white slaves from across Europe and colonial North America had been destroying families and wrecking innocent lives.

One of the newly captured men – Captain John Pellow of the *Francis* – had been forewarned of the perils of his trading voyage to the Mediterranean. Yet he had shunned the danger with characteristic bravado, sailing from Cornwall to Genoa in the summer of 1715. His six-strong crew included his young nephew, Thomas Pellow, who was just eleven years old when he bade farewell to his mother, father and two sisters. It would be many years before his parents would receive news of their unfortunate son.

Two other ships were captured on the same day. Captain Richard Ferris of the *Southwark* had attempted to rescue the *Francis*'s crew, but had also been captured by the corsairs. So, too, had the good ship *George*, which was making its return voyage to England. The terrified crews of these three vessels now stood side by side in the palace courtyard.

'Bono, bono,' cried the jovial sultan as he inspected his slaves. He passed along the line of men, poking their muscles and examining their physique. The captives were still reeling from the treatment they had received on their arrival in the imperial city of

Meknes. Crowds of townspeople had gathered at the palace gates to abuse them, 'offering us the most vile insults . . . and giving us many severe boxes'.

The sultan, oblivious to their fears and anxieties, was delighted to see that these hardy mariners were in good shape and noted that many years of service could be expected of them. He paused for a moment as he sized up the young Thomas Pellow. There was something about the boy's plucky demeanour that intrigued the sultan. He muttered a few words to his guardsmen, at which young Pellow was seized and taken to one side.

As the rest of the men were led away by a black slave-driver, Pellow prayed that his nightmare would soon come to an end. In fact, he was beginning twenty-three years of captivity as one of North Africa's forgotten white slaves.

I travelled to Meknes in the spring of 1992 when the Boufekrane valley was carpeted with wild mint and the little river was brimful with icy water. My travelling companion belonged to another world – an eighteenth-century padre, whose colourful account described the city at its apogee. His duodecimo volume – bound, appropriately enough, in tooled morocco – evoked a city of unparalleled grandeur. But it also revealed a far darker and more sinister story.

When my padre travelled here, the imperial palace of Meknes was the largest building in the northern hemisphere. Its crenellated battlements stretched for mile upon mile, enclosing hills and meadows, orchards and pleasure gardens, its sun-baked bulwarks looming high over the river valley. This impregnable fortress was designed to withstand the mightiest army on earth. Each of its gates was protected by a crack division of the black imperial guard.

The sultan's palace was constructed on such a grand scale that it came to be known simply as Dar Kbira, The Big. Yet Dar Kbira was just one part of a huge complex. A further fifty palaces, all interconnecting, housed the sultan's 2,000 concubines. There were mosques and minarets, courtyards and pavilions. The palace stables were the size of a large town; the barracks housed more than 10,000 foot soldiers. In the sprawling Dar el Makhzen – another vast palace-town – scheming viziers and eunuchs kept their courts. The fabled hanging gardens, perpetually in blossom, rivalled Nebuchadnezzar's fantasy in Babylon.

My padre had never seen anything like it and returned home with tales of bronze doors cast in fantastical arabesques and porphyry columns that sparkled in the sun. The courtyard mosaics were wrought with geometric perfection – a dizzying chiaroscuro of cobalt and white. There were slabs of jasper and Carrara marble, costly damasks and richly caparisoned horses. The Moorish stucco was most extraordinary of all; chiselled and fretted into an intricate honeycomb, it appeared to drip from the cupolas like snow-white stalactites.

Every inch of wall, every niche and squinch, was covered in exquisite ornamentation. The glasswork, too, was extraordinarily fine. Chinks of azure, vermilion and sea green were designed to catch and refract the brilliant African sunlight. In the hours before sundown, they scattered hexagons of colour over the tessellated marble paving.

Palace doorways were emblazoned with the emblem of the sun, prompting visitors to wonder whether the sultan was vying to outdo his French contemporary, King Louis XIV, the Sun King. In truth, the megalomaniac sultan hoped to build on a far grander scale than the recently constructed palace of Versailles. His vision was for his palace to stretch from Meknes to Marrakesh – a distance of 300 miles.

Three centuries of sun and rain have not been kind to this sprawling palace, built of pisé, a mixture of earth and lime. The winds of the Atlas Mountains have blasted the pink walls, reducing them in places to a powdery heap. Arches lie broken and towers have been eroded to stumps. The earthquake of 1755 caused the greatest devastation: the fabric of the great palace shuddered, groaned and expired. What had taken decades to construct was torn apart in minutes. Cedarwood ceilings were ripped from their rafters, and stucco crumbled and collapsed. Whole quarters of the palace slumped in on themselves, crushing furniture and antiques. The court fled in panic, never to return. The broken imperial shell, reduced to a sorry hodgepodge of roofless chambers, was quickly colonised by the poor and wretched of Meknes.

I approached the city through the Bab Mansour, the greatest of all Meknes' ceremonial gateways. It opened the way to a world of giants, where ramparts towered over palm trees and courtyards were as big as the sky. A second gateway led to a third, which contracted into a series of alleyways. These labyrinthine passages, festooned with telephone wires and cables, plunged me deep into the heart of the palace. To this day, people – indeed, whole families – live in the ruins of Dar Kbira. Front doors have been carved into the bulwarks and there are windows hacked out of the pisé. Ancient chambers have become modern bedrooms; courtyards are strewn with marble rubble.

I squeezed through a fissure in the battlements and found myself in a whole new jumble of ruins. A shattered porphyry column lay half embedded in waste, casually discarded like household junk. A twirl of acanthus betrayed its Roman past, pillaged from the nearby ruined city of Volubulis.

I wondered if this lost quarter had once been the forbidden harem, whose looking-glass ceiling was propped up by just such columns. Arab chroniclers speak of crystal streams and tinkling fountains; of sculpted marble basins filled with brightly coloured fish. Pausing for a moment in this roofless chamber, I scooped up a handful of the cool earth. As the powdery dust filtered through my fingers, a precious residue remained: fractured mosaic tiling in a myriad of shapes – stars, oblongs, squares and diamonds.

If my padre was to be believed, these tiny chunks were evidence of one of the darkest chapters in human history. Every hand-glazed mosaic in this monumental palace, every broken column and battlement, had been built and crafted by an army of Christian slaves. Flogged by black slave-drivers and held in filthy slave pens, these abject captives were forced to work on what the sultan intended to be the largest construction project in the known world. Moulay Ismail's male slaves were said to have toiled for fifteen hours a day and were often forced to work at night as well. The female captives were even more miserable. Dragged to the harem and forcibly converted to Islam, they had the dubious honour of indulging the sultan's sexual whims.

Morocco was not the only place in North Africa where white captives were held as slaves. Algiers, Tunis and Tripoli also had thriving slave auctions, in which thousands of captives were put through their paces before being sold to the highest bidder. These wretched men, women and children came from right across Europe – from as far afield as Iceland and Greece, Sweden and Spain. Many had been seized at sea by the infamous Barbary corsairs. Many more had been snatched from their homes in surprise raids.

Almost six years were to pass before I first began to search for written records of the Barbary slaves. I had assumed that such archives – if they had ever existed – would have disappeared long ago. But it gradually became apparent that a great many letters and journals had survived. There were plaintive descriptions of the ordeal of slave labour and blood-chilling reports of audiences with the Moroccan sultan. There were anguished recollections of the macabre humour of the slave merchants and petitions from 'slave widows' that begged for mercy and relief. I even found missives written by the sultan himself – grandiloquent tracts demanding that the kings of Britain and France convert to Islam.

Many of these accounts were to be found only in manuscript. The extraordinary journal of John Whitehead, a British slave in Meknes, remains unpublished to this day. Others were printed in such small quantities that only a handful of copies survive. A very rare volume by the French padre, Jean de la Faye, turned up in St Anthony's College, Oxford.

The most fascinating testimonies were those written by the slaves themselves. The story of the white slave trade is one of individuals caught up in a nightmare far beyond their control. Most were to end their days in a hellish captivity, but a fortunate few managed to escape the clutches of their owners. Those who made it back to their homelands were invariably destitute. One of the ways in which they could restore their fortunes was to publish their tales, in the hope of earning a few shillings.

The white slaves who survived their ordeal invariably emerged from incarceration in deep shock. Writing helped them come to terms with the past and reintegrate themselves into a society they had thought to be lost to them for ever. All who recorded their stories had undergone raw and harrowing experiences, and they left tales that even today have the power to be profoundly moving. They rarely make for pleasant reading, yet are illuminated by flashes of heroism and selflessness. A touch of kindness from a slave guard; the warm embrace of a padre. Such gestures reminded the captives that they were still a part of humankind.

One of the most remarkable stories of the white slave trade centres around Thomas Pellow and his crewmates on the *Francis*. Pellow would be witness to the barbaric splendours of Sultan Moulay Ismail's imperial court and would experience at first hand the ruthlessness of this wily and terrifying ruler. But his story was to prove far more extraordinary than that of a mere observer of events. As a personal slave of the sultan, Pellow unwittingly found himself thrown into the very heart of courtly intrigue. Appointed guardian of the imperial harem, he would also lead slave-soldiers into battle and take part in a perilous slave-gathering expedition to equatorial Africa. He would be tortured and forced to convert to Islam. Three times he would attempt to escape; twice he would be sentenced to death.

Pellow's tale is filled with a colourful cast of characters. He writes of lusty eunuchs and brutal slave-drivers, imperial executioners and piratical scoundrels. At the heart of his story is the towering figure of Sultan Moulay Ismail, who through the course of his long reign became increasingly obsessed by his opulent fantasy palace.

It was long believed that Pellow's *Adventures* – reworked for publication by a Grub Street editor – strayed far from reality. It is now clear that this is not at all the case. The early chapters are corroborated by letters written by his own shipmates, while the later years accord with reports written by European consuls who met him in Morocco. Arab records, too, support his version of events. The newly translated *Chronicles* of Muhammad al-Qadiri reveal that Pellow's account of the Moroccan civil war is remarkable for its accuracy. His revelations about life in Meknes also tally with Moroccan sources. Both Ahmed ez-Zayyani and Ahmad bin Khalid al-Nasari paint a strikingly similar picture of life in the imperial capital.

Thomas Pellow and his fellow shipmates were captured at a time when North Africa's slave population had diminished, but conditions were as wretched as ever. Their incarceration coincided with one of the last great flurries of slave trading, when virtually every country in Europe found itself under attack. But the story of the white slave trade begins almost ninety years earlier, when the Barbary corsairs launched a series of spectacular raids on the very heart of Christendom.

1 A New and Deadly Foe

The pale dawn sky gave no inkling of the terror that was about to be unleashed. A sea mist hung low in the air, veiling the horizon in a damp and diaphanous shroud. It enabled the mighty fleet to slip silently up the English Channel, unnoticed by the porters and fishermen on Cornwall's south-western coast.

The lookout who first sighted the vessels was perplexed. It was not the season for the return of the Newfoundland fishing fleet, nor was a foreign flotilla expected in those waters. As the mists lifted and the summer skies cleared, it became apparent that the mysterious ships had not come in friendship. The flags on their mainmasts depicted a human skull on a dark green background – the menacing symbol of a new and terrible enemy. It was the third week of July 1625, and England was about to be attacked by the Islamic corsairs of Barbary.

News of the fleet's arrival flashed rapidly along the coast until it reached the naval base of Plymouth. A breathless messenger burst into the office of James Bagg, Vice Admiral of Cornwall, with the shocking intelligence of the arrival of enemy ships. There were at least 'twentye sayle upon this coast' – perhaps many more – and they were armed and ready for action.

Bagg was appalled by what he was told. Over the previous weeks he had received scores of complaints about attacks on Cornish fishing skiffs. Local mayors had sent a stream of letters informing him of the 'daily oppression' they were facing at the hands of a little-known foe. Now, that foe appeared to be preparing a far more devastating strike on the south coast of England.

Bagg penned an urgent letter to the Lord High Admiral in London, demanding warships to counter the threat. But it was far too late for anything to be done. Within days of their being sighted the corsairs began to wreak havoc, launching hit-and-run raids on the most vulnerable and unprotected seaports. They slipped ashore at Mount's Bay, on the south Cornish coast, while the villagers were at communal prayer. Dressed in Moorish djellabas and wielding damascene scimitars, they made a terrifying sight as they burst into the parish church. One later English captive would describe the corsairs as 'ugly onhumayne cretures' who struck the fear of God into all who saw them. 'With their heads shaved and their armes almost naked, [they] did teryfie me exceedingly.' They were merciless in their treatment of the hapless congregation of Mount's Bay. According to one eye-witness, sixty men, women and children were dragged from the church and carried back to the corsairs' ships.

The fishing port of Looe was also assaulted. The warriors streamed into the cobbled streets and forced their way into cottages and taverns. Much to their fury, they discovered that the villagers had been forewarned of their arrival and many had fled into the surrounding orchards and meadows. Yet the corsairs still managed to seize eighty mariners and fishermen. These unfortunate individuals were led away in chains and Looe was then torched in revenge. The mayor of Plymouth informed the Privy Council of the sorry news, adding that the corsairs were steadily ransacking the surrounding coastline. The West Country, he said, had lost '27 ships and 200 persons taken'.

Far more alarming was the news – relayed by the mayor of Bristol – that a second fleet of Barbary corsairs had been sighted in the choppy waters off the north Cornish coast. Their crews had achieved a most spectacular and disquieting coup: they had captured Lundy Island in the Bristol Channel and raised the standard of Islam. It had now become their fortified base, from which they attacked the unprotected villages of northern Cornwall. They had 'seized diverse people about Padstow' and were threatening to sack and burn the town of Ilfracombe.

These two-pronged attacks caught the West Country completely unprepared. The Duke of Buckingham despatched the veteran sea-dog, Francis Stuart, to Devon, with orders to root out and destroy this menacing new enemy. But Stuart was dismayed to discover that 'they are better sailers than the English ships'. His letter to the duke, admitting defeat, expresses his fear that the worst was yet to come. 'Theis picaroons, I say, will ever lie hankering upon our coastes, and the state will find it both chargeable and difficult to cleere it.' The long coastline had few defences to deter the North African corsairs, who found they could pillage with impunity. Day after day, they struck at unarmed fishing communities, seizing the inhabitants and burning their homes. By the end of the dreadful summer of 1625, the mayor of Plymouth reckoned that 1,000 skiffs had been destroyed, and a similar number of villagers carried off into slavery.

These miserable captives were taken to Salé, on Morocco's Atlantic coast. This wind-blown port occupied a commanding position on the north bank of the great Bou Regreg river estuary. Her massive city walls were visible from far out to sea, and her turreted battlements and green-glazed minarets sparkled in the North African sunshine.

Just a few decades earlier, these landmarks had been a welcome sight for England's seafaring merchants. Lace-ruffed Elizabethans had come to Salé to exchange silver and woollens for exotic produce, brought in by desert caravans from the steaming tropics of equatorial Africa. In the overcrowded souks and alleys, they had jostled and traded with Moorish merchants dressed in flowing djellabas. After much haggling and bartering, they loaded their vessels with ivory and skins, wax, sugar and amber, as well as the fragrant Meknes honey that was famed throughout Europe.

On the south bank of the estuary, directly opposite Salé, lay the ancient town of Rabat. This, too, had been a 'great and famous towne', boasting beautiful palaces and an extraordinary twelfth-century mosque. But Rabat had fallen into slow decay. By the early 1600s it was scarcely inhabited, and most of the dwellings had been abandoned. 'It was in a manner desolate,' wrote an anonymous English visitor, 'abandoned by the Arabs because of wild beasts.'

Rabat would have fallen into complete ruin had it not been for a most unexpected circumstance. In 1610, King Philip III of Spain expelled all one million Spanish Moors from his land – the final chapter in the reconquest of southern Spain from the infidel. Although these Moriscos had lived in Spain for generations, and many were of mixed stock, they were allowed no right of appeal.

One of the most enterprising of these émigré groups was known as the Hornacheros, after the Andalusian village in which they had lived. Wild and fiercely independent, they pillaged without scruple. One Englishman would later describe them as 'a bad-minded people to all nations', and even their fellow Moriscos viewed them as thieves and brigands.

Expelled from their mountain stronghold in Spain, this haughty clan of 4,000 men and women set their sights on the ruined settlement of Rabat. They restored the kasbah, or fortress, and adapted with remarkable ease to their new homeland, which they renamed New Salé. However, they continued to harbour a deep resentment against Spain and vowed to do everything in their power to strike back. To this end, they began to forge alliances with pirates from Algiers and Tunis who had been preying on Christian shipping in the Mediterranean for more than a century. Within a few years, hundreds of cut-throats and desperadoes – some of them European – began to converge on New Salé in order to train the Hornacheros in the black arts of piracy.

The Hornacheros and their cohort of renegades made a formidable fighting force. This highly disciplined band became known in England as the Sallee Rovers. But to their Islamic brethren they were called *al-ghuzat*, a title once used for the soldiers who fought with the Prophet Mohammed, and were hailed as religious warriors who were engaged in a holy war against the infidel Christians. 'They lived in Salé, and their sea-borne *jihad* is now famous,' wrote the Arabic chronicler, al-Magiri. 'They fortified Salé and built in it palaces, houses and bathhouses.'

The Salé corsairs rapidly learned mastery of square-riggers, enabling them to extend their attacks far into the North Atlantic, and soon assembled a fleet of forty ships. They plundered with abandon, attacking villages and sea ports right along the coasts of Spain, Portugal, France and England. One Salé corsair, Amurates Rayobi, led more than 10,000 warriors to Spain and ransacked the coastline without pity. Their success emboldened their co-religionists elsewhere in Barbary. The al-ghuzat from Algiers targeted vulnerable merchant vessels passing through the Straits of Gibraltar. They were fortunate that their attacks coincided with the beginnings of the mercantile age, when there were rich pickings to be had on the open seas. Between 1609 and 1616, they captured a staggering 466 English trading ships.

Kings and ministers across Europe were paralysed by a sense of helplessness. Sir Francis Cottingham, one of King James I's clerks of the council, bemoaned the fact that 'the strength and boldness of the Barbary pirates is now grown to that height . . . as I have never known anything to have wrought a greater sadness and distraction in this court than the daily advice thereof.'

The lack of any co-ordinated defence encouraged the Sallee Rovers to widen their attacks. One of Salé's most infamous renegade captains, the Dutchman, Jan Janszoon, laughed in scorn at the ease with which he could seize European shipping. Known to his comrades as Murad Rais, he had first cocked a snook at the Channel defences in 1622, when he sailed to Zeeland in order to visit his estranged wife. A few years later, he embarked on a remarkable voyage of pillage to Iceland. His three-strong fleet dropped anchor at Reykjavik, where Murad led his men ashore and proceeded to ransack the town. He returned to Salé in triumph, with 400 enslaved Icelanders – men, women and children.

Wales, too, was hit on several occasions, while the fishing fleets of the Newfoundland Banks suffered several devastating raids. In 1631, Murad Rais set his eye on the richly populated coasts of southern Ireland. He raised a force of 200 Islamic soldiers and they sailed to the village of Baltimore, storming ashore with swords drawn and catching the villagers totally by surprise. He carried off 237 men, women and children and took them to Algiers, where he knew they would fetch a good price. The French padre, Pierre Dan, was in the city at the time, having been granted permission by the authorities to tend to the spiritual needs of his enslaved co-religionists. He witnessed the sale of new captives in the slave auction. 'It was a pitiful sight to see them exposed in the market,' he wrote. 'Women were separated from their husbands and the children from their fathers.' Dan looked on helplessly as 'on one side, a husband was sold; on the other, his wife; and her daughter was torn from her arms without the hope that they'd ever see each other again.'

Murad Rais's bravado was fêted in Morocco, and he was accorded the singular honour of being made governor of the port of Safi, some 200 miles to the south of Salé. His daughter visited him soon afterwards and found that power had quite gone to his head. He was 'seated in great pomp on a carpet, with silk cushions, the servants all around him'. When he took his leave, it was 'in the manner of royalty'.

Murad Rais was just one of many European renegades to strike an alliance with the fanatical corsairs of Barbary. The English apostate, John Ward, headed to Tunis shortly after King James I signed a peace treaty with Spain. Forbidden to attack the Spanish treasure fleet, Ward vowed to 'become a foe to all Christians, bee a persecuter to their trafficke, and an impoverisher of their wealth'. He and his locally recruited crew wreaked such havoc in the Mediterranean that his name was celebrated all along the coast.

This so delighted the ruler of Tunis that he gave Ward an abandoned castle and a large plot of land. Ward converted it into his principal residence, 'a very stately house, farre more fit for a prince than a pirate'. He lived 'in a most princely and magnificent state', according to Andrew Barker, one of his English captives. Barker was stunned by the wealth that Ward had accrued and said he had never seen 'any peere in England that beares up his post in more dignitie, nor hath attendants more obsequious'.

Like so many Christian renegades, Ward had originally turned to piracy in order to seize treasure. But he quickly realised that the merchants of Barbary were more interested in human booty and would pay huge sums to acquire Christian slaves as labourers, domestic servants and concubines. Ward began to focus on capturing ships' crews, who were taken to Tunis, Algiers or Salé to be sold in the slave markets.

The Sallee Rovers were particularly successful in seizing men, women and children, growing fabulously wealthy and powerful from their traffic in captured Christians. In about 1626 – the year after their raids on Cornwall and Devon – they cast aside all pretence of owing any allegiance to the Moroccan sultan and declared their intention of ruling themselves. '[They] resolved to live free,' wrote the French slave, Germain Mouette. 'Finding themselves more numerous than the natives of Salé oblig'd them no longer to own any sovereign.' Salé became a pirate republic and was henceforth governed by a twelve-strong divan – slave-trading corsairs – who were overseen by a grand admiral.

Few in England had any inkling of the fate of captives seized by the corsairs. They disappeared without trace and the majority were never heard from again. But one of them did manage to get a letter smuggled back to England. Robert Adams, who was seized in the first wave of raids in the 1620s, managed to relay news to his parents in the West Country. 'Lovinge and kind father and mother,' he wrote, '. . . I am hear in Salley, in most miserable captivitye, under the hands of most cruell tyrants.' He explained that he had been sold in the slave market soon after being landed in the town and was subjected to the harshest treatment by his owner. '[He] made mee worke at a mill like a horse,' he said, 'from morninge untill night, with chaines uppon my legges, of 36 pounds waights a peece.'

Adams ended his letter with a desperate plea for help. 'I humbly desire you, on my bended knees, and with sighs from the bottom of my hart, to commiserat my poor distressed estate, and seek some meanes for my delivery out of this miserable slavery.'

Adams' parents must have been appalled by what they read, but any appeals for help from the authorities fell on deaf ears. The lords of the Privy Council displayed a callous lack of concern for the enslaved mariners, while Church leaders were powerless to do anything more than organise collections for the families of captured seamen. Eventually, the 'slave widows' themselves were galvanised into action. They drafted a petition, signed by the 'distressed wifes of neere 2,000 poore marriners', and sent it to the Privy Council. The petition reminded the lords that their captured husbands had 'for a longe tyme contynued in most wofull, miserable and lamentable captivitie and slavery in Sally'. It also informed them that they were enduring 'most unspeakable tormentes and want of foode through the merciles crueltie of theire manifolde masters'. Their continual absence was not only a source of grief, but also threatened the very survival of their families. Many women had 'poore smale children and infantes' who were 'almost reddie to perrish and starve for wante of meanes and food'.

Their request was straightforward and emotionally charged. '[We] most humblie beseech Your Honours, even for Christ Jesus sake . . . to send some convenient messenger unto the Kinge of Morocco . . . for the redemption of the saide poore distressed captives.'

What these women did not realise was that King Charles I had already started to tackle the problem of the captives being held in North Africa. Within months of acceding to the throne in 1625, he despatched the young adventurer John Harrison on a secret mission to the infamous city of Salé.

Harrison's voyage was one of extreme danger. He was required to land in Morocco without being captured by the corsairs, and then travel to Salé undetected where he had to contact the ruling divan. He was given full powers to negotiate the release of all the English slaves being held by the town's corsairs. This latter point had provoked much heated debate among the inner circle of King Charles's advisors. Sir Henry Marten, an eminent lawyer and Cornish Member of Parliament, was appalled by the idea of entering into dialogue with the Sallee Rovers, stating bluntly that they were 'a company of pirates, with whom there is no treating or confederacy'. He argued that Harrison should parley only with the Moroccan sultan, even though he had virtually no influence over the Salé corsairs. King Charles himself was rather more pragmatic. Although he penned a long letter to the 'high and mightie' sultan, Moulay Zidan, he suggested that Harrison might have more success if he negotiated directly with the corsairs who were terrorising English shores.

Harrison landed secretly in Tetouan in the summer of 1625

and set out for Salé disguised as a Moorish penitent. Lesser men might well have balked at such a hazardous assignment, but Harrison was in his element. He relished the opportunity to smuggle himself inside one of the most dangerous cities in the world. Nevertheless, the overland journey stretched him to his physical limits, 'the greatest parte on foote, bare-legged and pilgrime-like'. It was blisteringly hot, and Harrison suffered from the dusty air and a constant lack of water. He would later describe it as 'a most desperate journey', yet he took a perverse pleasure in travelling undercover.

Harrison could have been forgiven for a failure of nerve on his arrival at the great walls of Salé, whose array of bronze cannon gave a hint of the menacing threat within. His orders were to penetrate the inner sanctum of this nest of corsairs, who held all Christians in the utmost contempt. Their spiritual leader was Sidi Mohammed el-Ayyachi, a wily *marabout*, or holy man, who was revered by the Salé slave traders. Pious and politically adroit, he had a personal magnetism that inspired fanatical loyalty. He was particularly revered for his hatred of Christianity and would later brag of having caused the deaths of more than 7,600 Christians.

Harrison abandoned his disguise on arriving at Salé and tentatively made contact with the ruling divan. To his surprise, he was greeted with the greatest courtesy. Sidi Mohammed invited Harrison to visit his residence and proved most attentive to his guest, 'entertayning me verie kindlie'. For all his religious fanaticism, Sidi Mohammed was also a pragmatist. He was willing to release his English captives if he stood to benefit, realising that Harrison's mission could be made to work in his favour.

Harrison met Sidi Mohammed on several occasions during his first week in Salé. After a few days of pleasantries, the marabout turned to the matter at hand. He expressed approval of Harrison's mission and promised 'to releasse all Your Majestie's subjects made captives', including those who had been 'bought and solde from one to another'. But there was a high price attached to his offer. He expected English assistance in attacking the hated Spanish and demanded a gift of heavy weaponry, including '14 brasse peeces of ordinance and a proportion of powder and shott'. He also asked whether some of his own cannon, which were 'broken and unservicable', could be taken to England for repair.

Harrison's instinct was to conclude a deal and free the slaves. But he knew that Sidi Mohammed's offer was tantamount to a declaration of war against Spain, and it could not be agreed to without the consent of the king. He had no option but to return to London, where the marabout's offer was discussed at length by the king and Privy Council. They eventually agreed that freeing the English slaves was imperative, but also decided to play games with the Moroccan marabout. They deliberately misread the number of cannon he requested – sending four instead of fourteen – and also scaled down the quantity of powder and shot. Harrison was told to make encouraging noises about an attack on the Spanish, but offer no firm commitments.

A weary Harrison landed back at Salé in March 1627 and was given a lavish welcome. He presented the four cannon with all the pomp he could muster and was surprised when Sidi Mohammed accepted them without a quibble. Harrison informed the corsairs that King Charles I was eager to attack the Spanish and would soon be preparing for war. Sidi Mohammed was so delighted that he vowed to release the English slaves immediately.

Harrison's sense of triumph was somewhat dented when he came to view the slaves. He had expected to be presented with at least 2,000 captives, and was concerned about how he would ship them all back to England. In the event, a mere 190 were released from their underground dungeons. Harrison accused Sidi Mohammed of trickery, but soon discovered that the majority of captives were no longer being held in Salé. Large numbers had been shipped to Algiers – the principal entrepôt for European slaves – while others had been acquired by the sultan. Many more had been 'carried into the countrie' and sold to wealthy traders. But by far the largest number had 'died of the late plague', which had ravaged Morocco in both 1626 and 1627, leaving less than 200 for Harrison to take home with him.

These ragged survivors were a picture of human suffering. Kept in underground cells for months, they were pale, malnourished and weakened by dysentery. According to Robert Adams whose testimony is one of the few from this period to have survived, they had been held in virtual darkness, forced to live in their own squalor and excrement. Their diet was appalling – 'a littell coarse bread and water' – while their lodging was 'a dungion under ground, wher some 150 or 200 of us lay, altogether, havinge no comforte of the light, but a littell hole'. Adams himself was in a terrible state. His hair and ragged clothes were 'full of vermin' – lice and fleas – 'and, not being allowed time for to pick myself . . . I am almost eaten up with them'. Worse still, he was 'every day beaten to make me turn Turk'.

John Harrison returned to England with the released slaves in the summer of 1627. The stories of their experiences in Morocco are no longer extant, and it would fall to a new generation of English captives to chart the full horror of life as a Christian slave. But Harrison's own writings offer a glimpse of the daily torments to which they were subjected. In his book, *The Tragicall Life and Death of Muley Abdala Melek*, he said that violent beatings were commonplace and revealed that many of the slaves had been acquired by the sultan. These were treated with even greater brutality than those held in Salé. 'He would cause men to be drubbed, or beaten almost to death in his presence,' wrote Harrison, '[and] would cause some to be beaten on the soles of their feet, and after make them run up and downe among the stones and thornes.' Some of the sultan's slaves had been dragged behind horses until they were torn to shreds. A few had even been dismembered while still alive, 'their fingers and toes cut off by everie joint; armes and legs and so head and all'.

When the sultan was in a black humour, he took great delight in torturing his Christian slaves. 'He did cause some English boyes perforce to turne Moores,' recalled Harrison, 'cutting them and making them *capadoes* or eunachs.' Others were beaten and mocked. When one English slave complained that he had nothing to eat except barley, the sultan ordered that his horse's food bag was 'hanged about the Englishman's necke, full of barlie . . . and so made him eate the barlie like a horse'.

The sultan's slaves, whom Harrison had not managed to free in his several missions to Salé, eventually managed to despatch a petition to King Charles I, asking him to 'think . . . upon the distressed estate of us, Your Majesty's poor subjects, slaves under the king of Morocus'. They reminded him that they had been in captivity for so long that they had almost forgotten their homeland: 'some twenty years, some sixteen, some twelve, and he that hath been least, seven years in most miserable bondage'. The king read their petition, but declined to act. The truce with Sidi Mohammed was being more or less observed and the attacks on England's coastlines had been temporarily halted. Preoccupied with troubles elsewhere, he abandoned the sultan's English slaves to their fate.

The uneasy peace was not to last long. The Salé corsairs, who depended upon slave trading for their livelihood, pleaded with Sidi Mohammed to abandon the truce. They argued that King Charles I had not respected his side of the agreement, having sent just four cannon, and reminded the marabout that the English king had displayed a singular lack of interest in attacking the Spanish. When it dawned on Sidi Mohammed that no military assistance was to be forthcoming, he ordered a series of spectacular new raids on England's southern coast. Within a few months, Salé's dungeons were once again filled with English captives. In one month alone – May 1635 – more than 150 Englishmen were seized 'and eight of them in Morocco circumcised perforce, and tortured to turne Moores'.

The king's patience finally snapped. When he learned that there were almost 1,200 captives in Salé, 'amonge which there is 27 woemen', he vowed to crush the slave traders once and for all. Diplomacy had failed. Now, the only answer was war.

In the sharp winter of 1637, a bullish sea captain named William Rainsborough was ordered to prepare a fleet of six warships and lead them towards the corsair stronghold of Salé. The town was to be bombarded until it was reduced to rubble. Captain Rainsborough was sanctioned to use whatever force he thought necessary, so long as it was 'for the advantage of His Majestye's honour and service, the preservacion of his territories, and the good of his subjectes'. He was also to keep a lookout for any corsairing vessels at sea. 'If you shall meet with any pyrattes or sea-rovers,' said the king, 'yow are to doe your best to apprehend or sincke them.'

Rainsborough's bellicose temperament was perfectly suited to such a mission and he relished the opportunity to destroy the corsairs. He assembled his fleet at Tilbury, in the Thames Estuary, and set sail in February 1637. He arrived in Salé within a month, having failed to capture any corsairs en route. This disappointment was more than compensated for by the providential timing of his arrival. Salé's slave-trading corsairs 'had made ready all their ships to go for the coast of England', and their huge fleet lay at anchor in the harbour.

Rainsborough was shocked at the number of vessels under their command. More than fifty had been made ready for action and their captains were preparing to launch attacks on both England and Newfoundland. One of Rainsborough's lieutenants, John Dunton, learned that the corsairs were expecting to seize more captives than ever before. 'The governor of New Salé [has] commanded all the captains . . . that they should go for the coast of England,' he was told, '. . . and fetch the men, women and children out of their beds.' Rainsborough was in no doubt that they were in deadly earnest. 'The last yeare, by this time, they had brought in 500 of his Majestie's subjects,' he wrote, 'and I veryly beleve, had wee not come, they would have taken many more this yeare.'

Most of the previous year's captives were no longer being held in Salé. When Rainsborough made discreet enquiries ashore, he was told that they had been auctioned in the slave market. 'All that I could heare,' he wrote, 'is that many English have been transported to Algiers and Tunis.' These unfortunate individuals had been 'sould for slaves, and there doth not remaine here [in Salé] above 250'. Although this news dismayed Rainsborough, he was pleased to learn that the town's corsairs had split into two rival factions. One group was led by Sidi Mohammed, who was attempting to consolidate his grip over the republic of Salé. The other was led by a rebel named Abdallah ben Ali el-Kasri. He was 'an obstinate fellow', according to Rainsborough, '[and] puffed up with his luck in theeving'. He had seized the ancient kasbah, where he was holding 328 Englishmen and 11 women 'in great misery'.

Rainsborough decided to exploit the divisions in the town. Concerned that a general assault on Salé might unite the rival factions, he proceeded to make overtures to Sidi Mohammed and suggested a joint attack on the kasbah with the aim of expelling the rebel corsairs. This would restore the prestige of Sidi Mohammed – who, Rainsborough believed, could be contained – and would also enable him to free the English slaves held by el-Kasri. Rainsborough noted the advantages of the scheme in his journal: 'a meanes that wee shall recover His Majestie's subjects,' he wrote, 'and keepinge this towne from ever haveinge any more men of warre'. It would not just benefit the English, but be 'a happie turne for all Christendome'.

Sidi Mohammed agreed to Rainsborough's plan and released seventeen of his personal slaves as a sign of goodwill. Rainsborough, meanwhile, prepared to open hostilities, priming his heavy weaponry and training it on the clifftop kasbah. The ensuing bombardment caused total carnage. 'We shot at the castle,' wrote John Dunton, 'and into it, and over it, and through it, and into the town, and through the town, and over it, and amongst the Moors, and killed a great many of them.'

As the dust settled, Rainsborough landed a troop of men and ordered them to dig a system of trenches. This allowed him to bring his heavy cannon ashore and fire on the ships that belonged to the rebel forces. 'Our men did sink many of their ships,' wrote Dunton, 'and shot through many of their houses, and killed a great many men.' If the English reports of the battle are correct, the rebels were taken aback by the accuracy of the attacking guns. 'We did so torment them by sinking and burning their ships,' wrote Rainsborough, 'that they were stark mad and at their wits' end.' The English commander was thoroughly enjoying himself. He revelled in the bloodshed and, when two Salé caravels opened fire on his fleet, he showed them no mercy. '[We] set upon them . . . and did heave fire pots [primitive explosives] unto her, and did burne three men of them to death, and did kill fifteen men of them outright.'

While Rainsborough sank ships in the harbour, Sidi Mohammed attacked the kasbah from the land. 'He hath beleagred it with 20 thousand men, horse and foote,' wrote Rainsborough, 'and burnt all theire corne.' It proved harder than expected to capture the castle, but after three weeks of intense bombardment the rebellious Hornacheros were a spent force. Weary of fighting and almost starved of provisions, they had no option but to capitulate.

Their first act was to release the English slaves. John Dunton compiled a list of these men and women, recording their names and the places from which they were seized. His information reveals that the Salé raids had affected every corner of the kingdom. Although the majority had been taken from the West Country – thirty-seven from Plymouth alone – there were captives from as far afield as London, Hull, Jersey and Cardiff.

By mid-August, William Rainsborough felt that he had achieved all he could. The rebel Hornacheros had been crushed, and their vessels were totally destroyed. Sidi Mohammed's prestige had been greatly enhanced, while Rainsborough was convinced that the marabout could be restrained from attacking English villages and shipping with the occasional gift of weaponry and gunpowder. After receiving solemn assurances from Sidi Mohammed, Rainsborough set sail for England in the autumn of 1637, with 230 of the surviving slaves on board.

He was given a warm reception when he arrived back home. There was a widespread feeling that the Salé menace had at long last been neutralised, and that the West Country was once again safe. There was additional cause for joy when King Charles I signed a treaty with the Moroccan sultan. The fourth clause of the treaty stated that 'the King of Morocco shall prohibit and restrayne all his subjects from takeinge, buyinge or receaveinge anie of the subjects of the said King of Great Brittainie to be used as slaves or bondmen in anie kind.'

No one in England paused to consider that their concern for the white slaves was not matched by a similar compassion for the black slaves being brutally shipped out of Guinea, on Africa's western coastline. Although England was not yet the principal slave nation in Europe – that dubious honour went to Portugal – an increasing number of blacks were being despatched to her fledgeling colonies in the Caribbean and North America. The suffering endured by these captives during the middle passage – the Atlantic crossing – was truly appalling. They were packed into unsanitary vessels and often forced to lie in a space smaller than a coffin. There was neither sanitation nor fresh food, and dysentery and fevers were rife. Sailors said that a slave ship could be smelled from more than a mile away at sea.

Reports of this trade, which would eventually lead to the capture and sale of some 15 million Africans, troubled few consciences in England. It was seen as altogether different from the capture and sale of men and women from their own country. Indeed, most viewed the enslavement of black Africans as a legitimate and highly profitable branch of England's growing international trade. More than a century would pass before people first began to draw parallels between the two slave trades and question whether or not the trade in black slaves could be morally justified.

King Charles I's attitude was no different from that of his subjects. Unmoved by the plight of Africa's black slaves, he nevertheless abhorred the trade in white slaves and greeted William Rainsborough's return with great joy. But the king soon discovered that the truce he had signed with the Moroccan sultan was to last just a few months. When he failed to stop English merchants trading with Moroccan rebels, the sultan tore up the peace treaty. The Sallee Rovers, too, found reasons to recommence their attacks on English shipping. By 1643, so many new slaves had been captured that Parliament was forced to order churches to collect money in order to buy the slaves back from their captors. 'It is therefore thought fit, and so ordained by the Lords and Commons in Parliament, that collections be made in the several churches within the City of London and Westminster, and the borough of Southwark.'

Redeeming slaves was a costly business, for markets extended all along the coast of North Africa. By the 1640s, at least 3,000 Englishmen and women had been taken to Barbary, where they were languishing 'in miserable captivity, undergoing divers and most insufferable labour, such as rowing in galleys, drawing carts, grinding in mills, with divers such unchristianlike works, most lamentable to express'.

The crisis was at its most acute in the Moroccan port of Salé, and in the Turkish regencies of Algiers, Tunis and Tripoli. These three maritime cities were nominally under the control of the Ottoman sultan, but real power was more often wielded by local admirals and slave-trading sea captains, who sold their European captives to merchants and dealers from right across the Islamic world. White slaves, who continually changed hands, were soon to be found not only in the great cities of Alexandria, Cairo and Istanbul, but also in dozens of smaller towns and ports. Some had even been enslaved in the remote Arabian peninsula. In one infamous incident that had occurred in 1610, Sir Henry Middleton and his crew had the misfortune to be seized in Aden and taken in chains to the inland city of Sana'a. It had required concerted military action to finally win their release.

In 1646, a merchant named Edmund Cason was sent by Parliament to Algiers to buy back as many English slaves as possible. An initial search located some 750, while many more were said to 'be turned Turkes through beatings and hard usage'. Cason bargained long and hard, but was obliged to pay an average price of £38 per slave. Female captives proved a great deal more expensive to redeem. He paid £800 for Sarah Ripley of London, and £1,100 for Alice Hayes of Edinburgh, while Mary Bruster of Youghal cost a staggering £1,392 – more than thirty-six times the average. These were huge sums of money; the average annual income of a London shopkeeper was just £10, while even wealthy merchants were lucky to make more than £40 in a year. The cost of ransoming each female slave was more than most Londoners would earn in a lifetime. It helps to explain why the Barbary corsairs were more interested in ships' crews than in their cargoes.

Cason's funds were soon exhausted, and he returned to England with just 244 freed captives. Those left behind in Algiers feared they had been abandoned to their fate and sent anguished letters to their loved ones. 'Ah! Father, brother, friends, and acquaintance,' wrote Thomas Sweet, 'use some speedy means for our redemption.' He begged that 'our sighs will come to your ears and move pity and compassion', and he ended his letter with a plea: 'Deny us not your prayers, if you can do nothing else.'

The Barbary corsairs had by now extended their attacks across the whole of Europe, targeting ships from as far afield as Norway and Newfoundland. The Portuguese and French suffered numerous hit-and-run raids on their shores and their shipping. The Italian city states, too, were repeatedly attacked, with the coasts of Calabria, Naples and Tuscany enduring particularly aggressive strikes. Russians and Greeks were also enslaved, along with noblemen and merchants from various parts of the Holy Roman Empire. The islands of Majorca, Minorca, Sicily, Sardinia and Corsica yielded particularly rich harvests for the slave dealers, while the citizens of Gibraltar were singled out so often that they wrote a desperate petition to the king of Spain, in which they bemoaned the fact that they never felt safe, 'neither at night, nor during the day, neither in bed, nor at mealtimes, neither in the fields, nor in our homes'.

Spain itself suffered the most devastating raids of all, and entire villages on the Atlantic coast were sold into slavery. The situation was even more critical on Spain's Mediterranean coast. When the town of Calpe was attacked in 1637, the corsairs made off with no fewer than 315 women and children. Life in Spanish coastal villages soon became so dangerous that new taxes had to be levied on fish, meat, cattle and silk in order to pay for constructing sea defences. But these proved of little use. By 1667, one of the Basque provinces had lost so many seamen to the corsairs that it could no longer meet its quota for the royal levy of mariners.

The Barbary corsairs were indiscriminate when it came to choosing their victims, seizing even merchants and mariners from the colonies of North America. In 1645, a fourteen-gun ship from Massachusetts was the first colonial American vessel to be attacked by an Islamic pirate vessel. The crew managed to fight off this assault, but many of their seafaring comrades were not so fortunate. By the 1660s, a steady trickle of Americans found themselves captured and enslaved in North Africa. The corsairs scored their greatest coup when they captured Seth Southwell, King Charles II's newly appointed governor of Carolina. It was fortuitous for the king that one of his admirals had recently detained two influential Islamic corsairs, who were released in exchange for Southwell.

The Sallee Rovers continued to plunder English shipping, in spite of the treaties they had signed. By the second half of the seventeenth century, the West Country fishermen were at their wits' end. Virtually every coastal port had been touched in some way by the white slave trade, and there seemed no hope of ending the crisis.

In 1672, there was – at long last – a glimmer of good news. The ruling sultan was dead and Morocco looked certain to plunge into civil war. It was hoped that in the ensuing chaos, the nations of Christian Europe could finally put an end to the trade in white slaves.

2 SULTAN OF SLAVES

THE MESSENGER GALLOPED THROUGH THE night, crossing rock-strewn wasteland and parched riverbeds. Dressed in a billowing djellaba and protected from the chill by a thick veil, he urged his dromedary onwards with a stout stick, beating the beast to ride faster and faster. Shortly before dawn on 14 April 1672, he at last glimpsed his goal. In the far distance, lit by a thin shard of moon, were the gates and minarets of Fez.

The messenger rode deep into the souk, pausing only when he came to the iron-studded doors of the viceroy's residence, a secretive palace whose inner courtyards were fringed with orange trees. After explaining his mission to the sleepy gatekeeper, the messenger was whisked inside and ushered into the presence of the city's acting viceroy, Moulay Ismail.

The twenty-six-year-old Ismail was not noted for his good humour, but he could scarcely refrain from smiling when he heard the messenger's news. His brother, the ruling sultan, was dead – killed by his own recklessness. He had been celebrating the end of Ramadan with customary abandon, carousing with friends and drinking deeply from the forbidden bottle. As he charged on horseback through the gardens of his Marrakesh palace, he had fallen from his stallion and 'dashed out his brains against an arm of a tree'. By the time his aides reached him, Sultan Moulay al-Rashid was bleeding to death.

Moulay Ismail knew he would have to act with speed and cunning if he was to secure the throne. He had no fewer than eighty-three brothers and half-brothers, as well as countless nephews and cousins. Although Ismail was one of the most plausible claimants to the throne, the death of a sultan in Morocco invariably signalled an outbreak of insurrection and fratricide as rival factions sought to eliminate one another. These orgies of bloodshed were unpredictable, and the favoured heir was by no means certain to succeed.

Moulay Ismail's first action was to seize the treasury at Fez. Once this was secured, he proclaimed himself sultan and reputedly celebrated his first day in power by slaughtering everyone in the city who refused to submit to his rule.

Deception and betrayal were second nature to Moulay Ismail. He had grown up in a land that was fractured into separate kingdoms and ruled by bitter rivals. Internecine feuds were commonplace; brutal warlords, mercenaries and fanatical holy men were continually butchering their rivals and installing themselves as petty despots. Ruling from mud-walled kasbahs, they were, for a time, absolute masters of all they could survey. They would plunder and pillage without mercy, and with teams of European slaves to serve them they would live in considerable splendour, until they found themselves evicted by a more successful – and less dissolute – princelet.

Moulay Ismail's patrimony lay in the sand-blown wastes of the Tafilalt, in southern Morocco. It was 'an extremely sandy and barren country', according to the French slave, Germain Mouette, 'because of the excessive heat which continues throughout the year'. The natives of this dusty backwater scratched a living as best they could, but remained a 'wild, savage and cruel people'.

For centuries, Moulay Ismail's family had ruled the Tafilalt with carefree indolence, stirring from their torpor only to murder a rival or despatch an interloper. Their power did not extend beyond the palm-fringed oases of the desert, and there was little sign that they were about to thrust themselves into the imperial pleasure palaces of Fez and Marrakesh. Yet they were a family with noble roots and an illustrious pedigree. One of their forebears, al-Hasan bin Kasem, was a *sharif* – a descendant of the Prophet Mohammed. This imbued them with a sacred piety, which Moulay Ismail would later exploit with aplomb.

Many of Morocco's bandit rulers could command small armies of European slaves and renegades, and Ismail's family were no exception. Moulay Ismail himself had been given his first slave when he was just three years of age. Dom Louis Gonsalez was a Portuguese cavalry officer who had been ambushed and captured while serving in the garrison of Tangier, at that time held by Portugal. Dom Louis soon found himself playing father to the toddler: 'he had him continually in his arms,' wrote one, 'and gradually won the affection of the little prince.' In later years, Moulay Ismail 'would always have him in attendance' and would eventually free Dom Louis after he had served more than thirty years in captivity. He was one of the few slaves who would ever escape his grasp.

The clan into which Ismail was born had become unruly and quarrelsome, and their hands were steeped in fratricidal blood. In 1664, Moulay Ismail's brother, Moulay al-Rashid, had wrested the family lands from a rival sibling, murdering him in the process. After installing himself as ruler of the Tafilalt, he led his army north towards the Rif and added this mountainous domain to his fiefdom.

Soon after, he captured the populous city of Fez and tortured its governors with such enthusiasm that the terrified townsfolk of nearby Meknes immediately capitulated. Moulay al-Rashid, feeling that his hour had arrived, promptly declared himself sultan of all Morocco and installed his young brother, Ismail, as governor of Meknes and viceroy of Fez. In the space of two bloodstained years, the family's fortunes had been transformed.

Moulay al-Rashid had gained his kingdom through terror, and he vowed to rule by terror as well. Germain Mouette, who witnessed him in power, was appalled by his unstable temperament. 'If I were to undertake the narration of all the cruelties and massacres he has committed,' he wrote, 'of all the human blood he has shed for trifling faults . . . the story would make a great volume.' Rashid hoped to extend his frontiers even farther and acquired bands of European slaves to fight his battles. These unfortunate captives proved invaluable in his struggle to pacify the land; many were expert gunners who were able to reduce mud-walled kasbahs to dust with a few well-placed cannon-balls. Moulay al-Rashid's victorious army swept southwards to the pink-walled city of Marrakesh, which was captured after a token resistance. The sultan was so 'inflated with prosperity' that he began to plan the conquest of the southern Sahara. But before this could be achieved, his life was cut short amidst the lemon groves of his Marrakesh palace.

The weary European slaves welcomed his death, hoping that the constant battles would at long last come to an end. So did the sultan's *kaids*, or lords, who had been relieved of much of their wealth during his reign of terror. What neither the slaves nor the kaids foresaw was that a far more tyrannous individual was waiting to wrest the reins of power. According to Mouette, 'it was as if nature, before giving birth to so exceptional a being, had attempted first to sketch the model.'

The news that Moulay Ismail had proclaimed himself sultan infuriated many members of his extended family. One of his brothers, Moulay al-Harrani, also declared himself sultan, as did his nephew, Moulay Ahmed. Other factions rose up in rebellion and attempted to carve out fiefdoms from the rapidly disintegrating empire.

Moulay Ismail's forces proved more than a match for these fledgeling armies, and he was encouraged by a number of decisive victories. His military successes – like those of his late brother – were due in part to the services of the European slaves he had managed to capture. 'Having some Christian slaves which he took from the Jews,' wrote one of England's few Islamic scholars, Simon Ockley, 'that were very skilled in managing his cannon, he soon became formidable to the enemy.'

Moulay Ismail rarely showed magnanimity towards the slaves he captured in battle. When the town of Taroudant fell to his troops, he seized 120 French slaves. Having poked and prodded these miserable captives, he declared them to be overfed and ordered them to be denied rations for a week. Then, when they were crying out for food, he sent them on a long march to Meknes.

One of these slaves, Jean Ladire, would later recount the woeful story of his life to the French padre Dominique Busnot. Ladire had by then spent more than three decades in slavery, yet he still had vivid memories of that dreadful march. It was almost 300 miles from Taroudant to Meknes, and many of the chained and shackled captives were suffering from a debilitating sickness – probably dysentery. Several of them dropped dead of fatigue, and 'the survivors were oblig'd to carry their heads, cut off by their conductors, for fear they should be accus'd of having sold, or suffer'd them to escape.'

After five years of warfare and unrest, Moulay Ismail brought much of Morocco under his control. Even the Salé corsairs, who had proved a thorn in the side of successive sultans, now realised that they had met their match. Fearful of Moulay Ismail's growing power, they elected to submit themselves to his rule. But they soon learned that Moulay Ismail had no intention of disarming them, rather, he wished to utilise them for his own sinister purposes. They were to become an instrument of his regime, providing him with a constant stream of slave labour.

When Moulay Ismail felt his grip on power was secure, he returned to the provincial city of Meknes, where he enjoyed 'all the sweets of ease and voluptuousness of vice'. He also began to turn his attentions to rebuilding a country that was in a truly desperate plight. For centuries, Morocco had see-sawed from extraordinary richness to catastrophic decay. Now, it was in one of its darker periods. Once-fertile fields had been laid to waste and the greatest imperial cities had been denuded by slaughter and famine.

Fez had traditionally been the most opulent city in the kingdom. When Leo Africanus wrote his description of the metropolis as it was in about 1513, Fez was still of a size and grandeur to make a lasting impression. 'A world it is to see,' wrote Africanus, 'how large, how populous, how well fortified and walled this city is.' Fez in its heyday was the greatest city in western Islam. Its sumptuous mercantile palaces offered the comforts of secluded courtyards and shaded walkways, and the richest merchants had enchanting walled gardens adorned with pavilions and tea houses. Designed to delight both the eye and the ear, their focal point was 'a christall-fountaine environed with roses and other odoriferous flowers and herbes, so that in the spring-time, a man may both satisfie his eies and solace his mind'.

In Africanus' day, there were 700 mosques in the city, as well as scores of colleges and *madrassas* or religious seminaries. Fez had also boasted hospitals, bathhouses, and 200 *fondouks* or hostelries. Africanus, who had travelled widely in Europe, was impressed. 'Never, to my remembrance, did I see greater buildings,' he wrote, 'except it were the Spanish college at Bologna, or the palace of the Cardinall di San Giorgio at Rome.'

By the time Moulay Ismail seized power, Fez had fallen into a terrible state of dereliction. Many of the great palaces were in ruins, and weeds ran riot in the sunken Andalusian gardens. According to an anonymous English account, written in the early 1680s, whole quarters of the city had been abandoned, and the scholars and theologians of old had long since fled. 'Former ages have had the honour to find this famous city in great beauty and glory,' reads the account, 'but time hath laid a rough hand upon it, and render'd it so deformed that her founders would not in the least know her again.'

The author added that although the decaying ruins were testimony to the ingenuity of Morocco's architects, 'true religion and learning has deserted this people, so has all manner of art to that degree that, by their neglect and laziness, they must in half another age become a heap of rubbish and confusion.'

Not everything in Morocco lay in ruins when Moulay Ismail acceded to the throne. As he toured his newly won kingdom, he glimpsed the broken vestiges of past architectural glories. Many of the greatest monuments had been built under the aegis of the medieval Merenid kings and the sixteenth-century Saadians. In the desert city of Marrakesh lay the fantastical palace of this latter dynasty, whose sultans had lavished a veritable fortune on beautifying their imperial capital. The result was al-Badi – The Marvellous – a palace whose exquisite beauty was to haunt Moulay Ismail for many years. 'All other palaces seem ugly,' wrote one visitor. 'Its appearance is fairy-like, its waters are pure, its earth is perfumed, and its walls rise proudly into the air.' The palace interior was encrusted with powdered gold, carried across the Sahara from the fabled cities of Djenne and Timbuktu. The floors were paved with slabs of polished marble. When a Spanish ambassador visited al-Badi in 1579, he penned a breathless description of its priceless silks and costly damasks, its glittering fountains and Turkish carpets.

Moulay Ismail was similarly entranced; al-Badi was a world away from the dusty kasbah in which he had been raised. The sight of its dappled courtyards and shaded pavilions was forever etched on his mind, inspiring him to begin a project that would change the lives of thousands of Europeans. Shortly after securing the throne, the sultan conceived the idea of building an imperial palace on such a vast scale that even the fabled al-Badi would pale into insignificance.

Moulay Ismail also harboured vainglorious dreams of restoring Morocco to a position in which the country would be considered the equal of the great powers of Europe. He realised that capturing large numbers of white slaves would provide him with precisely the leverage he wanted over the great powers of Christendom. He could hold European monarchs to ransom and force them to send emissaries to Meknes with begging bowls in hand.

The sultan trusted his Salé corsairs to garner a regular supply of captives from the North Atlantic and Mediterranean. But he also had his own, more tantalising vision of how to acquire large numbers of European slaves. Morocco's coastline was dotted with enclaves and fortified settlements, occupied by garrisons of Spanish and Portuguese troops. The Spanish held the towns of Ceuta, Larache, Mamora and Arzila, while the Portuguese controlled Mazagan. Their other Moroccan stronghold, Tangier, had been ceded to England in 1661, when King Charles II was betrothed to Catherine of Braganza, Infanta of Portugal. Together, these enclaves had a combined population of about 10,000 men – soldiers and civilians whom Moulay Ismail intended to capture and retain as slaves.

He was particularly attracted to the idea of attacking Tangier, which stood guard over the Straits of Gibraltar. The English had hoped to use the port as a base from which to eradicate the Salé corsairs. But this had proved almost impossible, and the garrison had singularly failed to halt the capture of English slaves. Instead of spearheading raids on Moroccan soil, the troops now found themselves facing an increasingly hostile and dangerous sultan.

In the dying days of 1677, Moulay Ismail ordered his trusty commander, Kaid Omar, to launch an offensive against Tangier. The kaid was told to seize captives whenever the opportunity arose and send them in chains to Meknes. He was also to attempt to capture the city itself. Moulay Ismail was confident of success, for the English troops were half starved and stricken with disease. But Kaid Omar quickly discovered that capturing a city was altogether more difficult than defending it, and that his hope of seizing Tangier's 2,000-strong garrison was steadily receding.

On a bitter January morning in 1681, a young English soldier could be seen pacing the battlements of Tangier. Colonel Percy Kirke made quite a spectacle as he marched up and down in his flamboyant uniform. He wore a long frock coat with slashed shoulder pads, while his chemise was decorated with lace ruffs and frilly sashes. His most foppish accessory was the dainty silk ribbon tied around each knee.

In normal circumstances, Colonel Kirke would not have dared to poke his head above the parapet in his formal dress uniform. For almost five years, the Moroccan forces had led charges against the citadel of Tangier and wreaked carnage among Kirke's fellow soldiers. In 1678, Kaid Omar's men had managed to destroy two of the outlying forts and had taken prisoner eight of the defenders, who were promptly led off to Meknes in chains. Delighted by his success in seizing these men, Kaid Omar launched a spectacular new wave of attacks and captured a further fifty-seven Englishmen. These, too, were shackled and sent to a gleeful sultan in Meknes.

Kaid Omar's warriors showed such resolution that there was a very real fear among the English that the entire garrison would be overpowered and taken into slavery. In the event, a fortuitous arrival of reinforcement troops saved the day. Kaid Omar's forces were beaten back, and the English and Scottish musketeers scored a decisive victory. 'The attacque prov'd a very hott and bloody piece of service,' wrote one of the English soldiers, '. . . comeing to push of pike and handy blowes in severall places.' After a severe struggle, Kaid Omar's troops were forced to abandon their offensive.

The garrison soldiers were elated by their victory, but their jubilation was tempered by the knowledge that large numbers of their countrymen – including some seventy members of their own garrison – were being held as slaves by the sultan. King Charles II, anxious to release these captives as soon as possible, decided to send an embassy to Moulay Ismail. Its purpose was to demand the immediate release of the slaves and discuss the terms of a lasting peace.

It was widely assumed that the slaves would be home within a matter of months. King Charles's ministers were buoyed by the recent triumph over the Moroccan forces and spoke of Moulay Ismail as if he were a simpleton. One Tangier veteran, Colonel Edward Sackville, was appalled by their dismissive comments and warned them not to underestimate the Moroccans. 'They discourse and debate matters calmly and judiciously,' he said, 'and therefore I see not where the reason of this contempt of them lyes.'

The ambassadorial delegation was led by the trusty Sir James Leslie, who was specially knighted for the mission. He arrived in Tangier in December 1680 and was anxious to head directly to Moulay Ismail's court. But his gifts for the sultan – transported on a separate vessel – had been delayed at sea. Since it was unthinkable for a foreign ambassador to arrive in Meknes empty-handed, Leslie decided to send a messenger to the sultan with an explanation of the delay.

The man chosen was most unsuitable for such an important role. Colonel Percy Kirke, a spineless individual, was a drunkard and a braggart who would later find himself castigated for his appalling lack of judgement. When Samuel Pepys met him in Tangier, he was horrified that such a man could be given a position of responsibility. 'The tyranny and vice of Kirke . . . is stupendous,' he wrote, and added that he was saddened 'to see so great a villain in his place [position]'.

Colonel Kirke headed towards Meknes in January 1681. His

experience of Moroccans had hitherto been limited to action on the battlefield, where he had been impressed by their skill and brutality. Now, as he travelled towards Meknes accompanied by a locally raised guard, he was startled to discover that the sultan's fearsome warriors could be quite charming in times of peace. 'I am among the most sevilisde pepell in the worlde,' he wrote, 'and iff ever I have a sone, I will rether choose to send him hether for breadin then to the cort of France.' His hosts took him hunting for wild boar and antelope, and grilled large quantities of meat for him to dine on each evening. 'Wee have in a prodigall manner more meate than wee can tell what to doe withall,' wrote Kirke.

He arrived in Meknes in February and was immediately invited to a personal audience with Moulay Ismail. The sultan was the personification of charm at this first meeting. Kirke was 'received by the king in his garden, being accompanied with four of his chiefest councillors and kaids, his bashaws and general officers'. Overawed by the formality of the occasion, he nervously handed Sir James Leslie's letters of apology to Moulay Ismail. The sultan smiled graciously '[and] returned more favourable answers than could be expected from a prince so haughty'.

He was extremely hospitable towards Kirke, offering him a tour of his lion den and laying on a dramatic display of Moroccan horsemanship. 'We owe him great acknowledgements for his kind usage of us,' wrote one of the Englishmen in Kirke's little entourage, 'not only supplying us plentifully with necessaries, but in as much fashionable ceremony as could come from any well bred man.'

Moulay Ismail proved adept at flattering his English guests and took particular care to woo and manipulate Colonel Kirke. He invited him to tea in his exquisite pleasure gardens and gave him a tour of the sweet-scented orange groves, glittering pavilions and pools of cool water. The two men 'discoursed very morally of trust and honour', and when Kirke lamely raised the vexed question of the peace treaty, Moulay Ismail smiled capriciously and proposed a four-year truce. He swore to Kirke that 'thare never should be bullet shot against Tangier so long as I was in it'.

Kirke was delighted with the success of his meeting and congratulated himself on his skills as a diplomat. He was convinced that the sultan was not only a man to be trusted but was keen to forge a closer relationship. When Moulay Ismail asked his new friend whether he could supply the Moroccan army with ten big guns, Kirke was only too happy to oblige, promising to 'help him with everything he lacked'.

The colonel was breathtakingly naive in his negotiations with the sultan and completely overstepped his duties. He had been despatched to Meknes as a mere emissary, yet he had assumed the role of an ambassador. Leslie might have forgiven him this transgression, were it not for the fact that Kirke displayed a total lack of regard for the English slaves being held in Morocco. These numbered at least 300, perhaps many more, and were being kept in pitiful conditions. Kirke almost certainly saw them at work, for Moulay Ismail relished the opportunity to display his slaves to visiting emissaries. Yet Kirke made virtually no mention of them in his despatches. Instead, he penned a letter to London – where news of the slaves was anxiously awaited – extolling the sultan's virtues. 'I must tell the holle world,' he wrote, 'I have met with a kinde prince and a just generall.'

Sir James Leslie remained in Tangier for two months, awaiting the vessel carrying the sultan's presents. It was not until March that it finally arrived, and he was able to set off for Meknes. Leslie proved a rather better judge of character than Kirke and quickly realised that while the sultan was all too quick to make promises, he was rather less eager to follow them through. Leslie tried his best to negotiate a release of the slaves, but Moulay Ismail washed his hands of the whole affair and asked Kaid Omar – the very man who had been defeated by the English – to draft a truce.

When the ambassador returned to the issue of redeeming the English slaves, Moulay Ismail was even less willing to negotiate. Leslie's first hurdle was to ascertain exactly how many slaves were in the sultan's possession. Moulay Ismail admitted to having just 130 Englishmen, of whom seventy were former members of the Tangier garrison. A further sixty belonged to members of his entourage, bringing the alleged total to 190. Yet the actual number of slaves was a great deal higher, as Leslie well knew. Scores of English ships had been seized in the preceding years, and their crews had disappeared without trace.

With sinking spirits, Leslie tried to buy back the seventy slaves captured from Tangier. But Moulay Ismail laughed in scorn at the sum he was offered and demanded 200 pieces of eight per slave. He added that the sixty slaves owned by his courtiers would be even more expensive. The total sum was far more than Leslie had available and, after months of fruitless negotiations, he was obliged to leave the court empty-handed. When the money was eventually raised and sent to the sultan, Moulay Ismail said that he had meant 200 ducats – an even greater sum – not pieces of eight.

Leslie's sojourn at the court of Meknes left him exhausted. He felt that the Moroccan sultan had consistently got the upper hand and bemoaned the fact that he had failed to free a single slave. 'I have beene a very unfortunate man in this businesse,' he wrote, '. . . [and] all I desire is that I may not be blamed before I am heard.'

Moulay Ismail, too, was most unsatisfied by the outcome. He had anticipated an array of presents from the English ambassador and was disgusted to discover that many of them were of inferior quality. The costly cloths and silks had been spoiled by the rain, and the English muskets exploded on being fired. When the sultan came to view the 'six Gallway naggs' – specially selected for their 'long tailes' – he found them fit for nothing but the knackers' yard.

Sir James Leslie continued to object to Moulay Ismail's obfuscation throughout 1681 and repeatedly demanded the return of the English slaves. Although the sultan refused to accede to their release, he did agree to despatch an ambassador to London. This ambassador was given plenipotentiary powers, enabling him to negotiate the terms by which all the English captives would be freed.

The man chosen to represent Moulay Ismail was Kaid Muhammad ben Haddu Ottur, a Moroccan nobleman whose mother was rumoured to be an English slave. Colonel Kirke had met the kaid on several occasions and believed him to be 'a person of a good temper and understanding'. He was alone in holding such a view. The French emissary, Pidou de St Olon, warned the English to treat the kaid with extreme caution. 'His ways and discourse discover a great deal of cunning,' he wrote. 'He is deceitful and wicked to the highest degree.' The ambassador's retinue was held to be even less trustworthy. One of his advisors, Hamet Lucas, was a renegade Englishman who had deserted from Tangier's garrison some years earlier. Even Kirke called him 'a subtile and impudent vilain' and stressed the importance of secrecy whenever Hamet was within earshot. 'Our affairs in England . . . ought as carefully to be concealed from these people as they endeavour to keep us ignorant in theirs.'

The embassy sailed from Tangier in December 1681 and arrived in London after a three-week voyage. There was great excitement in England about the arrival of the ambassador and his retinue, particularly among the West Country communities who had lost so many of their menfolk to the Salé corsairs. The king and his ministers also looked forward to face-to-face talks with their Moroccan counterparts, hoping to secure a deal that would lead not only to the slaves being freed, but would also end years of enmity between the two nations.

On 11 January 1682, the ambassador and his entourage had their first audience with King Charles II, a splendid affair that was held in the Banqueting Hall of Whitehall Palace. As the ambassador entered the hall, the assembled courtiers were enchanted by his exotic demeanour. Only one shrewd observer – the diarist, John Evelyn – expressed any disquiet at the manner of his entrance, noting that the kaid was haughty in his bearing and approached the throne 'without making any sort of reverence, not bowing his head or body'.

King Charles himself did not care one jot. The Merry Monarch was so excited by the occasion that he flung off his hat in an exuberant display of joy and welcome, a gesture that would later have important ramifications for the ambassador. Evelyn described Kaid Haddu Ottur and his men as 'all clad in the Moorish habite, cassocks of coloured cloth or silk, with buttons and loops'. To keep out the winter chill, they also wore a 'white woollen mantle, so large as to wrap both head and body'. On their heads were small turbans, while their arms and legs were bare, except for their thick leather socks. The ambassador was the most resplendent, wearing a delicate string of pearls 'oddly woven in his turban'. Evelyn found him 'an handsome person, well featur'd, of a wise looke, subtill, and extreamly civil'. He brought two lions as a gift for the king, as well as a number of ostriches, whose humorous facial expressions caused the assembled courtiers to chuckle.

London society extended every possible courtesy to the Moroccan entourage, hoping that their hospitality would help win the release of the slaves. King Charles II's French mistress, Louise de Kerouaille, Duchess of Portsmouth, prepared a 'great banquet of sweetemeates and musiq' in their honour and invited all of London's leading courtiers to welcome them to the capital. The English guests dressed in the most outlandish costumes and looked 'as splendid as jewells and excesse of bravery could make them'.

The Moroccan ambassador and his retinue looked on in bemused disbelief as the revelry rapidly degenerated into bacchanalia and saucy frolicking. Declining to join the fun, they 'behav'd themselves with extraordinary moderation and modesty', wrote Evelyn, '. . . neither admiring nor seeming to regard any thing'. They turned down the opportunity to engage in raucous dancing and turned up their noses at the offer of wine.

'They dranke a little milk and water', wrote Evelyn, 'but not a drop of wine; they also dranke of a sorbet and jacolatt [chocolate].' Evelyn was surprised that they retained their sobriety for the entire evening '[and] did not looke about, or stare on ye ladies, or expresse the least surprise'.

In the days that followed the banquet, the ambassador and his men spent much of their time in Hyde Park, 'where he and his retinue shew'd their extraordinary activity in horsemanship, and flinging and catching their launces at full speede'. The kaid was taken to the theatre on several occasions, where, 'upon any foolish or fantastical action, he could not forbear laughing, but he endeavour'd to hide it with extraordinary modesty and gravity.'

The Moors thoroughly enjoyed themselves in London, becoming a regular fixture on the social circuit. They showed no inclination to discuss the English slaves in Morocco, and the king's ministers decided not to press the issue until they could be sure of meeting with success. Instead, they took the Moroccans on sightseeing expeditions, making short excursions to Windsor, Newmarket, Oxford and Cambridge. Everywhere they went, huge crowds gathered to greet them. It was as if the whole of England wanted to glimpse a representative of the nation that had for so long been attacking their shipping and enslaving their mariners.

In Cambridge, the ambassador was invited to a banquet presided over by the Vice-Chancellor and heads of colleges. Here, for the first time since arriving in England, he allowed himself to join in the merriment. He munched his way through so many 'soused eeles, sturgeon and sammon' that he felt 'a little indisposed' and had to lie down in the Provost's lodgings at King's College.

In February, the ambassador was back in London, visiting Westminster Abbey, where the young Henry Purcell had just been appointed organist. In April, he was the guest of the Royal Society, whose president was Sir Christopher Wren. He was elected honorary fellow and took great delight in inscribing his name in the charter book 'in fair character in Arabic'. The following month, the ambassador was off again, this time to Oxford. He was given lodgings at the Angel, where he was visited by the Vice-Chancellor and various doctors, some of whom spoke Arabic. Dr Edward Pocock made a speech in Arabic, 'which made him laugh' – probably because of the numerous mistakes.

The ambassador beguiled all whom he met and proved no less skilful when – after enjoying almost six months of lavish hospitality – he sat down to discuss the slaves being held in Morocco. King Charles II had done all he could to welcome the ambassador with 'more than ordinary form', hoping that it would result in a lasting and advantageous peace. The negotiations he conducted with the ambassador were held behind closed doors, and details of the diplomatic wrangling were never set down on paper. But the resultant treaty – signed in March 1682 – was proof enough that the king had been worsted. The key concern had been the release of the English slaves in Morocco. Although the kaid agreed to sell back these captives at a cost of 200 Spanish dollars each, he said that this would need ratification by the sultan in person. Another priority had been to bring to a halt the depredations of the Salé corsairs, who continued to ransack the West Country and seize fisherfolk. Yet the treaty signed by King Charles had 'nothing in it of the sea, the ambassador professing utter ignorance of sea affairs'. It also permitted the Moroccans to continue to buy weaponry from the English – a clause that raised many an eyebrow in London – and sanctioned the release of seventy-nine Moroccan prisoners of war being held in Tangier. This was done in the belief that Moulay Ismail would display a similar magnanimity towards his English, Scottish, Welsh and Irish slaves.

The Moroccan ambassador returned home in September 1682 and immediately headed to Moulay Ismail's court to report on his triumph. Shortly before arriving in Meknes, he and his retinue were greeted by ten of the sultan's black guard. Far from congratulating the men on their success, they 'apprehended the embassador and his camerades [comrades], putting them immediately into irons'. They were then marched to the sultan, who expressed great anger at their conduct. According to Hamet Lucas, Moulay Ismail shouted at them, called them dogs and reproached them for being overly friendly to their Christian hosts. He then ordered the ambassador to be 'dragged by mules for the space of twelve leagues through a country of stones and bryers'.

The reason for the sultan's fury soon became apparent. In the hope of advancement, one of the ambassador's retinue had told Moulay Ismail that Muhammad ben Haddu Ottur had spent his time in England drinking and consorting with bad women. The ambassador retorted that he had been the very model of probity, but added that the others had indulged in 'whoring, and mixing pagan rumps with Christian giblets'. In the end, it was one man's word against another. The sultan was inclined to believe his ambassador and released him from his irons, confessing later that he had spared him only when he learned that King Charles II had saluted him by taking off his hat. The rest of the retinue were condemned for consorting with prostitutes and were ordered to strip naked. 'Their principle evidence was cut off,' reads one English account of the incident, 'which it is thought will spoil their whoring for the future.'

The ambassador never repaid the kindness he had been shown in England and certainly made no effort to persuade Moulay Ismail to release the English slaves. Thomas Phelps, one of the English captives in Meknes, wrote that 'the dog has returned to his vomit . . . and now improves his knowledge of English affairs to the detriment and ruin of all the king's subjects.' He added that whenever Muhammad ben Haddu Ottur passed the slaves as they worked, he would 'salute them with a devillish curse, which to the best of my remembrance, was expressed thus: Alli hazlebuck, i.e. God, roast your father'.

Moulay Ismail, too, was as vehemently anti-English as ever. He disowned all of the ambassador's work in England, including the treaty, and declined to inscribe his signature alongside that of King Charles II. He also refused to release his English slaves, even though the Tangier garrison had freed all of their Moroccan captives. When the English protested, Moulay Ismail demanded that another ambassador be sent to Morocco to renegotiate the treaty.

King Charles II himself despatched a letter in Arabic to Moulay Ismail, but the sultan was indignant that 'its tone was not more flattering and servile'. He replied with a stinging rebuke, informing the king that he would not rest 'till I have sat down before Tangier and filled it with Moors, and reduced it to my possession by the favour of God'. On the unresolved issue of peace at sea, he could scarcely have been less willing to compromise. 'We have no need of it,' he wrote in his letter, adding that Moroccan corsairs would continue to harass English shipping.

The sultan soon fulfilled his promise to fill Tangier with Moors, although not through military victory. With the peace treaty in shreds, King Charles II lost interest in his Moroccan outpost. Instead of pouring yet more money into the costly Tangier experiment – which had singularly failed to stop the depredations of the Salé corsairs – he ordered the evacuation and destruction of the town. During the winter of 1683, Tangier's harbour and fortifications – built at such a huge cost – were systematically demolished. The following February, the last English troops were pulled out.

The abandonment of Tangier did not change Moulay Ismail's attitude towards the English, nor did it encourage him to release any of his slaves. King Charles II died in 1685. During the short reign of King James II, many hundreds of English captives languished in their underground cells, alongside thousands of French, Spanish, Portuguese, Dutch and Italians. No attempt was made to win their freedom and the first news of them for many a year was received in 1689, when a Dutchman, Jan Smit Heppendorp, managed to visit a cell containing 400 English and North American captives. He wrote to William of Orange, England's Dutch-born monarch, informing him they were 'in great misery and servitude, such as there is no resemblance of in any other part of the world'.

King William III's conscience was pricked by this news and he began a series of discussions about their liberation. For five long years he attempted to haggle and negotiate, but the sultan kept demanding an increasingly large ransom. King William was so anxious to free the slaves that he eventually agreed to the extortionate sum of £15,000 and 1,200 barrels of gunpowder, sending Captain George Delaval to Morocco with both. 'The ship was so full of pouder,' wrote Delaval, 'that we were in continuall fear of her blowing up.'

Moulay Ismail began disputing the terms of the agreement within hours of the English captain landing in Tetouan. Delaval was exasperated but displayed commendable spirit in refusing to hand over the money until he had tangible evidence that the slaves were going to be released. His persistence – and presents – eventually bore fruit. In December 1701 the sultan agreed to free 194 of his English slaves, leaving just 30 in Meknes.

These last few captives were still being held by the sultan when Queen Anne came to the throne in 1702 and they looked set to spend the rest of their lives as slaves. But when the queen hinted that she might be interested in joining Moulay Ismail in an Anglo-Moroccan attack on the Spanish enclave of Ceuta, they were suddenly – and unexpectedly – released.

Their arrival in London was greeted with an outburst of public rejoicing, for it seemed as if the menace of the Salé corsairs had lifted at long last. The queen's ministers, too, breathed a collective sigh of relief. For the first time in 150 years, not a single English slave was being held on Moroccan soil. But Moulay Ismail had no intention of forging a lasting peace with Queen Anne. When the queen eventually declined to provide troops for the sultan's offensive against Ceuta, he told his Salé corsairs that British vessels were once again legitimate targets. After a truce that had lasted just three years, several trading vessels were seized and the fifty-five mariners on board found themselves incarcerated in Meknes. 'Pray God incline you to pitty us,' wrote James Hill, one of the slaves. '[We are] naked and abused, in prisons, without close [clothes] or any other necessaries.'

Moulay Ismail's formula of capture, ransom and occasional release was to set the pattern for the rest of Queen Anne's reign. He only ever redeemed slaves if he thought he stood to profit and always used his captives as instruments of his foreign policy. In the spring of 1714, he once again released his English slaves, signing yet another treaty of peace and friendship. Under the terms of this agreement, the English promised to send Moulay Ismail a large quantity of chinaware and cloth, as well as twelve spotted deer.

When the queen died in the summer of 1714, these presents had still not been sent. To Moulay Ismail, this was a deliberate snub that needed to be punished at all costs. By the spring of the following year, he was ready to order his Salé corsairs back to sea. At the very same time, England's West Country merchants – unaware of the sultan's change of heart – were also preparing to set sail.

3 Seized at Sea

The *Francis* slipped almost unnoticed out of Falmouth harbour. There were no crowds to see her off, no weeping wives and mothers. The farewells had been said on the previous evening. Now, in the absence of well-wishers, the crew went about their business with unusual efficiency. Dripping ropes were hauled to the decks and musty canvas unfurled. A sharp gust of wind was all it took to propel the little vessel into the English Channel. Within less than an hour, the Cornish coastline lay far behind.

The departure of the *Francis* in the year 'of our Lord Christ, 1715' was so unremarkable that it escaped the notice of all except the port's harbourmen and stevedores. The vessel was owned by a local merchant named Valentine Enys, an enterprising individual who had built up an extensive trading network that stretched as far afield as the Baltic and the Canary Islands. His fortune rested on the prosaic trade in pilchards, which abounded in the rich seas around Penryn. It was pilchards, dried and salted, that the *Francis* was carrying to Genoa, on the north-west coast of Italy.

The crew numbered just six men – seven including the captain – all of whom were experienced mariners. Captain John Pellow was a gruff sea-dog who had spent much of his life on the high seas. He was sufficiently educated to be able to read and write – skills that would prove invaluable in the years to come. The other six were familiar faces in the sea-swept taverns that lined Falmouth's harbour. They came from such humble and impoverished backgrounds that virtually nothing is known of them other than their names: Lewis Davies, George Barnicoat, Thomas Goodman, Briant Clarke, John Crimes and John Dunnal.

There was also a newcomer on board the *Francis* for this particular voyage. Thomas Pellow, just eleven years of age, had never before been to sea. He lived with his parents and two sisters in the thriving fishing port of Penryn, 'a pleasant, agreeable town', which lay just four miles from Falmouth. According to one of its most famous inhabitants, Peter Mundy, Penryn resembled a miniature Constantinople. It was embraced by two arms of the sea, like the Ottoman capital, and the meeting point of these arms was a place of recreation in both places. 'As in Constantinople, the grand seigneur's seraglio or place of pleasure stands on the point that divides them,' wrote Mundy, 'so we in like manner have a pleasant place for recreation . . . a fine bowling green and two brooks.'

Penryn's prosperity was inextricably linked to the sea, but the inhabitants were also acutely conscious of the dangers that lay just beyond the horizon. Corsair vessels had frequently been sighted in the past, and it was perhaps in reference to the Barbary pirates that the townsfolk had chosen to place a Saracen's head on the arms of their town.

Thomas Pellow was a pupil at the Latin School in Penryn. He was a bright and enterprising lad who might have improved his lot had he shown more enthusiasm for his studies. But he disliked the dawn start to each day, as well as the 'most severe discipline of the school', and decided to run away to sea – albeit with the permission of his family. He paid a visit to his uncle, Captain John Pellow, who he knew was about to sail to Genoa, and begged to be allowed to take part in what was sure to be an exciting adventure. '[I] so far insinuated myself into my uncle's favour,' he later wrote, 'as to get his promise to obtain the consent of my parents for me to go along with him.'

That consent was not readily forthcoming. Thomas's parents wished their headstrong son to continue with his education and repeatedly pointed out the hardships, 'which probably I might, in my so tender years, undergo thereby'. They also told him that school discipline was nothing when compared to the captain's lash and warned him that once he had felt the ship's cat-o'-nine-tails, he would soon be wishing he had never left Penryn. When Thomas persisted in his demand to be allowed to put to sea, his parents confided their 'ominous fears of our falling into the hands of the Moors' who had ravished the Cornish coastline for so long.

Thomas's obstinacy eventually paid off; his parents were no longer prepared to argue. 'I obtained their consent,' he later wrote, '. . . and was soon rigged in my sailor's dress.' After a 'long, long farewell' at the family home in Penryn and tearful goodbyes to his two younger sisters, Thomas walked the four miles to Falmouth and boarded the *Francis*. He hoped to return a sailor in six months; in fact, he was embarking on an adventure that was to last for the next twenty-three years.

Thomas's parents were wise to fear the Moorish pirates and might have done well to remind the captain and crew of the extreme dangers of the voyage they were about to undertake. They knew that large numbers of captives had until very recently been held in Barbary – many of them from Cornwall – and had a genuine anxiety that their son would meet a similar fate. But Valentine Enys, the owner of the *Francis*, felt that such concerns were misplaced. He knew that the Moroccan sultan had signed a treaty of peace and commerce with the British just a year previously. He also knew that this treaty had brought to an end the Salé corsairs' long reign of terror. They were forbidden to attack English vessels and prohibited from sailing anywhere near the English coastline. The sultan himself had warned that 'he who deviates may blame none but himself, and injures no head but his own.' He had added, somewhat cryptically, that if and when the truce came to an end, any mariner caught at sea would be 'deprived of our protection, shall enjoy no pact, and his hopes shall be in vain'.

Captain Pellow and his crew had no reason to suspect that the sultan was on the point of tearing up the treaty. They were unaware that the gifts promised by Queen Anne to the Moroccan sultan had never been sent. Nor did they know that Moulay Ismail was incensed at the way in which the English had reneged on their agreement to send these gifts.

Other English merchants were similarly ignorant of the sultan's change of heart and were preparing to take advantage of this window of peace. All over southern England, harbours were busy as ships were made ready for trading voyages to Spain, Portugal and the colonies of North America. A veritable flotilla of fishermen, traders and merchants had already hoisted their sails and pushed their vessels into the North Atlantic. The *Sarah*, with her crew of fifteen, was sailing from Bristol to Barbados. The *Endeavour* from Topsham was heading to Newfoundland with a cargo of salt, while the *David* – also of Topsham – was on course for Lisbon. The *Catherine* of Hampton and the London-owned *George* were heading for Spain, while the *Rebecca and Mary* of Hull was bound for Leghorn with a cargo of corn.

It was not just the English who had put to sea during the lull in piracy. Merchants from colonial America, who had been the victims of previous attacks by the Salé corsairs, had also set sail with cargoes to sell in the great markets of southern Europe. One of their vessels, the *Prosperous*, had recently left New England with a load of salt fish. Her crew of six included a young boy of Pellow's age called Abraham Kemach. A second New England vessel, the *Princes*, was also preparing to sail into the troubled waters of the North Atlantic. Her ten-strong crew, who included a fare-paying passenger, had no idea of the dangers that lay ahead.

The crew of the *Francis* had only the sky for company as they headed into the choppy Atlantic waters. The men, happy to be back at sea, were looking forward to brief dalliances with the raven-haired strumpets of Genoa. But young Thomas soon regretted his decision to set sail. His uncle proved an extremely hard taskmaster and afforded no special favours to his nephew. 'I had very little or no time allowed to play,' Thomas later complained and added that if he slacked in his work, 'I failed not of a most sure payment by the cat of nine tails.' To instil discipline in him, Captain Pellow ordered his nephew 'to go up to the main-top mast-head, even in all weather'.

Captain Pellow may have known how to turn young lads into mariners, but he had a cavalier attitude to the safety of his vessel. He had taken no precautions against the possibility of a rupture in the recent peace and had neglected to stow aboard a single musket. If the *Francis* were to come under attack, she would have absolutely no means of defence.

The most dangerous part of the *Francis*'s voyage was the passage through the Straits of Gibraltar. This was a favourite haunt of corsairs from Salé, Algiers, Tunis and Tripoli, who lurked in concealed coves until their prey was within easy reach. On this occasion, the corsairs remained hidden from view, and Captain Pellow and his men passed through the straits without any trouble. They pushed on eastwards towards Italy and arrived safely at Genoa, where the crew quickly sold their cargo of pilchards. With the money they made from this sale, they acquired goods that would fetch a good price in the West Country.

As the *Francis* began her return voyage to England, the crews' thoughts turned to their homecoming. Having received no hint of the menace that was brewing in the port of Salé, they were unaware that the corsairs had spent the last few months equipping their vessels for a season of piracy on the high seas.

One of these corsairs was the fearsome Captain Ali Hakem. Like his fellow pirates, he had been forbidden to seize English vessels ever since Moulay Ismail had signed the peace treaty with Queen Anne. He and his corsairs had continued to put to sea, concentrating their efforts on capturing vessels belonging to the Spanish, Portuguese or French. All knew that it was only a matter of time before the sultan tore up his treaty with the English, and her ships would once again be a legitimate target for their piracy.

Captain Hakem probably learned of the sultan's decision from Abderrahman el-Mediouni, the admiral of Salé, who had a nominal authority over the corsairs. The news led to feverish activity on the Salé waterfront, as the corsairs began immediate preparations to set sail. There were many practical hurdles to overcome. A crew needed to be hired, weaponry had to be cleaned and serviced, and the ship made ready for action. The Salé corsairs' preferred vessel was the xebec, a small, lateen-rigged ship that was extremely fast in the water. Captain Hakem and his men knew that they would have to depend upon speed and surprise if they were to catch any prizes. Their ships' hulls were greased with such care that they were said to glide through the waves like fish.

There were also religious rituals to be undertaken before a vessel could leave port. A curious mix of superstition and lore, these had been adhered to for so long that they were steeped in tradition. 'The *rais* [captain] never fails to visit one of the more famous marabouts,' wrote Father Pierre Dan in 1637, 'to ask him about his travels and to ask for his prayers.' Advice would be offered and donations given in return. The marabout would then present the captain with the gift of a sheep, which would later be sacrificed at sea.

Captain Pellow and his men were blithely unaware of the terror that was about to be unleashed on them. Their voyage had gone well – better than anyone could have expected – and they had been lulled into a false sense of security. They crossed the treacherous Bay of Biscay without any difficulties, and their spirits were raised even higher when they sighted another English vessel on the horizon. The *Francis* gave friendly chase, and there was a great cheer when the two vessels came alongside. The *George* belonged to Captain Robert Fowler of Topsham. Her five-strong crew were also looking forward to returning to their homes, having successfully acquired a large cargo of oil in Genoa. As the two ships passed the rocky headland of Cape Finisterre, their crews celebrated their trouble-free passage: 'our cargoes out and in,' wrote Thomas Pellow in his account, 'and by God's providence bound home'.

Captain Ali Hakem had sailed from Salé in the company of Admiral el-Mediouni. The two corsair vessels had been stalking the English ships for several hours. They knew that surprise was their most devastating weapon and continued to monitor the movements of the *Francis* and the *George* for some time, safe in the knowledge that their low-sided ships were invisible to their English prey.

In the tense hours that preceded an attack, it was customary to slaughter the sheep that had been given by the marabout. This was a solemn, if bloody, affair. According to Joseph Pitts, an English captive who witnessed one of these sacrifices, the captain first chopped off the head of the sheep. Then, the crew 'immediately take out the entrails and throw them and the head overboard'. After skinning the legs and belly, 'they cut the body in two parts by the middle.' One part was thrown over the right side of the ship, and the other was thrown over the left. This was done, wrote Pitts, 'as a kind of propitiation'.

Once the sacrifice was complete, the corsairs closed in on their prey. It had long been their custom to raise false colours in order to lure their unsuspecting victims to within striking distance. Only when the target vessel was at close quarters did the corsairs reveal their true intent by dramatically switching flags. Unfurled by the wind, these piratical banners usually depicted an arm brandishing a curved scimitar and were designed to frighten the hapless mariners into submission.

Captain Pellow and his crew were caught completely off guard by the two Salé xebecs. Young Thomas would later note that none of the crew had spied their pursuers until it was too late and they were 'very unhappily surprised'. He writes little of the ensuing attack, perhaps because almost a quarter of the century would pass before he recorded the story of his capture. Other victims recalled their sheer terror at the sight of the corsairs, whose shaved heads, bare arms and flashing scimitars left them quaking with fear. To Joseph Pitts, a cabin boy like Pellow, the experience was forever seared into his memory. 'The enemy seemed to me as monstrous ravenous creatures,' he wrote, 'which made me cry out "Oh master! I am afraid they will kill us and eat us."' The ship's captain had replied with uncanny prescience: '"No, my child, . . . they will carry us to Algier and sell us."'

The unarmed *Francis* stood absolutely no chance against Captain Hakem and Admiral el-Mediouni. Nor did Captain Fowler's boat, which was also without weaponry. But as the two English ships made 'such small resistance as we could both make', a sharp-sighted lookout caught sight of a much larger vessel heading towards them at full speed. It was the London sea-dog Captain Richard Ferris, 'in a ship of much greater strength, having twenty men, eight swivel and eight carriage guns'.

Captain Ferris's vessel, the *Southwark*, was indeed a great deal larger than either the *Francis* or the *George*. This sturdy merchant ship had been carrying a cargo of wheat from Portsmouth to Leghorn. She had no fewer than eighteen men aboard, and her captain was a bullish individual who was spoiling for a fight. He had no intention of allowing the *Francis* and the *George* to be carried off to Salé and vowed to use all the firepower he could muster to rescue the crews of the two captured boats.

The Salé corsairs were unused to their victims fighting back.

Their strategy was to attack with such ferocity that they overwhelmed their enemy before they had time to load their guns. Over the previous decades, only a handful of English vessels had attempted to defend themselves, even though they knew that capture would almost certainly lead to a long period of slavery. Those who did resist the corsairs found themselves facing a truly formidable foe. In 1655, the American colonist Abraham Browne had urged his men to fight back against their attackers. 'I fetcht up a bottell,' he wrote, 'and made every man to drinke, encoraging them in the best manner I could.' The ensuing battle had been ferocious, and Browne and his men had quickly found themselves forced from the exposed quarterdeck. 'Ther muskett shott . . . came soe thick [that] wee could staye their noe longer.'

This was a classic tactic of the Salé corsairs that would soon be repeated on the *Francis*, the *George* and the *Southwark*. It had certainly cost Browne and his men their freedom, and very nearly their lives. As they recharged their muskets, the corsairs had boarded the vessel and cut down the rigging in order to disable her. Next, wielding axes, they smashed through the woodwork and doors, steadily gaining control of the ship.

More than six decades after the capture of Browne and his men, Captain Ferris found himself in a very similar predicament. His sixteen heavy guns were more than enough to sink Captain Hakem's vessels, and his crew were motivated by the knowledge that they would certainly be sold into slavery if they lost the battle. But the size of the *Southwark*, which towered over the corsairs' xebecs, was to prove her greatest disadvantage. The ship's great guns were unsuited to firing low in the water, and Captain Ferris realised that if the Salé corsairs managed to grapple his vessel, there was every chance that they would be able to board her.

The men on the *Francis* and the *George* watched the unfolding battle with feverish anxiety, aware that their own lives were at stake. Thomas Pellow, too, looked on in tense excitement as the *Southwark*'s crew fired their muskets at the two xebecs. 'They behaved in the bravest manner,' he wrote, 'fighting ten hours, and with a noble resolution.'

Captain Hakem's men proved extraordinarily daring in their attack. They manoeuvred their xebec close to the *Southwark* and managed to secure themselves to the English ship with their grappling irons. As this exposed them to shot, Captain Ferris's men took full advantage of their position, 'putting the Moors off after boarding them three times, and killing many of them'. As the day wore on, Captain Ferris's men continued to prime and fire their guns, causing mayhem and bloodshed on the Salé vessels. But the corsairs fought with deranged fury, seeming oblivious to the carnage. Indeed, they appeared to be energised by the intensity of the battle and fought with gritty determination. For hour after hour they pressed home their attack, hacking their way on to the lower deck of the English vessel for a second, third and fourth time. Eventually, their numerical advantage began to tell. Captain Ferris's men were exhausted by the fight and their resolve was broken by the continual wave of assaults. As the day wore on, their strength failed and they lost control of their vessel little by little. After an entire day's battle, they had no option but to capitulate. 'Being overpowered by a superior force,' wrote Pellow, 'they were also obliged to submit.'

Crews of ships who resisted capture were accorded little mercy and were often executed on the spot. When the Englishman, Captain Bellemy, had tried to defend himself against a band of Salé corsairs, he met with a swift and violent end. 'The pirate cut him down with his cutlas,' wrote his captured crewmate, Francis Brooks, 'and rip'd him open, and said "there was an end of a dog" [and] so threw his murdered body into the sea.'

Captain Ferris was fortunate to be spared such a terrible fate, although he quickly discovered that the crews of all three captured vessels faced a grim future. Thomas Pellow provides scant information about the terrors endured by the men in the hours that followed their capture. He recalled only that the crews were 'closely confined and treated after a barbarous manner'. To an eleven-year-old boy, the experience of capture must have been quite terrifying. 'It is impossible for me to describe the agony I was then in,' he later wrote, 'being separated from my uncle.'

A sense of helplessness and despair was the first response of most captured mariners. Captain Pellow and his crew were no exception. Just a few hours earlier, they had been free men. Now, they had lost all hope of liberty, and their captors were terrifying in their foreignness. Abraham Browne described Salé's corsairs as 'mor like ravones beasts then men' – a sentiment echoed by many other victims – and said that they fell upon their captives with great savagery, 'striping of us all stark naked, having noe respect to any of us that weare wonded'. Such harsh treatment was by no means exceptional. When Joseph Pitts had been captured in 1678, he and his crewmates were chained in irons and denied all but subsistence rations: 'only a little vinegar . . . half a spoonful of oil, and a few olives, with a small quantity of black biscuit'.

The captured crews of the *Francis*, the *George* and the *Southwark* found themselves separated into small groups. Captain Pellow and three of his crew were ordered aboard Captain Hakem's vessel. Young Thomas was sent aboard the xebec commanded by Admiral el-Mediouni, along with his other three fellow shipmates. The Salé captains, realising that they had not enough space aboard their vessels to accommodate all of their captives, decided to place some of the Englishmen on board those they had seized. These were then despatched to Salé with a prize crew.

In the hope of capturing yet more ships, they spent the next month 'in looking sharp out after other prey, and examining into the value of our cargoes'. Although they failed to repeat their spell of good fortune, other Salé xebecs met with continued success. Many of the English vessels that had put to sea in 1715 found themselves ransacked by the corsairs. Captain John Stocker's ship, the *Sarah*, was captured at the end of March. Her fifteen crew members were seized and carted back to Salé. The *Endeavour* of Topsham was taken on the same day. Her nine-strong crew, which included a young boy, were also taken captive. Other seized vessels included the *Union* of Plymouth and the Hull-registered *Rebecca and Mary*.

Many of the colonial American merchants who had put to sea soon wished they had stayed at home too. Captain Benjamin Church's ship, the *Prosperous* from New England, was seized in the spring of 1716, just a few months before the *Francis*. Shortly after, the Salé corsairs captured a more profitable prize, the *Princes*, also from New England. All the crew members of these vessels would later meet – and become comrades in adversity – in the dreaded slave pens of Meknes.

Captain Hakem and Admiral el-Mediouni eventually tired of roaming the empty Atlantic. 'Seeing no likelihood of any more prizes, and their provision growing short, they followed the prizes and found them safe at anchor on the outside of the bar at Salé.' This shifting bank of sand, created by silt carried downstream by the Bou Regreg river, was extremely hazardous, especially for inbound vessels laden with cargo. Yet it also provided Salé with a natural defence from the sea and had long hampered large-scale military operations against the corsairs. Large craft were unable to enter Salé's harbour, and even smaller xebecs – like Captain Hakem's ship – were obliged to wait for high tide before they could nudge over the bar.

While the two captains waited for the tide to turn, they congratulated themselves on their good fortune. Knowing that Moulay Ismail would be delighted with the season's haul of slaves, they looked forward to receiving payment for their human catch. But the two men soon had a rude awakening. At about noon, '[they] were all on a sudden in an extreme hurry on their discovery of a sail standing right in from sea upon them'. According to Thomas Pellow, the captains feared that it was commanded by Captain Delgarno, 'who they knew then commanded a British man of war of 20 guns'.

The British captives could scarcely believe their unexpected good fortune. If this was indeed Delgarno, then his timely arrival presented them with a very real hope of rescue. The captain had made a name for himself by successfully attacking vessels belonging to the Barbary corsairs. Over the previous months he had seized two such ships. One had been taken in triumph to the British naval base at Gibraltar. The other had been shot to pieces and had sunk in the deep waters of Cape Cantin. It was now a race against the tide to see if the British captain could prime his guns and disable the Salé xebecs before the corsairs managed to reach the harbour.

The two corsair commanders acted with characteristic swiftness, trusting that the incoming tide was sufficiently advanced to allow them passage into the harbour. In this they were sorely mistaken. 'Medune weighing his anchor, and Ali Hakim slipping his cable,' wrote Pellow, 'they ran both aground on the bar.'

What happened next is not altogether clear. According to Salé's French consul, Monsieur le Magdeleine, who watched the scene from the distant shoreline, the corsair xebecs were smashed to pieces by the wind and waves. Thomas Pellow tells a rather different story. He says that the British ship – whose identity was never confirmed – began to close in on the stricken vessels with the clear intention of trying to sink them.

As the attacking ship neared the xebecs, the captain opened fire with the heaviest weaponry, 'some of his shot flying about them . . . [and some] far beyond them, insomuch that they were both . . . soon beat to pieces'. As the wind increased in velocity and the blustery squall developed into a spectacular storm, huge breakers began crashing over the sandy bar. The full force of the sea was now unleashed on the fractured xebecs, plucking at their timbers and steadily wrenching them apart. Their end was not long in coming. They spectacularly broke their backs and, as the foaming waters sluiced into their holds, the crews and prisoners were forced to swim for their lives.

'But for my part,' wrote Pellow, 'I could swim but very little, and which, had I attempted, the merciless sea must have overwhelmed me.' In his desperation, he begged his crewmate, Lewis Davies, to help. But Davies shook his head sadly, telling Thomas 'that all his strength was highly necessary towards his own preservation; and that should he take me on his back, it would in all likelihood lose both our lives'.

Pellow was still clinging to the wreck – with all hope almost gone – when a tremendous wave brought down the ship's mast. Realising that this was his last hope of saving himself, he leaped into the water and lunged for the mast. As he flailed about in the choppy waves, he was spotted by a lookout and was 'taken by some people in a boat from the shore'. Half drowned and trembling in terror, he watched in amazement as the Moorish crew swam calmly ashore. '[They] were under no apprehension of danger from the sea,' he wrote, 'leaping into it and swimming to shore like so many dogs.' His crewmates had also done well to save themselves. All of the men from the three captured ships managed to struggle through the breakers to safety, where they were picked up by agents working for the corsairs. As they sat on the foreshore recovering from their ordeal, they saw the British vessel slip quietly out to sea. Within minutes, she was little more than a shadow in the dense sea mist.

Thomas Pellow's first glimpse of Salé in the summer of 1716 revealed a town originally built for defence. Over the previous decades, each side of the river estuary had been enclosed by stout battlements, and the two castles were bristling with weaponry. There were also gun emplacements mounted on the rocky shoreline, providing defence against any enemy ships attempting to enter the harbour. Towers and minarets poked above the ramparts, and in places there were orchards and vegetable gardens that stretched down almost to the sea. When the orange and lemon trees were in blossom, Salé looked quite enchanting.

Yet the great wealth enjoyed by the slave traders and corsairs was rarely apparent to newly arrived captives. Although vast sums of money were lavished on the opulent interiors of the merchants' houses, the streets and alleys were filthy and half engulfed by rubbish. When the Frenchman, Germain Mouette, was taken there as a slave in the early years of Moulay Ismail's reign, he was disgusted to find that the city walls were used as a public latrine. 'There are many heaps of dung and earth as high as they,' he wrote, 'which would render the entrance very easy.' Others found the souks dirty and claustrophobic, and 'so narrow that a cart can scarce pass through them'. Many buildings appeared to be on the verge of collapse, and even the town defences were said to be in a pitiful state of disrepair. The walls were 'demolished and broken down in a great many places', according to one English witness, who concluded that ''tis a place of no great strength'.

Captain John Pellow, his young nephew and the other captives now had their first taste of life as slaves. It was a custom, throughout Barbary, for a large iron ring to be riveted to the ankle of each new arrival. In Algiers, these rings weighed one and a half pounds and were attached to a long chain, which the slave was obliged to drag behind him. The Salé slave traders often imposed far harsher conditions. One English slave said that his captor 'gave order that shackles should be made for each slave, weighing fifty pound weight'.

The captives were also ceremoniously marched through the town on their first arrival, so that the locals could curse them and offer degrading and hostile treatment. When the English captive, George Elliot, had been first brought ashore, he was surrounded by 'several hundreds of idle, rascally people and roguish boys'. As they lunged at him and made 'horrod, barbarous shouts', Elliot and his comrades were 'forced like a drove of sheep through the several streets'.

For Thomas Pellow, the experience of this public humiliation was extremely frightening. 'It may easily be imagined what sad terror and apprehension I was under in so dangerous a situation,' he later wrote; '. . . I could see nothing else by being delivered from death than the more grievous torments in my becoming a slave.' He and his crewmates were still in shock from the disaster they had suffered at sea; now, in a 'very low and feeble condition', they were led to the infamous *matamores*.

The matamores were underground cells, which each accommodated some fifteen or twenty slaves. The only light and ventilation came from a small iron grate in the roof; in winter, rain poured through this opening and flooded the floor. The grate provided the only access to the outside world. On the rare occasions when slaves were allowed out, a rope was suspended from the iron bars and they had to clamber up, using muscles that had often not been exercised for many weeks. But the luxury of fresh air was rare indeed. For weeks on end – until the next slave auction – the pitiful captives were held underground in overcrowded and unsanitary conditions.

Many slaves left accounts of these horrendous places, but only one – written by Germain Mouette – charts the full horror of life in this subterranean hell. The largest of Salé's subterranean dungeons, which was often used for the most recently arrived captives, was supported by brick pillars. It was so deep in the earth that water and sewage frequently bubbled up from the mud floor in the wet winter months. 'In this, the Christians for the most part cannot lye on the ground as they do in the others,' wrote Mouette, 'because there is water in it knee deep, six months in the year.' To avoid getting soaked, 'they make a sort of hammocks, or beds of ropes, hanging by great nails one above another, in such manner, that the lowermost almost touch the water with their backs.' All too often, the topmost hammock would come crashing down, 'and then he and all under him certainly fall into the water where they must continue the rest of the night'.

Although the smaller dungeons were not so deep in the earth, they were overcrowded and extremely claustrophobic. Mouette said that there was so little room in the cells that the captives were forced to lie in a circle with their feet meeting in the middle. 'There is no more space left,' he wrote, 'than to hold an earthen vessel to ease themselves in.'

The arrival of Captain Pellow and his men coincided with the worst of the summer humidity, which covered the rush matting they were given as bedding with a thick layer of mould. According to Mouette, these mats had 'such a noisome scent caus'd by the dampnes of the earth that the place becomes intolerable when all the slaves are in, and it grows warm'. The smallest of the matamores were usually 'filthy, stinking and full of vermin', and death was all too often a blessed release.

Thomas Pellow was led to one of these small matamores, where he was locked up with three of his shipmates – Lewis Davies, Thomas Goodman and Briant Clark – as well as with twenty-six men from the *George* and the *Southwark*. They were soon joined by seventeen French captives, who had also been seized at sea, and a group of slaves from elsewhere in Europe. 'For three days,' wrote Pellow, '[we were] closely shut up there, and our allowance by the Moors nothing but bread and water.' The men were extremely fortunate that a few European merchants – who had been granted exceptional permission to trade in Salé – brought other food, 'which was to us, in our so weak and disconsolate condition, of very great service'.

Tired, hungry and clothed in rags still stiff with sea salt, the men stood in fear of the day when they would be hauled from their cell and put up for sale. Salé's slave market had traditionally been the largest and most profitable on Morocco's Atlantic coast. Like its counterparts in Algiers, Tunis and Tripoli, it did a brisk trade in European slaves, many of whom were pounced on by dealers and later sold elsewhere. In each of the auctions, the overriding goal of the corsairs was to make as much money as possible out of their miserable captives. The fittest men and most beautiful women were eagerly snapped up by private buyers. The old and the sick, who were almost valueless, were sold for a pittance and spent the few months that they survived doing hard labour.

Salé had two slave markets, one on the north bank of the river – now the town's principal souk – and one on the south. Of the latter market, which was held in the shadow of the magnificent Oudaia Gate, not a trace remains. A gnarled tree spreads shade over the broken ground where slaves once stood in chains, and a whitewashed *koubba*, or domed sanctuary, marks the shrine of a holy marabout. It requires a leap of imagination to picture the scene as it was some three centuries ago.

Testimonies of slaves held throughout North Africa reveal a trade that was brutal and devoid of any moral scruples. In the days that preceded the auction, the strongest men often found themselves being treated to unusually generous rations. Abraham Browne was fed 'fresh vitteles once a daye and sometimes twice in abondance, with good white breade from the market place'. He rightly suspected that the bread was 'to feed us up for the markett, [so] that wee might be in some good plight agaynst the day wee weare to be sold'. As the sun rose on the day of the auction, the slaves were released from their dungeons and taken to the market place. 'We were driven like beasts thither and exposed to sale,' wrote William Okeley, who was auctioned at Algiers. 'Their cruelty is great, but their covetousness exceeds their cruelty.'

Just a few days earlier, these men had been masters of their own destinies. Now, they were stripped and put through their paces. They were made to jump and skip to test their agility; they had foreign fingers poked into mouths and ears. The experience of being auctioned was both terrifying and humiliating, and every individual had his own tale of suffering. George Elliot had been distressed by the way in which he was jostled through the crowd of dealers. He was chained to a black slave-driver, who 'coursed me up and down, from one person to another'. Joseph Pitts was appalled to discover that the dealers in Algiers had a sales patter that was similar to that of the traders peddling onions and aubergines in the weekly vegetable market. '"Behold what a strong man this is! What limbs he has! He is fit for any work. And see what a pretty boy this is! No doubt his parents are very rich and able to redeem him with a great ransom."'

Most of the slave dealers were keen to examine the teeth of their captives. 'Their first policy is to look in their mouths,' wrote Okeley, 'and a good, strong set of grinders will advance the price considerably.' There was a clear, if disturbing, logic to their interest in teeth: 'they [know] that they who have not teeth cannot eat; and that they that cannot eat, cannot work; and they that cannot work, are not for their turn; and they that are not for their turn, are not for their money.'

Once the slave dealer had satisfied himself that the slave was in good physical shape, he would make an offer. Prices varied enormously and were largely dependent upon the age and fitness of the slave. But family background also played a role, for many dealers bought slaves in the hope that they came from a rich family and could be ransomed for a large sum. Browne records that the common seamen on board his ship changed hands for between £30 and £35, while the two boys 'weare sold for £40 apice'. Browne himself was judged to be worth a mere £15 – 'a very low rate' – although that price rose dramatically during the course of the slave auction. 'Some Jews rise me up to 75£,' he wrote, 'which was the price my paterone [owner] gave for mee.'

Captain Pellow and his men feared much the same fate, for they were all too familiar with stories of slaves being bought and sold in Barbary. In the years prior to the capture of the *Francis*, there had been a flurry of publications written by escaped slaves, and many had enjoyed a wide circulation. William Okeley, Thomas Phelps and Joseph Pitts had all published long and fascinating accounts of their years in slavery, while many other stories circulated in the dockside taverns of the West Country. What the newly captured men probably did not realise was that the great slave market at Salé had become a thing of the past. While the auctions remained a regular fixture in Algiers, Tunis and Tripoli, the Salé market had undergone great changes since Moulay Ismail had acceded to the throne. One of his first acts had been to close the market – not out of charity or human kindness, but because he wished to keep all the slaves for himself. All recently seized men, women and children were taken from Salé to Meknes, where they were presented with all due pomp to their new owner, the sultan of Morocco.

This is what happened to the survivors captured from the *Francis*, the *George* and the *Southwark*. After four days of misery in Salé's underground matamores, 'we were all, in number fifty-two, taken out thence and sent prisoners to Meknes.' The men were fearful of the long walk, for many had lost their footwear, and their clothes were in tatters. But they were treated unusually well on the 120-mile trek to the imperial capital, 'some being put on mules,' wrote Thomas Pellow, 'some on asses, and some on horses; on one of which my uncle and I were mounted together'.

Their journey took them first through the ancient forest of Salé. Thomas Pellow would later remember it as being 'plentifully stored with most stately timber trees, of oaks, and vast quantities of wild hogs, lions, tigers [leopards] and many other dangerous creatures'. The forest was so dense that those who were ignorant of its tracks would hesitate to enter; whenever the sultan's tax collectors came to the region, the local merchants would disappear into the unmapped interior, safe in the knowledge that they would never be found.

Guided by Captain Hakem and Admiral el-Mediouni, Captain Pellow and his men passed safely through the forest and continued with their odyssey, 'all the way lodging in tents, as being in that parts of the country the only habitations'. The local peasant farmers resented the presence of Christians on their land and often made their grievance known. According to Father Dominique Busnot, who had travelled the same road a few years earlier: 'as soon as we were gone, they burnt branches of white osiers . . . and set up great cries, to purify the place.'

On the second day of their march, the men crossed the River Tiflit and pushed on towards Dar Oumm es-Soltan. By their fourth day on the road, the weary men at last came within sight of the imperial capital of Meknes.

'At our arrival to the city,' wrote Pellow, 'or rather indeed a mile before we reached it, we were commanded to get off our beasts.' All of the men were ordered to take off their shoes, 'that is to say, as many of us as had any', and they were told to put on yellow pumps 'which were brought to us by the Moors for that purpose'.

Hitherto, the men had been reasonably well treated. Captain Hakem and Admiral el-Mediouni hoped to impress the sultan with their latest catch and wanted their captives in the best possible condition. Pellow's account contains none of the usual complaints about paltry rations and brackish water, nor were his comrades beaten during the enforced march to Meknes. But the men knew they were unlikely to meet with friendly treatment once they passed through the city gates, for it was customary for captured Christians to be jostled and even assaulted on entering Meknes.

As the sun rose spectacularly over the city's eastern ramparts and the men were led through the principal gate, they were tormented by jeering, hostile Moors. 'We were met and surrounded by vast crowds of them,' wrote Pellow, 'offering us the most vile insults.' As word of their arrival spread through the souks, more and more people flocked to the city gate in order to mock the hated Christians. They surged towards the frightened captives and tried to beat them with sticks and batons. 'They could scarcely be restrained from knocking us on the head,' wrote Pellow, '. . . [and] they certainly would have done had not the Emperor's guards interposed.'

The guards pushed back some of the rowdiest elements in the mob, but allowed several aggressive men to throw punches and lash out at Captain Pellow and his men. 'They would not hinder them from pulling our hair and giving us many severe boxes,' wrote Thomas Pellow, 'calling us *Caffer Billa Oarosole* [*kafer billah wa bi er-rasul*] which signified in English that we were hereticks and knew neither God nor Mahomet.' After a few terrifying minutes of abuse and violence, the men were whisked inside the imperial palace compound, which the crowd was forbidden to enter. Here, 'before we entered, we were obliged to take off our pumps.'

The captives were relieved that they no longer had to face the baying hordes outside but soon learned that they were about to experience something far more terrifying. That very morning – shortly after eight o'clock – the men were to be ushered into the presence of the sultan.

Moulay Ismail, the fearsome ruler of Morocco, wished to view his newly captured slaves.

4 Pellow's Torments

Moulay Ismail woke at the first cockcrow. He was a light sleeper, easily disturbed by noises outside the palace compound. Thomas Pellow would later note that he was also troubled by terrible dreams. 'Whether [this was] from his natural disposition, or the horror of the many murders, exactions and cruelties he had committed on his poor subjects and slaves, I cannot determine.'

The sultan's first act on waking was to go to prayer. Once his oblations were complete, he would embark on a daily inspection tour of the building works. These were spread over such a large area that they could not possibly be visited on foot. Moulay Ismail would therefore travel around on horseback, or in the chariot pulled by his wives and eunuchs. According to Pellow, he conducted courtly business while he was doing the rounds of his domain. 'He gave audiences to ambassadors, conversed sometimes sitting on the corner of the wall, walked often and sometimes worked.'

Having grown to love the pomp and trappings of power, Moulay Ismail delighted in the choreographed ritual of courtly life. He was accompanied by a personal bodyguard of twenty or thirty statuesque black slaves. These highly trained guards were armed with polished scimitars and firearms, which were kept drawn and cocked in case any attempt was made on the sultan's life.

It was also customary for two young blacks to be posted behind the sultan, one of whom held a parasol over his head to shade him from the sun. The parasol was kept twirling continually, in order to deter flies from settling on his sacred skin. In addition Moulay Ismail was flanked by another phalanx of ceremonial guards, called *msakhkharim*. These boys, between twelve and fifteen years of age, who had tonsured heads and wore white woollen robes, also served as bodyguards.

The sultan's imperial courtiers had learned through experience to treat Moulay Ismail with wary respect and approached with trepidation whenever they were summoned to an audience. 'They pull off their shoes,' wrote Pellow, 'put on a particular habit they have to denote a slave, and when they approach him [they] fall down and kiss the ground at his horses feet.' Whenever his kaids met him while he was touring the palace, they would immediately fling themselves into the dirt. Trembling with fear, they would remain prostrate until he had disappeared from view.

They had good reason to be frightened, for the sultan showed great contempt towards his kaids and courtiers. 'He treats all that belong to his empire not as free subjects, but as slaves,' wrote the French padre, Father Busnot. '[He] thinks himself absolute master of their lives, as well as their fortunes, and to have a right to kill them only for his pleasure, and to sacrifice them to his honour.'

This particular morning had begun with the usual routine. Moulay Ismail made his customary dawn tour of the palace works, and his courtiers fell to the floor in obeisance. But at some point during his inspection – probably at about seven o'clock – Moulay Ismail was brought news of the arrival of the crews of the *Francis*, the *George* and the *Southwark*. When he heard that they were assembled in the ceremonial parade ground close to the inner walls of the palace, he immediately set off to view them.

Thomas Pellow and his companions were hungry and frightened as they were lined up inside the imperial compound. They were still dressed in the filthy rags that they had been wearing for many months and had not been able wash since their desperate swim through the surf. The ill treatment to which they had been subjected on their arrival in Meknes had been a cause of considerable alarm. Now, stripped of their shoes and their dignity, they feared a far worse fate at the hands of the tyrannical sultan.

The men had been conducted into the palace by Captain Hakem and Admiral el-Mediouni. As they were led through the two inner gateways, they gazed in disbelief at the monumental agglomeration of gilded domes, mosques and pleasure palaces. Meknes palace was heavily fortified and 'prodigious strong', according to Pellow, who estimated that the battlements alone were 'twelve feet thick and five stories high'. The first block of palaces was larger than anything the men had ever seen, yet they could clearly see that the site stretched far into the distance. Much was still under construction, and there were scores of half-built walls and towers, which swarmed with a mass of ragged, half-starved humanity.

The men were led through yet another ceremonial gateway and found themselves in a large processional square. It was here, in the shadow of an exquisitely tiled pavilion, that Moulay Ismail's black bodyguards were accustomed to march, drill and engage in audacious feats of arms. It was here, too, that the sultan watched tournaments and fantasias, in which his crack horsemen – decked in bejewelled costumes – would chase each other through the dust, firing at targets as they rode.

Captain Pellow and his men were instructed to form a line in the sun and await the entrance of the sultan. They had heard many rumours about Moulay Ismail, yet nothing could quite prepare them for their first audience. The self-styled Prince of the Faithful and Overcoming in God cut an extraordinary figure, quite different from the copperplate engravings later produced in Europe. With his elfish chin, aquiline nose and spectacular forked beard, he had the air of an Old Testament prophet.

'His face [was] oval, his cheeks hollow, as well as his eyes, which are black and sparkling.' So wrote the French ambassador, Pidou de St Olon, when he met the sultan in the 1690s. He added that his pointed chin looked quite bizarre when set against his plump, fleshy lips.

On great state occasions, the sultan wrapped himself in fabulous silks and damasks, cutting a most resplendent figure. He liked to wear a voluminous silk turban, which was held in place by a sparkling jewel. His waist-length cloak, too, was quite spectacular, 'wrought all over with silver and gold', according to the British slave, Francis Brooks. It was left open at the neck to reveal a baggy undershirt 'with sleeves so large that will make any ordinary man a pair of drawers'. Moulay Ismail also wore elegant stockings with a flamboyant design that matched his breeches and bright red riding boots.

Although the sultan enjoyed the reputation of being a dandy, he did not always dress with such panache. He was notoriously unpredictable and occasionally appeared at the palace works in dishevelled rags. When Pidou de St Olon had first met him, he resembled the unkempt marabouts whose company the sultan so enjoyed. 'His face was muffled up in a snuff handkerchief, of a dirty hue, his arms and legs bare, sitting without matt or carpet.' On another occasion, the sultan invited the ambassador to an audience in his stables, 'with his clothes and right arm all imbru'd with the blood of two of his chief blacks, whom he had just butcher'd with a knife'.

Few foreigners realised that the colour of the sultan's clothes was an indicator of his mood and temperament. Father Busnot was the first to remark upon this disturbing feature. 'The passion that prevails on him may be seen by the colour of his garments,' he wrote. 'Green is his darling colour, which is a good omen for those that come to him.' But if he was wearing yellow, even his closest courtiers prepared themselves for an outburst of violence. 'When he wears yellow,' wrote Busnot, 'all men quake and avoid his presence; for that is the colour he puts on when he designs soe bloody executions.' Such attention to detail on the part of the sultan provides a chilling insight into the manner of his rule. Fear was his instrument of control, and he terrified his courtiers with capricious outbursts and acts of extreme violence. These appeared random to most European visitors, but Busnot's observation suggests that every action of the sultan – every word and deed, down to the colour of his cloak – was designed to keep total control over his often unruly subjects.

Moulay Ismail was in fine fettle on this particular morning – the colour of his dress is nowhere recorded – and was delighted by the arrival of so many new slaves. Captain Hakem had thrown himself into the dirt when the sultan first entered the parade ground. Now, he was ordered to his feet and greeted warmly by Moulay Ismail. '[He] received us from the hands of the Salleeteens,' wrote Pellow, 'giving Ali Hakem, in exchange for every one of us, fifty ducats.' This was a very low price for the corsairs, about £15 per slave, considerably less than the Salé pirates had been accustomed to receive from dealers in the years before the closure of the great slave market.

Captain Hakem had enough experience of the wily old sultan to know that any expression of dissatisfaction would be extremely unwise. He also knew that it would be foolish to pocket all of the money. 'Out of this was paid back again one-third, and a tenth as customary tribute.' The sultan was satisfied by this display of deference on the part of his corsair captain and turned towards Admiral el-Mediouni, ready to receive the second batch of captives. The admiral stepped forward in order to accept payment for his slaves, but there was something in his demeanour that caused a dramatic change in the sultan's humour. The British captives were uncertain as to how the admiral managed to offend Moulay Ismail, but what happened next sent a chill through all the men standing in the palace courtyard. The sultan unsheathed his huge sword and swung the polished blade through the air. Admiral el-Mediouni was decapitated on the spot.

The men were appalled by this gruesome display, and it was only much later that Thomas Pellow was told that the admiral had been executed for failing to attack the British vessel in the waters off the coast of Salé. 'For not fighting Delgarno,' wrote Pellow wryly, '[el-Mediouni] had the extraordinary favour bestowed upon him of losing his head.'

The execution also provided Moulay Ismail with the opportunity to demonstrate his physical prowess. Although he was seventy years old when Captain Pellow and his men first met him, he was as strong and energetic as a young antelope. 'Age does not seem to have lessen'd anything either of his courage, strength or activity,' noted Busnot just a few years earlier, '[and] he vaults upon anything he can lay his hand on.' He was always keen to show his dexterity with a sword, and the French padre had been as shocked as the British slaves to discover that 'it is one of his common diversions, at one motion, to mount his horse, draw his cimiter, and cut off the head of the slave who holds his stirrup.'

Moulay Ismail had received a large number of British and colonial American captives over the previous months, but he was nevertheless delighted by this new band of slaves. There were fifty-two in total, including three captains and two boys, and all were in good physical shape. This gave the sultan particular satisfaction, for each of these men represented an additional fifteen hours of hard labour per day.

He paused as he walked past Thomas Pellow, then ordered him to step to one side. Richard Ferris, James Waller and Thomas Newgent were also instructed to join the young Cornish lad, along with three more whose names Pellow does not record. When the sultan seemed satisfied that he had chosen all that

Salé's corsairs attacked with overwhelming firepower, before boarding enemy vessels. 'With their heads shaved and armes almost naked, they did teryfie me exceedingly,' wrote one captive.

Tangier's English officers wore outlandish uniforms which made them easy targets for Moroccan sharpshooters.

Kaid Muhammad ben Haddu Ottur led an embassy to London in 1681. He treated his European slaves with contempt, greeting them with 'God, roast your father.'

Slaves were marched inland to Meknes. Those who died en route were decapitated; survivors were forced to carry the heads as proof that they hadn't escaped. The slaves pictured here are British.

The weekly slave market terrified new captives. The fittest men were fattened with extra rations in the days preceding their sale.

Slaves were poked, prodded and subjected to a cheeky sales patter. 'Behold what a strong man this is! What limbs he has!'

Slaves were housed in matamores, or underground dungeons, that were 'filthy, stinking and full of vermin'. Captives wore chains around one ankle.

Sultan Moulay Ismail demanded absolute deference from both subjects and slaves. Anyone granted an audience had to fling himself into the dust at the sultan's approach.

I shall give you a small
Account of Our Sufferings here In Slavery: We
have been forced to draw Carts of Lead with Ropes
about Our Shoulders all one as horses, & further
We have Carry'd Great Barrs of Iron upon Our
Shoulders as big as we could well get up, & up to
our knees in dirt, & as slippery that we could
hardly goe without the Load: we have not had a bitt
of bread allowed us for Eight days togeather, but
What We have gone from Dore to dore a beging
of other Christian Slaves, & as for our Lodging it is
on the cold Ground, I have not had a shirt on my
back these 8 months & God knows When I shall. I

A few slaves wrote letters to their loved ones, detailing the sufferings they endured. This letter, written by John Willdon in 1716, reveals that he was harnessed like a horse and forced to pull carts of lead.

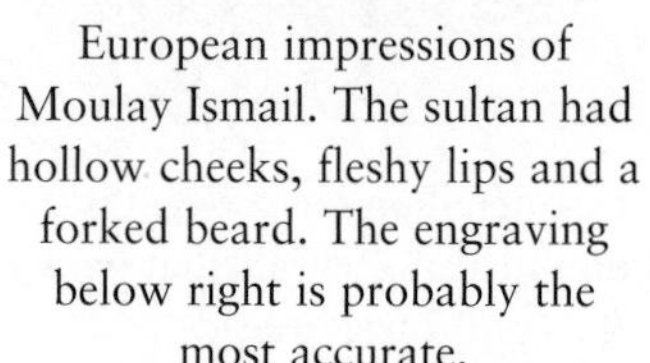

European impressions of Moulay Ismail. The sultan had hollow cheeks, fleshy lips and a forked beard. The engraving below right is probably the most accurate.

Slaves endured fifteen hours' hard labour each day. Their gruelling tasks included cutting stone and mixing pisé, an earth-and-lime cement.

Slaves were treated with great cruelty and public executions were commonplace.

The sultan's black guards were absolute masters of the European slaves. Reared from childhood in special schools, they were haughty and fiercely loyal.

Torture of slaves was commonplace. The bastinado (bottom right) was widely practised. The slave was held down and the soles of his feet were beaten until raw.

he needed, he instructed his black guards to take away the rest of the slaves. Pellow watched in fear and alarm as his uncle and the others were led out through the palace gateway. It would be several weeks before he received any news of them.

He and the other six were also placed under the command of a black guard. They were then marched across the courtyard and escorted to a large door that opened on to an underground passage. This, in turn, led into a storehouse called the Koubbat el-Khayyatin, a subterranean labyrinth 'where the tailors work and the armoury is kept'. Built on an impressive scale, it contained enough military hardware to equip the sultan's 150,000-strong standing army. A later English visitor described it as being 'near a quarter of a mile long' and filled with 'great quantities of arms in cases'.

Thomas Pellow and the others were 'directly employed in cleaning the arms'. Moulay Ismail was immensely proud of his arsenal, much of which had been pillaged from captured Christian vessels, and demanded that every pike and musket be kept in immaculate condition. From dawn till dusk, Pellow and his comrades worked alongside hundreds of other European slaves employed in repairing weaponry and cleaning gunlocks. The work was carried out in near-darkness, for the only light came from tiny holes that perforated the great vaulted ceiling.

Pellow was not kept in the armoury for long. Just a short time after he had been sent there, a guard arrived and ordered him to lay down his tools. 'I was taken out of the armoury,' he later wrote, 'and was given by the emperor to Muley Spha, one of his favourite sons.'

This was the worst possible news. Moulay es-Sfa was a most unsavoury individual who displayed a sneering contempt towards his European slaves. It is not clear as to why he selected young Pellow to join his household, for he had no need for any more slaves. Pellow was given futile tasks to perform, 'run[ning] from morning to night after his horse's heels'.

Moulay es-Sfa kept a close eye on his new captive and soon realised that he was an uncommonly bright young lad. Instead of beating him, as was his custom, he amused himself by trying to convince Pellow to convert to Islam. 'He often prompted me to turn Moor,' noted young Thomas, 'and told me, if I would, I should have a very fine horse to ride on and I should live like one of his esteemed friends.' But Pellow steadfastly refused to consider converting to Islam. He had been brought up in the Protestant faith of his forefathers and abhorred the idea of apostasy, even at the promise of better treatment.

Moulay es-Sfa grew irritated by Pellow's stubbornness and offered him bribes in return for his conversion. But still his young slave refused to countenance the idea and told him so quite bluntly. 'I used to reply that as that was the only command wherein I could not readily gratify him, I humbly hoped that he would be pleased, of his great goodness, to suspend all future thought that way.' He added that he was 'thoroughly resolved not to renounce my Christian faith' and said that he would continue to resist his pleas, 'be the consequence what it would'.

Pellow's obstinacy needled Moulay es-Sfa, who was accustomed to being obeyed by his slaves. One day, after Pellow had once again refused to convert, Moulay es-Sfa decided to punish his recalcitrant captive. '"Then", said he, in a most furious and haughty manner, "prepare yourself for such torture as shall be inflicted on you, and the nature of your obstinacy deserves."' Suddenly fearing for his safety, Pellow begged to be spared a beating. When Moulay es-Sfa dismissed his pleas with a contemptuous sneer, Pellow entreated him, 'on my knees, not to let loose his rage on a poor, helpless, innocent creature'. But Moulay es-Sfa had lost all patience with this pertinacious Cornish ship boy and relished the opportunity to make him suffer for his faith. 'Without making any further reply,' wrote Pellow, '[he] committed me prisoner to one of his own rooms, keeping me there several months in irons, and every day most severely bastinading me.'

This punishment, used widely throughout Barbary, inflicted terrible pain. Almost every surviving slave account mentions it, and there were very few captives who avoided a bastinading. The ankles of the condemned slave were strapped together with rope, and he was suspended upside down so that his neck and shoulders were just resting on the ground. 'Then comes another lusty, sturdy knave,' wrote William Okeley, a British captive in Algiers, 'and gives him as many violent blows on the soles of the feet as the council shall order.' Slaves elsewhere in North Africa were accustomed to receive forty or fifty blows; in Morocco, they were often given many more. On one occasion, Moulay Ismail ordered two slaves to be given 500 bastinadoes each. '[This] put the hip of one of them out,' wrote Father Busnot, who was a witness to the event, 'but it was set again some time after by the violent operation of a second bastinado.'

Pellow's beatings were brutal affairs. They were personally administered by Moulay es-Sfa, who took delight in thrashing him senseless. He would work himself into a terrible rage, 'furiously screaming in the Moorish language, "Shehed, shehed! Cunmoora, Cunmoora! In English, Turn Moor! Turn Moor," by holding your finger'. This simple signal – raising one finger to the sky – was all that was required by Christian slaves to show that they agreed to apostatise. To many Muslims, it was a signal that they denied the Holy Trinity.

For week after week, Moulay es-Sfa tormented his young slave, beating him until his skin was bruised and welted. 'Now is my accursed master still more and more enraged,' wrote Pellow, 'and my tortures daily increasing.' He was denied food for days on end. Then, when he was eventually allowed to eat, he was given only bread and water. 'I was,' wrote Pellow, 'through my severe scourging, and such hard fare, every day in expectation of its being my last.' After months of abuse, the prospect of death no longer frightened him. 'I should certainly then have dy'd a martyr, and probably thereby gained a glorious crown in the kingdom of heaven.'

Moulay es-Sfa's treatment of Pellow – and his desire to secure his conversion to Islam – was not unusual. Throughout Barbary, there were slave owners who pressurised their slaves into renouncing Christianity and adopting the religion of their new land. They paid particular attention to their younger captives and gained great kudos from owning slave converts, particularly if they were masons, blacksmiths or professional soldiers.

Pellow was unfortunate in having a slave master who was determined to achieve his conversion to Islam, even if it resulted in his death. 'My tortures were now exceedingly increased,' he wrote, 'burning my flesh off my bones by fire, which the tyrant did, by frequent repetitions, after a most cruel manner.' After months of ill treatment, young Thomas Pellow was unable to endure any more pain. Battered and half starved, his spirit was as broken as his wretched body. When Moulay es-Sfa next came to torment the lad, Pellow broke down in tears. 'I was at last constrained to submit,' he wrote, 'calling upon God to forgive me, who knows that I never gave up the consent of the heart.'

Pellow would always protest that he had converted under duress and that he had not wished to abjure his Christian faith. Yet he surely knew that this event marked a turning point in his life. In raising his forefinger to the sky, albeit unwillingly, he had forever turned his back on his family, his country and his past. He had also forfeited the right to be redeemed by his home government, who considered those who apostatised to be beneath contempt.

This was something that the Algiers slave, Joseph Pitts, had discovered to his cost. 'You must know,' he wrote, 'that when a Christian slave turns Mohammetan, there can be no ransom for him.' Nor was he likely to be set free by his owner, as many converts wrongly assumed. ''Tis an error among some,' continued Pitts, '. . . that as soon as ever a Christian turns

Turk, he [thinks he will be] emancipated or become free.' He said it was extremely rare for slave converts to be released. 'I have known some that have continued slaves many years after they have turned Turks,' he wrote, 'nay some, even to their dying day.' Very few were treated with any respect after converting to Islam; Pitts cited his own case as an example and a warning. '[I] suffered a great deal of cruel usage,' he wrote, 'and was then sold again.'

It was nevertheless common for slave converts to be accorded much pageantry on the day of their apostasy. Germain Mouette describes how in Morocco they were 'walk'd about the town on horseback in triumphant manner, with the noise of drums and trumpets'. In Algiers, and elsewhere in North Africa, such ceremonies were even more extravagant. The new convert was given splendid new clothes and loaned a finely caparisoned horse. 'He is also richly habited and hath a turbant on his head,' wrote Pitts.

He was then marched around the city accompanied by stewards and sergeants. These held 'naked swords in their hands, intimating thereby . . . that if he [the convert] should repent, and show the least inclination of retracting what he had declared . . . he deserved to be cut in pieces'. Some slave converts reported having to perform a humiliating renunciation of Christianity before the ceremonies were over. They were made to 'throw a dart to the picture of Jesus Christ in token of disowning him as the saviour of the world'.

Thomas Pellow's apostasy had been made under duress, depriving him of any right to such pageantry. The only tangible sign that he had converted was his enforced circumcision, a humiliating and painful operation that was often performed in public. Father Pierre Dan was the first to write about such surgery – more than eighty years earlier – informing his readers that in Algiers the surgeon 'cuts the foreskin of the unfortunate renegade in the presence of everyone'. He added that unlike the

Jews, who 'only cut a little bit of the skin of the foreskin', the Barbary Muslims were prone to 'cut it entirely, which is extremely painful'.

The operation was usually a botched affair and a cause of such loss of blood that the convert was obliged to take to his bed for several weeks. Only when fully recovered did he get to enjoy the Muslim slave woman he was invariably given as a wife.

Moulay es-Sfa continued to beat Thomas Pellow as he was recovering from his circumcision, in punishment for his refusal to wear Moroccan dress. 'I was kept forty days longer in prison,' wrote Pellow, 'on my refusing to put on the Moorish habit.' When fresh beatings opened old sores, he decided that his 'very foolish obstinacy' was futile. 'Rather than undergo fresh torments, I also complied with it [the dress], appearing like a Mahometan.' His head was shaved, his old clothes were taken away and he was given a long woollen djellaba.

News of Pellow's conversion eventually reached Moulay Ismail, who was always delighted to hear of slaves who had abjured their Christianity. He ordered him to be released from prison and suggested that Pellow should be 'put to school, to learn the Moorish language and to write Arabic'. But Moulay es-Sfa ignored this request and continued to mistreat his slave, cursing him for remaining a 'Christian dog' and thrashing him at regular intervals. This infuriated the sultan, who summoned Moulay es-Sfa to his palace. Scarcely a word passed between them before Moulay Ismail motioned to his black guard and Moulay es-Sfa was 'instantly despatched, by . . . breaking his neck'. Pellow suggested that this summary execution was punishment for the treatment that Moulay es-Sfa meted out to his slaves, but it is far more likely that the sultan was disgusted by his son's disobedience, which he would have viewed as a direct challenge to his authority. Anyone who refused to defer to Moulay Ismail was in danger of losing his head. Moulay es-Sfa was not the first of the sultan's numerous sons – nor would he be the last – to be killed on an apparent whim.

Sultan Moulay Ismail's slaves came from virtually every corner of Europe. There were Frenchmen and Dutchmen held in Meknes, as well as Greeks, Portuguese and Italians. A few came from Ireland and Scandinavia; some were from as far afield as Russia and Georgia. But the largest group was formed by the sultan's Spanish slaves, which usually numbered several thousand.

These men and women were also the most miserable. Many had been seized more than a decade earlier, and some of the younger captives had spent the greater part of their lives in Meknes. The most wretched of all was the handful of survivors who had been seized during the siege of Mamora. The stories of their capture – which had occurred in 1681, thirty-five years earlier – would haunt all who were brought to Meknes in the summer and autumn of 1716.

The garrison fortress of Mamora had been one of a string of Spanish settlements on the Moroccan coastline. Now known as Mehdiya, it occupied a strategic position on the country's Atlantic shore and also stood guard over the mouth of the River Sbu, which curled inland almost as far as Meknes. The troops posted to Mamora quickly discovered that they were encircled by well-equipped forces who launched constant attacks on their undermanned defences. They were also dependent on Spain for all their military supplies and provisions. Food was on occasion so scant that the soldiers only kept starvation at bay by eating dogs, horses, cats and rats.

In the blinding heat of midsummer, the sluggish river cast a terrible spell over the Spanish garrison. The sticky mudflats provided a breeding ground for swarms of malarial mosquitoes, and disease and sickness lurked in stagnant pools and marshy backwaters. 'The excessive heat renders the air very infectious,' wrote Simon Ockley, 'so that in summertime, 'tis a most unwholesome and pestilential place.'

According to the Mamora survivors, the story of their capture began in the spring of that fatal year. The heatwave had set in unusually early and men had begun to weaken before April had run its course. One member of the Spanish garrison was so fearful of a lingering death in this pestilential hell-hole that he defected to the Moroccans and confirmed to Moulay Ismail 'that most of the garrison was ill and dying of hunger, and with a little effort he could take it'. The sultan acted immediately. He ordered Kaid Omar – still smarting over his defeat by English forces outside Tangier – to head for Mamora with a battalion of crack troops.

Kaid Omar had learned much from his battles against the English. His tactic against Mamora was to break the enemy's spirit with a lightning attack on their outer ring of defences, then to offer the garrison inside the option of surrender or death. He advanced on the town with great swagger. First, 'he forced the spiked palisade which stretched from the city walls to the river banks.' Then, as darkness descended, he succeeded in capturing two of the shore-side towers.

The Moroccan commander knew that the garrison was demoralised and hoped to seize the rest of the town without firing another shot. He sent an extraordinary offer to Mamora's governor, Don Juan Penalosa y Estrada, promising that the Spanish soldiers would not be sold into slavery if they surrendered unconditionally. 'Although they would be captives,' he said, 'they would spend their days without working, until the first redemption.'

It was a shrewd move on the part of the kaid. When the sickly garrison heard they would be treated as prisoners of war, rather than slaves, they agreed with one voice to surrender. The Spanish governor was horrified and urged them to fight, but his remonstrance fell on deaf ears. So did the pleas of the resident monks, who warned the troops not to trust Kaid Omar's promises. They insisted that everyone would be put in chains and would 'either die in the irons of cruel captivity, like those in Meknes, or lose their souls'. The soldiers refused to listen, and the governor was left with no option but to hoist a white flag. Kaid Omar entered the city that same day and reiterated his promise to free all of his captives just as soon as ransom money arrived from Spain.

Moulay Ismail was delighted when he received the news of Kaid Omar's success. He presented the messenger with one hundred gold ducats, then set out with his cavalry for Mamora. The Spanish governor was forced to congratulate the sultan on his military success and suffered the indignity of having to kiss his boots. He then watched in silence as Moulay Ismail entered the citadel in triumph and formally took possession.

Moulay Ismail was amazed by the arsenal of captured weapons, which included eighty-eight bronze cannon, fifteen iron cannon, fire-pots, muskets and gunpowder. 'It was more,' wrote Mouette, 'than he had in the rest of his kingdom.' The sultan prostrated himself and gave thanks to God for his victory. He then sent the Spanish governor to Larache, sixty miles to the north, to inform the garrison that it was his next target.

Moulay Ismail was particularly pleased by the captured Spanish troops and civilians, who included 'fifty poor girls and women'. He saw no reason to honour Omar's promises and had no intention of allowing these 2,000 captives to be redeemed. He needed them for his construction works at Meknes and sent them to the imperial capital. The majority converted to Islam after being brutally beaten by their slave-drivers. A large number had died, but a handful of survivors were still being held in the slave pens when Captain Pellow and his men arrived in the autumn of 1716.

The capture of Mamora provided a huge boost to Moulay Ismail, for it proved that the great European powers were no longer invincible. The sultan's soldiers were exultant in victory and, according to one English witness, became extremely 'sawcy'. They began drawing up plans for the capture of Larache.

The Larache campaign was delayed by years of civil war and it was not until 1688 that the sultan was able to pitch his forces against the citadel. Hoping to cow the Spanish garrison into submission, he despatched a massive force under the capable command of Kaid Ahmad ben Haddu al-Rifi. The kaid ordered his forces to undermine a section of the battlements, then detonated a huge quantity of gunpowder. The ensuing fireball enveloped the Spanish powder magazine, causing a terrific explosion. As the dust settled, Kaid Ahmad's troops poured through a large breach in the walls.

What happened next is unclear. Several accounts assert that the town's Spanish priests urged the garrison to capitulate. The English writer, John Braithwaite, claimed that the most vocal calls for surrender came from 'the friars, who began to be a little pinched in their bellies'. Others blamed the Franciscan padre, Gaspar Gonzales, who had been sent to Meknes to negotiate with the sultan. He returned with the news that Moulay Ismail promised to release everyone in Larache if they handed over their citadel to his forces.

The 1,734 Spanish soldiers and civilians surrendered unconditionally – an indication of just how miserable conditions were in Larache. ''Tis a terrible life,' wrote Braithwaite, 'little better than slaving, to be obliged to live in such a small garrison, always in war . . . and no supplies of provisions but by sea.' The surrendering soldiers clung to the hope that the sultan would honour his word but soon realised that they had made a terrible misjudgement. They were 'disarm'd, beaten and very ill us'd', before being sent to Meknes under armed guard. These Moroccan guards forced their captives to drag behind them the great guns of Larache, along with all the other weaponry, muskets and powder. These war trophies included one monumentally large cannon, known to the Moroccans as al-kissab (the reed), which was thirty-five feet long and took four men – arms outstretched – to encircle its breech.

As the captives neared the imperial capital, they found themselves at the centre of a spectacular parade. The sultan had gathered 10,000 soldiers to help him celebrate in style, and bands played all day in commemoration of their historic victory. Several of the sultan's sons were exhilarated by the sight of so many captive Christians and began firing wildly into their ranks.

The festivities continued late into the night. Statues of the Virgin and saints were brought before the sultan so that he could spit on them, and there was a great fantasia to celebrate the triumph. Moulay Ismail issued an edict banning the wearing of black shoes, because the Spanish were said to have introduced the custom to Morocco when they first acquired Larache in 1610. The mufti of Fez was so elated by the victory that he was moved to poetry:

> How many infidels at dusk have had their heads
> severed from their bodies!
> How many were dragged away with the death rattle
> in their throats!
> For how many throats have our lances been as
> necklaces!
> How many lance-tips were thrust into their breasts!

Once the fantasia was over, Moulay Ismail separated the Spanish officers from the regular soldiers. He hoped to ransom the officers for a large sum, and they were lodged in secure cells. The rest of the men were cudgelled by the sultan's black guard before being sent to the slave pens. 'The negroes kept them at hard slavery,' wrote the British captive, Francis Brooks, 'beating and whipping them all day long; and at night they were to lodge underground; allowing them such bread as his other poor captives have, and water to sustain them alive.'

Such cruel treatment quickly took its toll on these sick and malnourished men. 'After the poor Christians had undergone their hard labour and cruel stripes for the space of five months time,' wrote Brooks, 'many of them fell sick and died.' When Moulay Ismail asked why so many were missing from the building works, he was informed that 500 had perished, while a further 700 had converted to Islam in order to escape punishment. By the time Captain Pellow and his men were brought to Meknes, only a handful remained alive.

Moulay Ismail was jubilant at his military triumphs and now turned his attentions to Ceuta, the largest and most formidable of Spain's possessions in Morocco. He had been told that the citadel's defensive walls were almost impossible to scale or mine, but nevertheless ordered his French slaves to dig deep tunnels under the walls. He also called upon the services of one of his Russian renegades, a blacksmith who was an expert at making powerful weaponry. But cannon proved of little use when it came to bringing down the city's stone ramparts, and the sultan instructed his gunners to destroy Ceuta's churches and mansions instead.

The attacks on Ceuta were to continue on and off for the next two decades. By 1716, the Spanish population had dwindled to a fraction of what it had been in former times and most of the buildings lay in rubble. Moulay Ismail nevertheless ordered yet another bombardment in the summer of that year, and a concerted campaign might well have won him the city. But he quickly lost interest when he learned that there were very few inhabitants left to capture. Besides, his new concern was how best to employ the growing number of captives already being held in the Meknes slave pens.

5 Into the Slave Pen

Captain John Pellow and his men had been horrified when they first entered the Meknes slave pen. It lay just outside the city walls but was a world away from the decorative splendours of the imperial pleasure palace. Built in the form of a square and surrounded by high ramparts, the slave pen looked like a military prison. It had four tall watch-towers, and its main gate was strongly fortified and protected by a thick iron grille. According to the French padre, Nolasque Neant, this was always locked and was 'closely guarded by the king's Moorish guards'. Once inside, the sultan's captives found themselves in a grim compound that contained four barrack-style buildings. 'Although they were very large,' wrote the Spaniard, San Juan del Puerto, 'they were very uncomfortable because of the growing number of slaves.'

Captain Pellow and his comrades were led into one of the barracks and lodged alongside the other British slaves. There were some 125 Britons being held in captivity – a number that was set to rise – as well as an estimated 3,000 slaves from elsewhere in Europe. These emaciated men shared stories with the new arrivals and told a woeful tale of the miseries they had endured since being brought to the imperial capital.

One of them, John Willdon, said that Meknes was 'the [most] barbarosy place of the whole world'. He and his comrades had 'been forced to draw carts of lead with ropes about our shoulders, all one as horses'. They had also been beaten and whipped until their skin was raw, and made to carry 'great barrs of iron upon our shoulders, as big as we could well get up, and up to our knees in dirt, and as slippery that we could hardly goe without the load'.

Another of the men, John Stocker, had been captain of the *Sarah* when his vessel was intercepted by the Salé corsairs. He had been brought to Meknes shortly before Captain Pellow and his company, and was already half starved by the terrible diet. 'I am in a most deplorable condition,' he wrote to a friend in England, '[and have] nothing but one small cake [loaf] and water for 24 hours after hard work.' He said that the slave lodgings lacked even basic sanitation and complained that his hair was crawling with lice. '[I] live upon the bare ground, and [have] nothing to cover me, and [am] as lousy as possible.' Like the other British captives being held in the slave pen, Stocker had fallen into a deep depression. Having listened to the tales of the Spanish slaves with a heavy heart, he feared that he would never be released. He confessed that 'when I think on my poor wife and children, and the hardship they will meet with in my absence . . . [it] almost drives me distracted.' Touchingly, he added that he had written to his wife 'in another stile, knowing her weak heart cannot bear to hear of the hardships I goes through'.

Captain Pellow and his men soon discovered that they were part of an organised, well-disciplined system that was designed to stretch each slave to his physical limits. On first arriving at the slave pen they had been given an old straw mat and were told to find themselves a place to sleep 'on the cold ground' of the barracks. The filthy floor was infested with fleas and cockroaches. The slaves ate and slept in these terrible conditions, and spent the short nights dreaming of their families back in England.

Each morning, as the fiery sun broke the dawn sky, one of their number was appointed to oversee thirty of his comrades for the rest of the day. Some days this role would fall to Captain Pellow himself. On other days, it would be undertaken by Briant Clarke or Lewis Davies. The duties of the overseer included emptying the slop bucket and filling the water pitchers. It was also his job to collect the stinking barley flour from the storehouse, make the dough, bake it, and distribute it evenly among the men.

The daily ration for each of the men was woefully inadequate – fourteen ounces of black bread and an ounce of oil. The oil was often exchanged for 'something to make us pottage at night'. Craving fresh meat, the men were sometimes able to acquire fat and gristle from one of the numerous European renegades in Meknes. These rancid scraps were used to make the evening gruel – the only hot meal that the slaves ever got to eat. If they were lucky, they could supplement this with any edible roots and weeds that they could grub out of the earth.

Their staple was bread made from barley that had lain for many months in damp storehouses. It was often so rotten that it could not be kneaded into dough. Worse still, the bread was only partially cooked in the middle, because the ovens were heated with damp reeds that produced very little heat. John Whitehead complained that 'many times it has had such a nauseous smell that a man could not endure it at his nose.' There were occasions when the supplies of barley ran low and Captain Pellow and his men were given nothing at all to eat. In one letter, John Willdon bemoaned the fact that 'we have not had a bitt of bread allowed us for eight days togeather, but what we have gone from dore to dore a-beging of other Christian slaves.'

Moulay Ismail was anxious that the slaves should eat in order to preserve their strength and had been known to visit the slave pens in order to ensure that the men were eating their pitiful rations. 'One day,' wrote Father Busnot, '[the sultan], finding some of that bread which a slave had hid in a hole of the wall,

[he] call'd Francis le Clerc of St Brieux [who had hidden it] and made him eat it by force, which he told us had been greater torment to him than if he had fasted three days.'

The French slaves were particularly disgusted with the food and complained bitterly about those who prepared it. 'Those poor cooks were subject to be affronted by all the gang,' wrote Germain Mouette, 'because sometimes the pot was too salt, or too fresh, or not well boil'd and everyone had something to say to vex them, so that sometimes nobody would serve the office.'

Life was miserable for everyone in the slave pen, especially in midsummer when it was airless and hot. There was a rank stench of unwashed bodies, and the slop buckets also contributed to the noxious air – particularly as many of the slaves were suffering from diarrhoea and dysentery. On their arrival at the pen, Captain Pellow and his company had each been handed a rough woollen djellaba with a huge hood. They made frequent complaints about this strange and uncomfortable garment, which they never had the opportunity to wash. It quickly turned fetid and rubbed against their broken skin, causing weals and livid blotches. 'In this habit,' wrote Simon Ockley, 'they are exposed to the scorching heat of the sun in summer, and the violence of frost, snow, excessive rain and stormy winds in winter.'

There was the occasional exception to the daily cycle of thirst and gnawing hunger. Moulay Ismail was accustomed to eat his lunch in full view of the slaves working on his building project. On one occasion, the platter of couscous and viands was larger than usual, and the sultan was unable to finish it. He bade his assembled kaids eat the remnants, but they attacked the food with a greedy relish that disgusted the sultan. He told them to stop 'and order'd it to be taken from them . . . [and] carry'd to the Christian slaves that worked close by'. The kaids thought that he was jesting and began picking out chunks of meat, tossing them to the slaves and 'alleging that the Christians were unworthy to eat in the same bason as the king had done'. But Moulay Ismail meant what he said and forced them to hand over the entire bowl, 'full of pullets, pigeons and rice, dress'd with saffron, which they eat with at least as good an appetite as the kaids would have done'.

Such unexpected supplies of food were rare indeed, and for month after month Captain Pellow and his men existed on starvation rations. Thomas Pellow said that many of his former crewmates grew quite desperate from the continual hunger. 'This scantiness,' he wrote, 'has put several upon hazarding a leap from very high walls only to get a few wild onions that grow in the Moor's burying place.'

The terrible food was not the only grievance of Captain Pellow and his men. The newly arrived slaves quickly discovered that the black guards appointed to oversee them were extremely violent. The guardian of the British captives lived in a small shack next to the main gate of the slave pen. He was responsible for discipline and punishment, and also kept a daily tally of the captives under his charge. '[He] locks them up every night [and] counts them out in the morning,' wrote John Whitehead. He also woke the men at dawn and led them to 'the several drivers or overseers, who carry them to their respective works, where they are kept labouring till the stars appear in the evening'.

The black guards were absolute masters of the slaves under their charge and most had been hand-picked by Moulay Ismail on account of their physical strength and willingness to thrash their captives. Germain Mouette penned a vivid description of his first meeting with the guardian of the French slaves, whose self-appointed role was to make the men's lives as miserable as possible. A 'black of prodigious tall stature, of a frightful aspect, and a voice as dreadful as the barking of Cerebus', he was also a harsh disciplinarian and always clutched 'a staff in his hand, proportionable to his bulk, with which he saluted every one of us, and then led us into the storehouses to chuse pickaxes of an extraordinary weight'.

Mouette's guard was accustomed to chain the men at night and took a sadistic delight in tormenting the French captives. 'Nothing was to be heard at night in our prisons but dismal groans,' wrote Mouette, 'occasion'd by the violent pains proceeding from our beating.' Every dawn, the guard would appear at the door with his staff and call the men to work. 'His voice put such life into us that the moment we heard him in the morning cry out at the door, "*eoua-y-alla crusion*", that is, "come out quick", every one of us throng'd to be foremost, for the hindermost always felt the weight of his cudgel.'

The repeated beatings, appalling diet and unsanitary lodgings caused many of the men to fall ill. Moulay Ismail required his sick slaves to continue with their work; only those too weak to stand were allowed to rest their broken bodies in the little infirmary that lay within the compound of the slave pen. This building had been established in the 1690s, when Moulay Ismail granted the king of Spain permission to endow a small friary in the captives' quarters. It housed up to twelve Franciscan fathers, whose safety was guaranteed by the sultan as long as the Spanish king paid protection money.

The sick who were sent to the infirmary were accorded few privileges. 'They are no better us'd in sickness than in health,' wrote Mouette. 'The common allowance to the king's slaves is only a porringer of black meal and a little oyl.' They were still required to perform chores and given precious little time to recover. 'No rest is allow'd them,' added Mouette, 'till they see they are not able to wag hand or foot . . . [and] cannot rise thro' weakness.' The Frenchman said that many slaves were terrified of being forced to undergo treatment by local physicians, whose homespun cures were primitive and painful. 'If the slaves complain of any pains in their body,' he wrote, 'they have iron rods, with buttons of the same metal at the end, as bigg as walnuts, which they make red hot and burn the wretched patient in several parts.'

Moulay Ismail rarely showed any sympathy towards slaves who fell ill and would often beat them for not working as hard as their healthy comrades. On one occasion, he exploded with rage when told that his building programme was being delayed by the fact that so many slaves were ailing. 'By the emperor's order,' wrote Francis Brooks, 'his negroes fell to haling and dragging them out of that place [the infirmary].' The sick slaves were brought before the sultan, who showed no mercy towards them. 'When, in that weak and feeble condition, [he saw] that they could not stand on their legs when dragged before him, he instantly killed seven of them, making their resting place a slaughter house.'

Captain Pellow and his men had been in captivity for just a few weeks when three of their number fell desperately ill. It was clear that they were unlikely to survive, and their shipboard companions looked on anxiously as they succumbed to a slow death. John Willdon wrote a desperate missive to England, warning that unless an ambassador was sent within the next few weeks to try to win their release, there would no longer be any English slaves alive in Meknes. 'If he don't come in a little time,' he wrote, 'he may abide where he is, for we have a distemper called the callenture, and our men dye almost every day for want of subsistance.'

Willdon's warning proved all too prophetic. Captain Richard Ferris of the *Southwark* was the first to die; he breathed his last in September 1716. John Osborne and John Foster died soon afterwards, while Matthew Elliot of the *George* succumbed to severe sickness in the spring of 1717. Thomas Pellow's shipmate, Briant Clarke, also died at about this time. Just six days later, he was followed to the grave by Captain Robert Fowler of the *George* and John Dunnal of the *Francis*.

John Dunnal was a popular crew member and the men

grieved deeply at his departure. Captain John Pellow gave a moving address on the day of his death, aware that many more of his British colleagues were likely to meet their end in the Meknes slave pen. Thomas Pellow managed to obtain permission to attend the little ceremony and was touched by his uncle's words. 'I shall never forget my uncle's tender behaviour at the interment,' he wrote. 'The corpse, being brought to the grave, and no particular person appointed to read the Christian ceremony of burial, my uncle took it upon him.'

Captain Pellow began reading the prayers, but the months in captivity and the overwhelming sense of loss proved too much for him to bear. In the midst of reading, he faltered and broke down. 'He was not able, through the abundance of tears flowing, to go through it.' The captain was so overcome with emotion that he had to pass the Bible to one of the crew. 'Never did I see such a mournful meeting,' wrote Thomas Pellow, 'every one catching the contagion and all standing for a considerable time in dead silence, quite overwhelmed with grief.'

Once the little ceremony was over, Dunnal's corpse was lowered slowly into the ground, in a plot that lay some distance from the city walls. This site had only been in use for a few years, for Moulay Ismail's Christian slaves had previously been buried close to the ramparts. But having decided to incorporate the Christian burial ground into his palace gardens, the sultan 'caus'd it to be dug six foot in depth, and all that earth to be carry'd three quarters of a league from thence'. Father Busnot said that 'of five thousand Christian slaves employ'd at that work, which lasted but nine days, fifty dy'd by the stink of the bodies newly bury'd'.

The black guards kept a meticulous note of the slaves under their charge and were careful to record any mortality. These daily tallies have long since been lost, and the surviving records are frustratingly incomplete. The accounts of visiting ambassadors, padres and the captives themselves suggest that at any given time there were up to 5,000 slaves being held in Meknes. But the Arabic sources tell a more troubling story. The nineteenth-century Moroccan historian, Ahmed ez-Zayyani, studied the archives in the royal collection and reckoned that at any one time there were at least 25,000 white slaves in Meknes. If so, the city's slave population was about the same as that of Algiers.

The slave pens would quickly fill after the capture of one of the Spanish presidios, but their numbers would soon be thinned by disease and sickness. The plague was a regular visitor to the slave pen, reaping a rich harvest among men already suffering from dysentery and malnutrition. Mouette said that in one particularly bad year, it killed one in four of the French slaves, and he added that there was very little they could do to halt the mortality. 'We doubled our usual daily prayers at that time, and for eight days said the whole rosary, instead of the third part repeated before.'

So many slaves died from sickness, disease and sheer exhaustion that even Moulay Ismail began to grow seriously alarmed. When he consulted his kaids, they told him there was a good reason for the high mortality rate. In the captives' own country, they said, Christians 'were much strengthen'd by drinking of wine and brandy'. They added that if Moulay Ismail wished to slow the death rate and encourage his slaves to work harder, 'he need only order every one of them three or four glasses of wine.'

The sultan took the kaids at their word. 'He sent for the clerk of the Jews, whom he order'd to bring four great pitchers of wine . . . [and] distributed [it] among the captives.' When he returned to the works a little later in the day, '[he] was amazed to see that the Christians had done more in two hours . . . than in three parts of the day before'. Henceforth, he ordered the Jews to supply the Christian slaves with 'one hundred weight of raisins, and the same of figs, in order that they might make brandy'. He even sanctioned the opening of a makeshift tavern in the slave pen, although he almost certainly failed to appreciate the irony of sick and dying men having access to eau-de-vie.

Captain Pellow and his men continued to suffer from disease and malnutrition, yet they soon discovered that the poor food was not their main grievance. The real source of woe – and the subject of endless complaints – was their punishing daily routine. It was at the building works of Meknes palace, where they spent up to fifteen hours of every day, that the men discovered the full horror of life as a slave of Sultan Moulay Ismail.

Meknes had been a provincial market town when Moulay Ismail acceded to the throne. It had never been an imperial capital, like the great cities of Fez, Rabat and Marrakesh, nor did it have an illustrious history. This was what made it so appealing to the new sultan. Moulay Ismail was acutely conscious of his place in history and wished to be remembered as the founder of a dynasty whose imperial capital was of a scale and grandeur that surpassed all others.

The monumental construction programme began shortly after he had secured the throne. 'He demolished the houses which neighboured the kasbah,' wrote Ahmed ez-Zayyani, 'and got the inhabitants to take away the rubble.' When this was complete, he ordered the entire eastern quarter of the town to be razed. The sultan was still not satisfied with the size of the area that had been cleared and demolished many of the other buildings that remained standing.

The extraordinary assemblage of fortifications and palaces that began to arise from the rubble were of a size that astonished all who saw them. The walls alone were planned to stretch for many miles, for Moulay Ismail wished his various interlocking palaces and chambers to march in endless succession across the hills and valleys around Meknes. There were to be vast courtyards and colonnaded galleries, green-tiled mosques and pleasure gardens. He ordered the building of a huge Moorish harem, as well as stables and armouries, fountains, pools and follies. He instructed his engineers to raid the Roman ruins of Volubulis for marble columns and slabs of dressed stone. He also took all the most precious adornments from the once splendid al-Badi palace in Marrakesh, including cartloads of marble columns and exquisite jasper. Other precious stones were specially imported from Pisa and Genoa.

Visitors to Meknes would later assert that Moulay Ismail was motivated by a desire to build a palace that was grander and more impressive than King Louis XIV's Versailles. The two monarchs – who reigned contemporaneously – certainly had much in common. Both personally supervised their building works and both treated their labourers with contempt. But Meknes was already under construction when Moulay Ismail was first brought news of the splendours of Versailles, and his rambling panoply of Moorish pleasure palaces could not have been more different from Versailles.

The French padre, Nolasque Neant, nevertheless insisted that the sultan had actually expressed the desire to outdo everything that the Sun King had achieved. One European visitor to Moulay Ismail's court even had the nerve to tell the sultan that if he wished to imitate the king of France, he should not have his subjects and slaves killed in his presence. 'This is true,' was the sultan's ready answer, 'but King Louis commands men, whereas I command beasts.' These 'beasts' were forced to work on Moulay Ismail's never-ending project, constructing walls, mixing mortar and heaving slabs of stone. Even though the sultan had thousands of slaves at his disposal, he was always short of manpower and had to issue a decree to the effect that every tribe in Morocco was obliged to furnish a fixed number of men and mules.

The first of Moulay Ismail's palaces to be finished was the Dar Kbira. This was completed in 1677, after three years' labour, and was opened with an impressive nocturnal ceremony attended by all of the sultan's kaids and governors. At the stroke of midnight, Moulay Ismail slaughtered a wolf at the main gateway, killing it with his own hands. Its head was chopped off and built into the centre of the gate.

The size and scale of the Dar Kbira was quite without precedent. '[It] makes a magnificent boundary for the city to the northwards,' wrote Father Busnot in 1714, 'the greatness of its enclosure, the whiteness of its lofty walls, the height of [its] several turrets.' The first section of gardens were also laid out on an impressively grand scale. Moulay Ismail ordered his slaves to transport mature trees 'of an extraordinary size' to decorate the Dar Kbira and also began planning a hanging garden in echo of the fabled Babylon.

The Dar Kbira was huge, yet Moulay Ismail conceived it as merely the first in an elaborate series of palaces. To the southwest of his private quarters, he began laying the foundations of a truly vast city of pleasure, the Dar al Makhzen, which was to consist of no fewer than fifty adjoining palaces, each with its own mosque and bathhouse. This was to be surrounded by three sets of defensive walls, with the outer ring flanked by crenellated towers. There was to be a storehouse – the *heri* – large enough to contain a year's harvest from the whole of Morocco. Moulay Ismail also ordered the construction of an enormous reservoir and boating lake, while the stables were intended to house up to 12,000 horses.

Undaunted by the scale of his project, the sultan began laying plans for a sprawling diplomatic quarter, the Madinat el-Riyad, where his viziers and officers were to have their residences, and a vast military barracks housing 130,000 of his black troops. Most fabulous of all was to be the Dar al-Mansur palace, which was to stand over 150 feet high and be surmounted by twenty pavilions decorated with glazed green tiles.

Moulay Ismail was the principal architect, engineer and

consultant of his building project. He would appear every morning, long before dawn, and give instructions for that day's work. He gave orders to the slave-drivers and watched in satisfaction as they thrashed their slaves in order to make them work harder. 'The sultan Moulay Ismail busied himself in supervising the construction of his palaces,' wrote Ahmed ez-Zayyani. 'As soon as he had finished one, he would start on another.' As the walls of imperial Meknes began to fill the skyline, visitors were awed by the scale of the project. 'Never,' wrote ez-Zayyani, 'had such a similar palace been seen under any government, Arab or foreign, pagan or Muslim.' The ramparts alone stretched so far along the valley that it required 12,000 soldiers to guard them.

The construction work had been under way for more than four decades by the time Captain Pellow and his men were brought to Meknes, yet there was no sign of any end to the project. Indeed, the sultan's plans became ever more fantastical as the palace grew in size. Thomas Pellow had been astonished at the size of the place when first led inside the ramparts and no less shocked by the manner in which his British comrades were beaten and thrashed by their black slave-drivers. 'At daybreak,' he wrote, 'the guardians of the several dungeons where the Christian slaves are shut up at night, rouse them with curses and blows.' Captain Pellow and his men were marched under guard to the latest section of palace walls and spent the next fifteen hours toiling under the burning African sun. 'Some are employed to carry large baskets of earth,' wrote Pellow. 'Some drive waggons drawn by six bulls and two horses.' Skilled labourers were given more taxing work – they had to 'saw, cut, cement, and erect marble pillars'. Those without skills were 'set to the coarsest works, as tending horses, sweeping stables, carrying burthens [and] grinding with hand-mills'.

Being unskilled, the crews of the *Francis*, the *George* and the *Southwark* were therefore given the most back-breaking tasks. Mixing the lime mortar was one of the most arduous of their jobs, and many of the slaves left accounts of the dangers involved. According to Thomas Phelps, they first had to construct large wooden boxes that were open at the top. These were then filled with 'earth powdered, and lime, and gravel well beat together'. The men next added water and mixed everything together until it had the consistency of thick soup. The liquid mortar was allowed to dry, 'which then will acquire an incredible hardness, and is very lasting'. Once the wooden boxes had been removed, the mortar was either coated in white plaster, or faced with polished marble.

Mixing the mortar was extremely hazardous. The slaves were frequently burnt by the lime and suffered great pain when it got into sores and cracks in their skin. Father Busnot was appalled that the slaves were not allowed even the most rudimentary safety precautions and were 'often burnt alive, as lately happen'd to six Englishmen and one Frenchman'. Their task was made all the more difficult by the fact that much of their work was undertaken on walls that were already thirty or forty feet high. Germain Mouette said that they were given neither scaffolds nor ladders and had to heave the mortar up by pulley and cord, 'which burns and cuts the fingers of such as pull at it'. He said that 'if those who work above cease but one moment pounding the earth that is between the planks, with heavy rammers, the overseers, who have quick ears, throw stones at them to continue their perpetual labour.'

It was clear to Captain Pellow and his men that the building work would continue for as long as Moulay Ismail was alive. The sultan was rarely satisfied with the finished buildings and would often order his slaves to tear down the entire edifice. 'The unsettled humour of the king of Morocco renders it [the palace] like unto the scenes in a theatre,' wrote Father Busnot, 'which change almost at every act.' He said that 'the slaves assur'd me that when a man had been ten years away, he cannot know them again, so great are the alterations that prince is daily making'. In one four-month period, Moulay Ismail forced his slaves to demolish twelve miles of palace walls and then ordered that the chunks of rubble be 'beaten to powder'. Once this work was completed, he told the slaves to rebuild the walls in exactly the same position. When the sultan was asked why he was constantly demolishing his newly constructed buildings, he explained that he viewed his slaves as scheming vermin who needed to be kept occupied. 'I have a bag full of rats,' he said, '[and] unless I keep that bag stirring, they would eat their way through.'

The black slave-drivers were extremely cruel to the men under their charge. '[They] immediately punish the least stop or inadvertancy,' wrote Thomas Pellow, 'and often will not allow the poor creatures time to eat their bread.' The drivers worked in shifts and, at the end of each shift, would tell their replacement which of the slaves had been slack in their work. The new driver would then raise his cudgel and beat the hapless slaves, 'which he always took care to bestow on those parts where he thought they would do most hurt'. Mouette said that most of the slave-drivers would strike at the head, 'and, when he had broke it, counterfeited the charitable surgeon, applying some unslacked lime to stanch the bleeding'. If any slave was beaten so badly that he was no longer able to work, the slave-driver 'had a dreadful way of enabling him, by redoubling the stripes, so that the new ones made him forget the old'.

The slave-drivers often amused themselves by waking the men at night. 'It frequently happens,' wrote Pellow, '[that] they are hurried away to some filthy work in the night time, with this call in Spanish, "Vamos a travacho cornutos", i.e. "Out to work, you cuckolds."' The exhausted men were beaten from their beds and obliged to do another few hours of hard labour.

The guard of the French slaves had been known to punish the men by reducing their already scant rations and sometimes ordered them to clean the city's sewers. '[He] made us empty all the privies,' wrote Mouette, 'and remove all the dunghills in the town, carrying all the filth in wicker baskets, so that it ran through and fell on us.' After several days of such treatment, the French slaves were in a terrible condition. 'Our hams [thighs] were all cut with the weight of our chains, and some of them, as well as mine, were a finger deep in the flesh.'

Moulay Ismail visited the construction site on a daily basis. According to Simon Ockley, he was accompanied by three palace servants: 'one . . . to carry his tobacco pipe (which has a bowl as big as a child's head) . . . another carries his tobacco, and a third a brazen vessel of hot water'. The slaves trembled as this entourage approached, for they knew that anyone considered to be slacking would be given a sound thrashing. 'His boys carried short brazil[wood] sticks,' wrote Pellow, 'knotted cords for whipping, a change of clothes to shift when bloody, and a hatchet.'

Moulay Ismail's inspections were punctilious and extremely thorough. He would shout orders, proffer advice and suggest new projects to be undertaken. If the work was not proceeding satisfactorily, he had been known to clamber on to the walls and start mixing the mortar himself. He could not abide poor craftsmanship and did not hesitate to punish slaves whose work was of an inferior quality. On one occasion, he was inspecting bricks when he discovered that some were very thin. He called for the master mason and, after admonishing the man for his poor work, ordered his black guard to break fifty bricks over the mason's head. When this was done, the blood-drenched slave was thrown into prison.

On another occasion, the sultan quizzed one of his slaves about the quality of the mortar. When the trembling slave admitted that it was indeed inferior, Moulay Ismail 'bid him hold his head fare to strike at; having strucken him, he knocked down all the rest with his own hands and broke their heads so miserably that the place was all bloody like a butcher's stall'.

The Spanish slaves suffered particularly harsh treatment. When one of their number walked past Moulay Ismail without removing his hat, the sultan 'darted his spear at him'. It pierced deep into the man's flesh and caused him considerable pain as he ripped the barbed tip out of his skin. The slave handed the spear back to the sultan, only to have it thrust repeatedly into his stomach.

The most feared punishment was known as 'tossing'. 'The person whom the emperor orders to be thus punished,' wrote Pellow, 'is seized upon by three or four strong negroes who, taking hold of his hams, throw him up with all their strength and, at the same time, turning him round, pitch him down head foremost.' The black guards who performed this punishment were 'so dexterous by long use that they can either break his neck the first toss, dislocate his shoulder, or let him fall with less hurt'. Pellow said that they would continue to toss the slave until the sultan ordered them to stop.

The continual cruelty took a severe toll on the slaves in Meknes, yet they knew that any resistance was futile. When the Spanish captives had attempted to assassinate the sultan, it had very nearly ended in disaster. According to Pellow, one of their number stole a musket and fired at the sultan's chest as he toured the building works. But his nerves got the better of him, and 'the two balls he had charged his gun with flew into the pommel of the emperor's saddle'. Moulay Ismail was incensed when he realised what had happened. The man was seized '[and] it was expected he would be put to a cruel death'. But the sultan – unpredictable as ever – was overcome by compassion. He asked the Spaniard 'what he had done to deserve being used so, whether he was no more beloved, and people were tired with him'. Then, with unusual clemency, he 'calmly sent him to the works among the rest of the Christians'.

The sultan's violent behaviour was a source of continual grievance for the slaves toiling on Meknes palace, and they feared that their friends and families in Britain were ignorant of their plight. Thomas Goodman, one of the *Francis*'s crew, wrote a letter to his family in November 1716, informing them of the terrible treatment he was suffering at the hands of the Moroccan sultan.

'I have undergone a great deal of hardship,' he wrote, 'for we are kept to work night and day; and drove like so many sheep.' He said that the hard labour was almost unendurable, and added that 'when we go out to work, we don't know whether we shall come in alive or not, for they are very barbarous people and give nothing but bread and water.' After begging his family to pray for him and his comrades who were currently alive, he ended his letter by revealing his sense of despair and depression. 'Nothing can be worse to me than to think how happy I have lived, and now live worse than a dog, and naked; not one rag of clothes to cover our nakedness.'

Another of the English captives, Thomas Meggison, begged that something be done to help him before the onset of winter, which he believed would kill many of his sick friends. 'Our poor men are in a very miserable condition, God knowes, and dyes every day almost for want,' he wrote. 'They will be starved this winter without God's great mercy, and all nations is provided for but the poore English has noe assistance for their nation but a parcell of lyes and storys.'

Meggison was right to fear the winter, which took its toll on men already weakened by sickness. At some point in early 1717, Thomas Pellow learned that his uncle was seriously ill with little hope that he would recover.

A few days later, Thomas was brought the terrible news that Captain Pellow had died, 'taken off by a violent flux'. He had survived some six months in captivity and had outlived four of the *Francis*'s seven-strong crew. But the cruel regime and pitiful diet had weakened his already broken frame. When he also contracted dysentery, his body was unable to fight off the disease.

The survivors were terrified that they would be next and wrote frantic letters to England, begging that something be done. But they feared that their cries for help were falling on deaf ears. 'I believe all Christian people have forgotten us in England,' wrote John Willdon, 'because they have not sent us any relief, never, since we have been in slavery.'

6 GUARDING THE CONCUBINES

ON A BRIGHT SPRING MORNING in 1717, a pale-skinned gentleman could be seen strolling purposefully through Whitehall. He looked quite the dandy in his velvet cloak and grey-blond wig, yet his face betrayed an air of disquiet. Joseph Addison, one of the two secretaries of state for foreign affairs, was on his way to a crisis meeting of the cabinet. He and his fellow ministers were gathering to discuss one of the most intractable problems of the age.

An increasing number of vessels were being captured by the Salé corsairs and there was no obvious way to curb the menace. The *Constant John*, the *Desire*, the *Henry and Mary*, the *David*, the *Abigail*, the *Catherine*, the *George*, the *Sarah*, the *Endeavour*, the *Prosperous* and the *Union*: all had been seized in recent months, and their captains and crews sent to Meknes in chains. Britain was being held to ransom – along with the rest of Europe – and something needed to be done.

The recently crowned King George I had displayed a remarkable lack of interest in the plight of the British slaves in Meknes. The German-born ruler of Hanover had been offered the throne on the death of the childless Queen Anne. He spoke only broken English and had come to his new kingdom with great reluctance. 'Our customs and laws were all mysteries to him,' wrote Lady Mary Wortley Montagu, 'which he neither tried to understand nor was capable of understanding.'

The king had caused quite a stir when he arrived in London three years earlier, accompanied by a vast retinue of German courtiers, including his prime minister, principal advisor and all his domestic staff. But what had particularly shocked the capital's populace was the fact that his household included two Turkish advisors, Mehemet and Mustafa. George's British ministers were also appalled that the king could place his trust in two 'Muslims' – they had, in fact, converted to Christianity – and that one of them had been made keeper of the privy purse. Within months of the king installing himself in Whitehall Palace, he was the subject of vicious ballads and xenophobic ditties. He stood accused of bringing his Turks 'for abominable purposes', and his German entourage in order for them to line their pockets at Britain's expense.

> Hither he brought the dear illustrious house
> That is, himself, his pipe, close stool and louse;
> Two Turks, three whores, and half a dozen nurses
> Five hundred Germans, all with empty purses.

In the spring of 1717, King George I received a desperate petition from the wives and widows of Captain Pellow and the other enslaved mariners. They begged him to help win their release, wording their petition in highly emotional language. It called upon the king to tackle the crisis without further ado, and 'most humbly beggs, implores and earnestly desire[s] a speedy reliefe to your afflicted subjects'. It also urged him to establish 'a charitable contribution' for the slave widows, many of whom were destitute and at risk of starvation.

The petition was presented to the king by Jezreel Jones, a clerk to the Royal Society. He warned that the British slaves were in a truly terrible condition and 'ready to perish with extream want, hard labour, in a naked condition, severe strokes and disability to work'. But King George showed so little interest in the fate of the captives that Jones turned instead to the newly appointed secretary of state, Joseph Addison, whose responsibilities included British relations with southern Europe and the Mediterranean.

Addison's appointment to this post had surprised everyone. Although he had been a Member of Parliament since 1708, he had singularly failed to shine in the chamber. He had attempted just one speech in the House of Commons, but was so terrified by the cries of 'Hear him! Hear him!' that he quickly returned to the benches. Yet he had a brilliant intellect and had long dazzled the capital's intelligentsia with his essays in *The Spectator, Tatler* and *Guardian*. When the Whig grandee, James Stanhope, was appointed first lord of the treasury and chancellor of the exchequer in the spring of 1717, he offered Addison the post of Secretary of State to the Southern Department.

Addison had been fascinated by Morocco ever since he was a child. His father had served in the Tangier garrison, and the young Joseph had been brought up on fireside stories of life in the land of the Moors. Old Lancelot's tales – which he had published in 1671 – were darkly romantic and peppered with stories of gallant warlords. He warned that Moorish warriors were treacherous and 'implacable in their hatred', but he took a rather more charitable view of their delectable womenfolk, whom he found to be 'well complexioned, full bodied and of good symmetry', hinting that he had tried to snatch a moment of intimacy with these beauties. But he had been prevented by their chary husbands, who 'keep [them] in great subjection and retirement which makes adultery a stranger to their beds'.

Joseph Addison was more interested in the character of Moulay Ismail, who intrigued and repulsed him in equal measure. In the year before he became secretary of state, he had written an essay on tyranny for *The Freeholder*. He cited Moulay Ismail as the very worst sort of ruler and compared his brutal despotism with Britain's enlightened parliamentary government. The sultan's subjects, he wrote, lived in constant fear of his unpredictable outbursts and were required to display absolute subjugation whenever they were in his presence. Even his advisors were unable to express their views openly. Addison said the sultan was accustomed to conduct his affairs while 'mounted on horseback in an open court, with several of his kaids, or governors, about him, standing barefoot, trembling, bowing to the earth, and at every word he spoke, breaking out into passionate exclamations of praise'.

In the same essay, Addison informed his readers that Moulay Ismail was forcing his Christian slaves to construct a pleasure palace on a truly monumental scale. He said that he was using 'many thousands in works of that kind', and added that 'it was usual for him to show the delicacy of his taste by demolishing the building and putting to death all that had a hand in it.'

Addison had spent much time reflecting on how best to proceed with Moulay Ismail. All previous attempts to deal with the sultan had ended in failure, and it was clear that there was no obvious solution to the crisis. Just a few months earlier, Admiral Charles Cornwall had been sent to Morocco with orders to 'demand satisfaction' for the depredations of the Salé corsairs and 'procure the release of all His Majesty's subjects now captive in Barbary'. Admiral Cornwall had presented this demand to the sultan, who replied that his only desire was to establish 'a lasting and profound peace between the two crowns'. Yet he declined to release any of his slaves, and Cornwall had responded by attempting to blockade the principal ports of Morocco. Although ineffectual, it was still in force when Addison attended the crisis meeting of the cabinet on 31 May 1717.

Addison had come well prepared. He was clutching a document entitled 'State of Barbary Affairs', which contained much information on how best to proceed with the sultan. The secretary of state believed that blockading Morocco's ports was not the answer. Although Admiral Cornwall had captured several corsair vessels, he had singularly failed to free any slaves. Indeed, his blockade had given the Moroccan sultan so little cause for concern that Addison said, 'it is to be question'd wether Moulay Ismail is thoroughly appriz'd of the loss of his vessels.'

The secretary of state believed that the sultan was unlikely to negotiate the release of any slaves unless an ambassador was sent to the imperial capital. Moulay Ismail himself had admitted as much in a letter to Admiral Cornwall, saying that he was tired of conducting negotiations from a distance. 'This is not the way you can achieve anything with me,' he wrote. 'If you have the will to speak with me, and have something to ask of me, then may you come to my High Palace of God.' He had added, with haughty disdain, that 'I, Servant of God, cannot talk with you by post and letters.'

Addison told his colleagues that it was imperative for an accredited ambassador to be sent to Morocco without delay. 'The English captives will not be sett att liberty unless some minister goes to Meknes with a handsome present for the emperor, and bribes for his favourites.' Yet he knew that there was a real risk attached to sending a high-ranking ambassador to Meknes. Moulay Ismail treated visiting envoys with contempt, and Addison had been appalled by stories told by previous ambassadors. When one of France's emissaries had been granted an audience, the sultan had 'received him in robes just stained with an execution . . . [and] was blooded up to his elbows by a couple of Moors, whom he had been butchering with his own imperial hands'.

Addison realised that the prospect of such humiliating treatment was unlikely to persuade the cabinet to despatch an ambassador. He admitted that 'the objections made against sending a minister to Meknes are the dangers of his being detain'd, the expence, and the little dependence that is to be had on any treaty made with the Moors.' Yet he urged the cabinet to agree to such a course of action, in spite of the risks. Someone had to be sent into the lion's den, and the secretary of state argued that 'one man would be very well sacrific'd for the prospect of redeeming so many of his countrymen.'

Addison's presentation of the crisis led to a lengthy debate. His fellow ministers considered the costs of sending an ambassador and weighed the expenses of maintaining Admiral Cornwall's fleet. They also looked into the benefits of a peace treaty with Morocco, which could lead to the opening of a new market for England's wool exports. Eventually, Addison's performance in cabinet won the day. His fellow ministers conceded to his demands, and the delighted secretary of state noted on his agenda: 'one to be sent to Meknes.'

The man chosen to lead the mission was Coninsby Norbury, one of the captains of Cornwall's fleet. A most inappropriate choice for such a delicate mission, he was arrogant and contumacious, as well as having the uncanny ability to cause offence wherever he went. How he came to be selected remains unclear. It is quite possible that none of his colleagues was willing to risk their lives on a visit to Meknes, and that Norbury was the only volunteer. Within hours of being rowed ashore at Tetouan, in northern Morocco, he managed to insult several of Moulay Ismail's most important officials. Chief among these was Kaid Ahmed ben Ali ben Abdala, the sultan's principal commander-in-chief.

Kaid Ahmed was accustomed to being treated with deference, especially by European emissaries. But Captain Norbury had no intention of abasing himself before the kaid. Indeed, he behaved with such an air of disdain that the kaid sent a complaint to the king's ministers in London. Its Arabic script was promptly translated and circulated among the cabinet. 'On Captain Norbury's arrivall,' wrote the kaid, 'I went to the seaside accompanied by a thousand people to meet him, ordering a tent to be pitched for the said captain and another for myself, in order to receive him with all tokens of friendship.' Kaid Ahmed relished the pageantry of an official visit, but quickly discovered that this particular embassy was to be rather different from most. 'I was surprised to see him [Norbury] in a passion about the form of his reception,' he wrote, 'thinking the ceremony was not attended with sufficient submission.' Norbury sniffed haughtily, expressed his displeasure and 'turn'd his backside to me and so return'd to his tent'.

This was a grave insult, and the kaid was deeply offended. He claimed to have done everything in his power to receive Captain Norbury with all due splendour and to have provided the English retinue with the finest horses in the area. Yet when he had asked to cast his eye over the presents Norbury had brought for Moulay Ismail, he was met with a blank refusal. 'He refus'd it,' wrote the kaid, 'saying nobody should see it till he came to Meknes.' Kaid Ahmed was exasperated, but was prepared to let the offence pass. He attributed Norbury's snub to 'bad pollicy and ill councill', yet he could not help noting that 'from the very beginning, till the day he left Meknes, he endeavoured to have piques and differences, not only with me on frivilous matters, but with the ministers there.'

Kaid Ahmed accompanied Captain Norbury to the imperial capital and presented him to the sultan. Moulay Ismail was courteous at the first meeting, for he was looking forward to receiving his gifts, but the British captain was brusque to the point of rudeness. '[He] demanded the slaves, saying that without them he'd make no peace, and would blockade all their sea-ports and destroy their commerce, with other threats of that kind.'

Norbury brushed aside complaints that he had breached courtly protocol. Indeed, he may well have argued that criticisms about his behaviour were deeply hypocritical, since Moulay Ismail and his ministers were constantly breaching the peace accords they had signed. The sultan was disgusted by Norbury's lack of respect, but the captain was not yet finished. Incensed that the sultan was holding so many of his countrymen as slaves, he began shouting and 'stamping on the ground three or four times before the emperor'. When Moulay Ismail attempted to calm him, Captain Norbury blurted out, '"God damn you", which the courtiers understood'.

Thomas Pellow was witness to this extraordinary incident and reported that Captain Norbury's behaviour 'put his majesty into an excessive passion'. The sultan was so furious that he lashed out at those who were closest to him. 'Many of the people about him bore the marks of his sword, lance or short sticks,' added Pellow. 'The face and arms of the negro who carried his umbrella when Captain Norbury was there was scarred all over with cuts that the emperor had given him.'

Whether or not Moulay Ismail intended to release his British slaves is not known, but he was certainly in no mood to free them after Norbury's arrogant display. He informed the captain 'that he had behav'd himself very ill' and added 'that strangers ought not to endeavour to gain the disgust of the people where they are'. One of the sultan's courtiers, Kaid Abdala, blamed the failure of the British mission squarely on Captain Norbury. 'If the said captain had behav'd himself as he ought to have done,' he wrote, '. . . he might have acquir'd what he desir'd.' In the event, his overweening 'avarice and covertousness' caused his mission to fail. Norbury was escorted empty-handed back to Tetouan and shortly afterwards rejoined Admiral Cornwall's fleet.

Captain Norbury's mission had been a disaster. Joseph Addison had hoped to sign a permanent truce with Moulay Ismail and at the same time free all the British slaves. In the event, his ambassador's sole achievement was to incense the sultan with his threats and boasts. The only positive outcome was the news that Moulay Ismail had agreed to the posting of a British consul in Morocco, probably because he saw it as a means of increasing the flow of gifts to his court. The man chosen for this office was Anthony Hatfeild, an enterprising merchant whose contacts in Morocco had enabled him to continue a trade of sorts with the port of Tetouan. Consul Hatfeild was to prove a diligent servant over the coming years and would do everything in his power to win the freedom of the British slaves. But, like Joseph Addison and Admiral Cornwall, he was to find it almost impossible to deal with the proud and unpredictable sultan.

While the British captives toiled on the walls and ramparts of Meknes, Thomas Pellow's circumstances had changed for the better. He was now about fifteen years of age and had been away from home for more than three years. Soon after Moulay es-Sfa's death, he was given to one of the sultan's courtiers, Ba Ahmed es-Srhir, 'whose business was to train up and instruct youth how they should speak and behave before the emperor'. Pellow was being groomed as a palace retainer – one of the army of servant-slaves who were in daily contact with Moulay Ismail.

Six hundred youths had been selected for such training, but few showed any aptitude or enthusiasm. It was not long before Pellow was singled out as one of the more competent in the group. Within two weeks of joining Ba Ahmed's household, he was given the rank of captain and put in charge of eight other renegades. They were sent to the imperial palace and told to 'clean the walks in the emperor's garden, where he and his favourite . . . were used to walk'.

The position was fraught with danger. Moulay Ismail had decreed that his wives should be seen by no one except the palace eunuchs, and the inhabitants of Meknes were instructed to remain indoors whenever the sultan and his entourage took their daily promenade. Father Busnot had observed one of these colourful spectacles from a distance and was astonished at the lengths to which the sultan would go to ensure that no one saw his wives. Whenever they left the palace compound, 'the eunuchs run before, firing their pieces several times, [so] that all persons may withdraw on pain of death.' He added that 'when anyone is surpriz'd, so that he cannot get away, he avoids the punishment by lying down with his face flat on the ground; for should he look upon one of these women, he would certainly suffer death.'

Pellow kept a careful eye on the entrance to the garden, but soon made an error that could have cost him his life. He was sweeping the gravel walkways when one of the sultan's four principal wives, Halima el-Aziza, unexpectedly entered the garden. 'The queen,' wrote Pellow, 'coming one day into the walks, before I had the power to hide myself in a little house set there for that purpose . . . happened to see me.' There was something about Pellow's plucky demeanour that aroused her curiosity. Instead of reporting him to the sultan – and demanding that he be punished – she asked to be granted him as a servant for her own household.

Moulay Ismail was anxious to please his favourite wife and gave his consent. '[He] ordered us immediately out, one by one, till she should see the same person.' As soon as Pellow appeared, the queen recognised him '[and] I was forthwith given her'. His new position was quite extraordinary and was to bring him into far greater danger. He was made chief porter to the innermost series of doors of the queen's palace – the entrance that ultimately led into one of the sultan's several harems. These inner quarters were controlled by a phalanx of black guards and eunuchs, and entry was forbidden to all but a chosen few. In these cloistered courtyards, which lay at the very heart of the palace, were the queen's private quarters. This was where she, 'with thirty-eight of the emperor's concubines, and several eunuchs, were closely shut up'.

The harem was a sumptuous mansion whose courtyards were adorned with polished marble columns. According to Francis Brooks, one of the slaves involved in its construction, a sculpted marble basin formed the centrepiece of the courtyard. This was filled with 'curious spring water . . . [which] boils up in the middle thereof, and comes from a fountain about two miles from the castle'.

The number of women in Moulay Ismail's several harems was a constant source of fascination for European visitors to the imperial palace. Pellow claims that the sultan had more than 4,000 concubines during the time he was in Meknes, all of whom were 'closely shut up in other houses allotted for them'. Such a number is impossible to verify, although Moulay Ismail is known to have sired a vast number of children. The birth of each child was marked by a special tax upon the country's Jews, in order that suitable gifts could be bought. The register of this tax suggests that the sultan had at least 1,200 children during the course of his long reign.

Pellow never glimpsed inside the harem, for to do so would have cost him his life. But a Dutch slave girl named Maria Ter Meetelen left a unique portrait of life in the quarter that Pellow was now set to guard. 'I found myself in front of the sultan,' she wrote, 'in his room, where he was lying with at least fifty women'. They were 'painted on their faces and clothed like goddesses, extraordinarily beautiful, and each with her instrument'. Maria listened in amazement as 'they played and sang, for it was a melody more lovely than anything I'd ever heard before'.

The ladies of the harem presented an extraordinarily rich spectacle. The sultan's principal wives were decked in gold drops and pearls, 'which were hanging from their necks and were very heavy'. They wore golden crowns interlaced with more pearls, and their wrists jangled with gold and silver bangles. Even their hair was pleated with golden thread, which sparkled in the brilliant sunlight, while their necklaces were so laden with gems 'that I was wondering how they could keep their heads straight with all that gold, pearls and precious stones'.

The sultan's concubines spent the greater part of their lives shut away from the outside world and rarely left this forbidden corner of the palace. Many grew so bored with life in the harem that they bribed their eunuchs into acquiring wine from the Christian slaves. Others sneaked out to visit friends elsewhere in the palace. Such clandestine sorties were made with great risk. When Father Busnot was in Meknes, he said that Moulay Ismail 'caus'd fourteen of them to have all their teeth drawn for having visited one another privately'.

The sultan's harem often contained European slave girls who had been captured at sea by the Salé corsairs. Francis Brooks had watched the arrival of four English women seized aboard a vessel bound for Barbados. The chief eunuch informed the sultan that there was 'a Christian virgin amongst the rest of the women', and a delighted Moulay Ismail urged her to renounce her faith, 'tempting her with promises of great rewards if she would turn Moor and lie with him'. The girl refused to apostatise, earning herself the full force of the sultan's wrath. '[He] caused her to be stript, and whipt by his eunuchs with small cords, so long till she lay for dead.' He then instructed his black women to take her away and feed her nothing but rotten bread. The poor girl's spirit was eventually so broken that she had no option but to 'resign her body to him, tho her heart was otherwise inclined'. The sultan, gratified, 'had her wash'd and clothed . . . and lay with her'. Once his desire was sated, 'he inhumanly, in great haste, forc'd her away out of his presence.' The lovemaking was perfunctory but productive. The girl became pregnant and eventually gave birth to a healthy child who was destined to a life of servitude in the great palace of Meknes.

The rules that governed the harem were strictly observed, and no one but the sultan and his eunuchs was allowed into the inner sanctum. Moulay Ismail himself was governed by a protocol that required prior warning before he could be granted entry. Pellow was informed of these rules and told that his function was to stop any visitor from entering these quarters between the hours of dusk and dawn.

It was not long before his resolve was tested to the limit. One evening, shortly after sundown, there was a loud knock on one of the doors that he was guarding. Pellow knew that most of the courtiers had already retired to their quarters; he also realised that whoever stood on the other side of the door had managed to evade several other guards. He feared that the sultan himself stood outside, yet he was under the strictest instructions not to open the door. 'I had positive orders,' he wrote, 'to admit none after such an hour, without being before advised of it, and of some certain signs to be given accordingly.' His orders were not merely to deny access to the person outside. 'In case anyone should attempt to enter at such an unseasonable hour, and not immediately depart . . . I should then fire through the door.'

There was a second knock, and Pellow demanded to know who was there. It was the answer that he most feared. Moulay Ismail was indeed demanding access to his harem and was furious that a palace slave was blocking his path. Pellow was momentarily in a quandary, aware that whatever course of action he chose was certain to lead to punishment. If he refused to open the door, he faced torture and execution for disobeying the sultan's command. If he opened the door, contrary to orders, he would be put to death for proving himself untrustworthy.

The guards at the outer entrance had panicked when they realised the sultan himself was demanding entry, so fearful of disobeying an order that they had meekly opened the doors. But Pellow had always displayed a great independence of spirit and was rarely prepared to compromise. It was this stubbornness that had enabled him to leave home against the wishes of his parents. It had also – by extension – led to his capture. Now, it would result in a very different outcome.

Pellow's masterstroke was to dissemble, telling the sultan 'that I very much doubted it [was him], for that I have never known His Excellency to come at such an unseasonable hour without my being pre-advised thereof'. He added that whoever stood on the other side of the door 'should at his peril be gone, or I would present him with half a dozen bullets through the door'.

Moulay Ismail ordered Pellow to hold fire and barked 'that if I would not let him in, he would certainly chop off my head the next day'. Then, changing his tone, he said that 'if I would admit him, he would give me such a fine horse . . . with all the rich furniture in the empire.'

Pellow instinctively mistrusted the sultan and, convinced that he was being put to the test, declared that he would not open the door, '[even] if he would give me all the horses and furniture in the empire'. He said that the reason for his refusal was simple: 'I was entrusted and commanded by the renowned Moulay Ismail, the most glorious emperor in the world, to keep that post inviolable against all imposters and intruders whatsoever.' He added that 'it was in vain for him any longer to persist.' Moulay Ismail was so infuriated by Pellow's words that he began banging wildly on the door.

Pellow knew that it was too late to backtrack. He also knew that he was under orders to fire his gun through the door if any uninvited guest continued to demand admittance. He was sure that the shot was unlikely to hurt the sultan. The door was made of heavily studded timber, and there were plenty of alcoves on the other side in which Moulay Ismail could take shelter. Yet he could scarcely believe that he – a palace slave – was about to turn his musket on the sultan of Morocco. Nervously, and half sick with fear, he began to charge his weapon.

As he pulled the flintlock, a huge blast reverberated around the palace. 'I fired all the bullets which I had ready by me in a blunderbuss,' he wrote, 'quite through the door.' The shot splintered the woodwork and peppered it with holes. It finally convinced the sultan to retreat. 'On his seeing my so resolute resistance, and no likelihood of his admittance, he returned as he came.' As Moulay Ismail left, he shouted wild threats at

Pellow, while at the same time commending the guards of the outer doors who had given him access.

Pellow was terrified as to what would happen in the morning. He was woken early, along with the other guards, and ordered into the presence of the sultan. Although certain that he would face execution for his behaviour, he soon discovered that the sultan's fury was directed towards the guards of the outer gates. 'All those who gave him admittance,' wrote Pellow, 'had some their heads cut off, others cruelly used.' Pellow himself received extravagant praise from Moulay Ismail. 'After being highly commended for my fidelity,' he wrote, '[I was] rewarded with a much finer horse than he offered to give me in case I would betray my trust.'

Pellow's bravura in facing down the sultan was to bring him into daily contact with the inner circle at court. He was first made an attendant to one of Moulay Ismail's sons, the unpredictable Moulay Zidan. 'He was by nature cruel enough,' wrote Pellow, who was horrified to witness him 'kill his favourite black with his own hand'. The man was murdered because he had accidentally disturbed a pair of pigeons that Moulay Zidan was feeding.

Pellow was next made an attendant to Moulay Zidan's mother, a kindly lady who found him 'a careful and diligent servant'. Soon after, when Pellow was about sixteen years old, Moulay Ismail took him directly into his service. Realising that this young Cornish slave was uncommonly bright and industrious, the sultan wanted to make use of his talents. Pellow was ordered 'to wait on him at his palace for such future commands as should be by him enjoined me'. His new servant was confined to the luxurious palace compound, where he was 'always ready in obedience to his commands, in receiving him bare-headed and bare-footed at his entrance in, or at his going out of the palace'. It was not long before the sultan ordered Pellow to serve as one of his personal attendants. '[I was] strictly charged to be observant of the emperor's commands only,' he wrote, 'and to wait on him on all occasions.' Whenever Moulay Ismail left his palace on horseback in order to inspect the workmanship of his white slaves, Pellow rode alongside. 'I was generally mounted on the fine horse he gave me for my fidelity in maintaining my post at the door.' On such occasions, he had to carry 'a club of about three feet long, of brazil-wood, with which he used, on any slight occasion, to knock his people on the head, as I had several times the pleasure of beholding'.

As Pellow accompanied the sultan on his courtly business, he was obliged to watch in silence as his master lashed out at his slaves. 'He was of so fickle, cruel and sanguine a nature,' he wrote, 'that none could be even for one hour secure of life.' Pellow watched in despair as Moulay Ismail ordered his black executioners to kill slaves who were slacking, giving them signals to show how he wanted them despatched. 'When he would have any person's head cut off,' wrote Pellow, '[he demonstrated] by drawing or shrinking his own as close as he could to his shoulders and then, with a very quick or sudden motion, extending it.' His sign for a slave to be strangled to death was 'by the quick turn of his arm-wrist, his eye being fixed on the victims'.

Pellow's loyalty to the sultan earned him better lodgings. Although his quarters were tiny, the cell had a tiled roof and was sheltered from the worst of the summer heat by the great walls of the palace. He was also entitled to a share of the daily feast that was prepared for the sultan's inner circle.

Everything in Moulay Ismail's palace was on a grand scale, and the meals were no exception. Pellow could scarcely believe his eyes on the first occasion when he ate at court. A giant platter, which held enough couscous to feed 900, was wheeled into the palace courtyard. The assembled company were divided into groups of seventy or eighty men, '[and] had all our messes served out from the cart in large bowls, and set in the middle of us'. Pellow had never eaten couscous before and was surprised to find it quite delicious. Soaked with melted butter and lightly perfumed with saffron and spices, it was 'very good, grateful and nourishing . . . and excellent eating'.

Many of Pellow's companions had been slaves for several years before they had converted to Islam and earned themselves a position at court. Accustomed to a diet of bread and oil, they were unable to restrain themselves when first presented with food from the palace kitchens. The men lunged at the platters, grabbing large chunks of meat and cramming it into their mouths. The attendant guards were appalled, especially when the food became lodged in the men's throats. Henceforth, they were attended 'by several persons with clubs in their hands, in case any should by chance swallow a piece too large for their gullets, and it should stick therein – which, through their greediness, often happened'. If they began to choke, 'one of those attendants gave the party a very hearty blow with his cudgel in the neck, by which means it was generally discharged either up or down.'

The better diet and enclosed lodgings caused a dramatic improvement in Pellow's health. He had arrived in Morocco suffering from the deprivations of many months at sea and had been further weakened by his time aboard Captain Hakem's vessel as well as his beatings at the hands of Moulay es-Sfa. Now, after a few months in the sultan's service, he was 'in pretty good plight'. The principal danger was no longer disease and starvation, but the capricious sultan and his wives. 'I was obliged,' wrote Pellow, 'to walk like one . . . on the brink of a dangerous precipice whence, should he happen to make but the least wry step, he is sure to tumble down and break his neck.' His situation became even more worrying when one of Moulay Ismail's wives displayed amorous intentions towards Pellow, who had no desire to reciprocate her affections. 'I thought it highly prudent to keep a very strict guard upon all my actions,' he wrote.

Moulay Ismail's behaviour was always unpredictable and he had been known to call for impromptu inspections of his household retinue. On one occasion, Pellow noticed that the sultan was 'on the merry pin' and anxious to be amused. With a malicious smile, he ordered 800 of his servant-slaves – including Pellow – to be brought before him. When they were assembled in the palace parade ground, he called for an equal number of women to be summoned from the palace. He then gave a brief address, informing the men that he had, 'on several occasions, observed their readiness and dexterity in obeying him'. As a reward for their loyal behaviour, he said, he had decided to present each one of them with a wife. The men assumed he was joking, but Moulay Ismail was in earnest. He entered the throng with great enthusiasm and began matching men and women, 'some by his own hand . . . and to others by the beckoning of his head and the cast of his eye, where they should fix'.

Pellow was horrified by the spectacle that followed, particularly when he realised that he was not immune from the sultan's grotesque matchmaking. 'I was also called forth and bid to look at eight black women standing there, and to take one for a wife.' Pellow looked them up and down, but found none to his taste. It was not their looks that he disliked. Pellow, filled with the prejudices of his age, objected to the colour of their skin. The women had been brought as slaves from tropical Africa and were all jet black.

'Not at all liking their colour,' wrote Pellow, '[I] immediately, bowing twice, falling to the ground and kissing it, and after that the emperor's foot . . . humbly entreated him, if, in case I must have a wife, that he would be graciously pleased to give me one of my own colour.'

Pellow was taking a great risk in making such a request. Yet Moulay Ismail was bemused by his entreaty and ordered seven half-caste slaves to be summoned from the palace. None of these pleased Pellow, 'at which, I again bowed to the ground, still entreating him to give me one of my own colour'. The sultan was all too familiar with Pellow's obstinacy, and his good humour prevailed. '[He] sent for a single woman, full dressed, and who, in a very little time appeared with two young blades attending her.' When Pellow was ordered to take her hand, he got a shock. 'I perceived it to be black also, as soon after I did her feet.' The effect was just as the sultan intended. He 'ordered me to lift up her veil . . . and look at her face'.

Doing as he was commanded, Pellow was surprised to discover that the girl was much paler than most, and that her hands and feet had been stained with henna. '[I] found her to be of a very agreeable complexion,' he wrote, much to Moulay Ismail's delight. 'The old rascal [was] crying out, in a very pleasing way, in the Spanish language, "Bono! Bono!" Which signifies "Good! Good!"' He decreed that Pellow and the girl should be married without further ado.

The sultan enjoyed marrying off his slaves and counted it as one of his chief pleasures. He often placed himself in the role of chief officiator, standing in front of the crowd and pointing to a male and female slave. According to Pellow, he would call out 'that take that', and the couple would march off 'as firmly noosed as if they had been married by the Pope'. Moulay Ismail paid particular attention to the skin colour of the children they would produce. He was particularly fond of mulattos, or half-castes, and 'always yokes his best complexioned subjects to a black helpmate, and the fair lady must take up with a negro'.

Moulay Ismail had hit upon the idea of breeding slaves early on in his reign. He found mulattos to be the most trustworthy of his servant-slaves and often forced his white slaves to wed black women in order to replenish his household of loyal half-castes. 'He took care to lay the foundation of his tawny nurseries,' wrote Pellow, 'to supply his palace as he wanted.' Pellow said that the offspring from these enforced unions were reared by Moulay Ismail's own officers, and 'taught to worship and obey that successor of their Prophet, and being nursed in blood from their infancy, become the executioners and ministers of their wrath'.

Such bizarre breeding programmes were by no means unique to Morocco. Mixed-blood slaves were also reared in Algiers, in order to increase the stock of half-caste servants of the regime. The French captive, Chastelet des Boyes, was bought by a slave master who kept fifteen or sixteen black women on his farm close to Algiers. He would regularly send his white slaves to breed with them and on one occasion selected Chastelet des Boyes. The Frenchman was taken to the farm by a eunuch, who ordered four of the women to strip him and set to work. 'Having spoken to them,' wrote de Boyes, 'he shut the door behind us, leaving me food . . . [and] a bottle of date brandy.' The eunuch remained close by and kept a watch on the sexual activity occurring within. 'He didn't fail,' wrote de Boyes, '. . . evening and morning, to give us serenades on his drum.' After six days of sexual activity, the eunuch entered the room and released de Boyes. 'He had a private talk with each one of the black women, and took me back to the patroon [slave owner] in the town.'

Thomas Pellow discovered that his new bride did much to improve his situation. The girl's brother-in-law was 'a man of very considerable authority' with some 1,500 young men under his charge. Other family members were also well placed; they, too, were generous to Pellow and his bride, and 'received us very courteously indeed'. They told him to 'always behave to her as a loving husband . . . and at the same time exhorting her no less duty to me'.

Pellow was given fifteen ducats by the sultan – as were the other newly betrothed retainers – but had to use some of this to buy his marital certificate. Once the certificate had been signed by the court secretary and presented to the couple, 'we were all dismissed to make merry with our friends, and celebrate our nuptuals.'

Pellow's adopted family did their best to organise a feast. One of his wife's brothers provided food, while Pellow himself borrowed enough money to buy 'a fat bullock, four sheep, two dozen of large fowls, [and] twelve dozen of young pigeons'. The wedding feast lasted for three days, and the family engaged in 'a great deal of mirth and friendly satisfaction'. But for Pellow himself, one important ingredient was missing: he was unable to acquire any wine or spirits to enliven the party. 'It [was] the soberest wedding you ever saw,' he wrote, 'for we had not, among all this great company, one intoxicated person.'

Pellow's unexpected marriage bound him ever closer to his adoptive home. His conversion to Islam meant he was most unlikely to be redeemed by his home government, and he now found himself with a family of his own in Morocco. With mounting despair, he realised that he was unlikely ever to return to his native village of Penryn.

7 Rebels in the High Atlas

THERE ARE FEW RECORDS FROM Meknes between the years 1717 and 1720. The surviving British slaves had begun to lose hope of ever being released from their misery. A lone anonymous letter, which appears to have been written in the spring of 1717, suggests that conditions were as appalling as ever.

'Ye rains are now pretty well gone,' it reads, 'so that it's now beginning to be hot and long days.' The writer added that it was enough 'to pierce a man to think of standing, sixteen hours or more, bare-headed in the sultry hot sun' and noted that forty-one of the British captives had recently died from hunger, sickness or the gruelling daily regime. The men were still working on the outer reaches of the imperial palace and were forced into 'carrying prodigious loads of dirt and stones from morn to night, without intermission, on our bare heads, without any difference twixt masters and men'. The same correspondent said that 'we are all alike miserable, and I run the risk of many bastinadoes for the present stolen moments.'

The men were probably working on the Dar al-Mansur, a monumental edifice that stood on the edge of the palace compound. Some of the slaves may also have been toiling on the enlarged stables, whose size and scale had already impressed Father Busnot when he visited them a few years earlier. The interior walls were almost a mile long and supported row upon row of arched galleries. Each arch was supplied with fresh running water, and there were fountains, pavilions and exquisite domed storehouses for the horses' bridles and saddles. Father Busnot thought that the stables were 'the beautifullest part of his palace'. By about 1719, they had become one of the largest.

Accounts vary as to how many horses were housed in them at any given time. Some visitors counted 1,000; others claimed to have seen more than 10,000 in the enlarged outhouses. The Moroccan chronicler, Ahmed ben al-Nasari, said the total number of horses was closer to 12,000.

Moulay Ismail was obsessed with the care of these horses and selected his most trusted slaves to pamper them. He decreed that every ten stallions should have two captives to care for them and provide them with every possible luxury. The sultan's favourite horses were fed with lightly perfumed couscous and camels' milk. Others were given sweet herbs that were gathered by the slaves each morning. Horses that made the pilgrimage to Mecca were given right royal treatment: they were exempt from labour, and the sultan himself declined to mount them. The slaves who cared for these sanctified animals were under the strictest orders and were punished with great severity if they slacked in their duty. Every time the horse urinated, they had to be ready with a vessel in order that the holy urine did not have contact with the earth. Some years earlier, the French ambassador, Pidou de St Olon, watched in bemused disbelief as he was shown a horse that had recently returned from Mecca. 'It was led in state just before him [Moulay Ismail],' he wrote. 'His tail was held up by a Christian slave, who carried a pot and a cloth to receive his excrements and wipe him. I was told that the king, from time to time, went to kiss that horse's tail and feet.'

A group of specially selected slaves was also charged with caring for the sultan's extensive menagerie. Many of these animals had been presented to him as gifts from various African rulers and included wolves, leopards, lions and lynxes. He was particularly attached to two of his camels, which were 'as white as snow', and instructed his slaves to wash them with soap every other day.

Moulay Ismail also had an obsession with cats and had forty of them as pets, 'all of them distinguished by their names'. He always visited them when they were being fed by the slaves and was accustomed to throw them 'whole quarters of mutton'. On one occasion, the sultan was horrified to discover that one of his favourite cats had snatched a rabbit from its warren and killed it. Instead of punishing the slave in charge, as everyone expected, the sultan ordered 'that an executioner should take that cat, that he should drag it along the streets of Meknes with a rope about its neck, scourging of it severely and crying with a loud voice: "Thus my master uses knavish cats"'. Once this gruesome spectacle had been performed, the unfortunate feline had its head chopped off.

The slaves were terrified of the sultan's whimsies – just as he intended – for they never knew who would be his next victim. The British and colonial American captives wrote little about how they found the inner strength to survive the daily horror of life in the slave pens. But when the Boston preacher, Cotton Mather, met a group of American slaves released from Algiers in 1681, they told him that communal prayer had done much to fortify their spirits. '[They] formed themselves into a society,' he wrote, 'and, in their slavery, enjoyed the liberty to meet on the Lord's Day Evening.' The men warned each other about the temptation of apostasy and even set out a code of conduct 'to prevent and suppress disorders among themselves'. Many of the slaves from the American colonies were deeply religious men, having been raised in strict Puritan households. Joshua Gee, a puritan from Boston, Massachusetts, admitted that prayer alone had enabled him to survive his suffering. 'I always found reliefe in seeking God, when I could find it nowhere else,' he wrote.

'It was a great relief to me that I had learned so much scripture by heart when I was young.'

The British slaves in Meknes also found strength in prayer. According to Francis Brooks, they prayed 'for the preservation of their own king and country, and that God would be pleased to open their hearts to remember them in this sad and deplorable condition'. They prayed for their families; they prayed for their comrades. But most of all, they prayed to be released from the appalling hardship and suffering.

These Protestant captives always looked with envy upon their Catholic counterparts. Moulay Ismail permitted his Catholic slaves a certain freedom of worship – as did the dey of Algiers and the bey of Tunis – and occasionally allowed the padres in the friary to celebrate religious festivals. The most colourful of these was the feast of Corpus Christi, when the padres would bribe the slave guards to allow all the Catholic slaves to participate. In the spring of 1719, Father Francisco Silvestre was one of those who helped organise the festival. 'On this day,' he wrote, 'the walls of the patio of the *sagena* [slave pens], where the procession begins, are decorated with green stalks.' Arches were bedecked with herbs and flowers, and all the slaves were given candles. 'A cleric leads . . . [and] all walk, chanting hymns appropriate to the day.' It was one of the few times in the year when the Catholic slaves could momentarily forget the miseries of their lives.

Moulay Ismail did not always allow the padres to celebrate such festivals. He gave 500 bastinadoes to one slave who asked if the men could celebrate the feast of St John the Baptist and showed even less inclination to offer concessions to his British and American captives. 'Some of them had asked him leave to keep their Easter,' wrote Father Busnot, 'as he had granted it ten days before to the French Catholick slaves.' The sultan pondered for a moment, then asked if they had fasted. When they shook their heads, he told them: 'Where there is . . . no lent, there is no Easter, and so he sent them back to the works.' It was a typically cruel but rational observation.

Thomas Pellow had changed beyond recognition in the five years since he had left Penryn, and his parents and sisters would scarcely have known him. He was no longer a boy – his wispy beard was testimony to that – and he wore a long djellaba with a pointed hood. He had also acquired a new language since leaving home. Although he had slacked in his studies while at grammar school in Penryn, he was a bright, quick-witted lad who had little trouble in mastering Arabic. If he remained in the country for many more years, there was every chance he would speak Arabic more fluently than his native English.

Pellow had certainly experienced more than most young lads of sixteen. He had witnessed appalling suffering, and had been beaten and tortured by his now-dead slave master. He had also found himself married, albeit unwillingly, and had been forced to change his religion. In the process, he had suffered the pain and humiliation of public circumcision. His experiences had transformed him into an outspoken young man, who was fêted among his fellow renegades for having dared to deny Moulay Ismail access to his own harem.

At some point in 1720 – the exact date is unclear – Pellow received some unexpected news. Moulay Ismail decreed that 600 apostates were to be sent to guard Kasbah Temsna, a fortified encampment that lay some 200 miles to the south-west of Meknes. Pellow himself was to be one of the captains of the troop – a polyglot band of former slaves from France, Spain and Portugal, along with men from several city states of Italy.

Pellow was pleased by the turn of events, for he was desperate to leave the imperial capital. The sultan's capriciousness terrified him, and he was depressed by the constant murders and beatings. Yet he feared that this new posting would bring its own dangers. Moulay Ismail had long used renegade Europeans to fight his battles and often ordered them to lead the first wave of attack against rebellious warlords. 'He takes 'em with him into the field,' wrote Pidou de St Olon, 'and, in the engagements, always places 'em in the front, where, if they betray but the least design of giving way, he cuts 'em up in pieces.'

Pellow and his men had received only cursory training in warfare before receiving orders to pack their belongings and prepare to depart. It was a dishevelled but well-armed band that assembled on horseback outside the walls of Meknes. Their wives waited beside them on mules, while scores of other pack animals carried food and supplies. The troop was led by one of the sultan's commanders, Hammo Triffoe, who had a further 2,000 men under his charge. His orders were to accompany Pellow and his men to Kasbah Temsna and leave them with enough supplies for six months.

The sight of such a large band of soldiers on the march terrified the inhabitants of the villages that lay on their route. Moulay Ismail's troops were often unruly and violent, and were given free rein to pillage their way across the landscape. Entire regions could be devastated by their passing, with farmers left destitute and peasants relieved of their belongings. Those who refused to hand over supplies would be 'plundered of all that they have, and cut in pieces themselves'.

The presence of the disciplinarian Commander Triffoe helped to keep order on this occasion, and Pellow makes no mention of any insubordinate behaviour. The men spent four uneventful days on the march before they sighted the great walls of Salé, where Triffoe hoped to stock up on provisions.

Their arrival at Salé brought back unpleasant memories for Pellow. This was where his captivity had begun five years earlier; this was where he had been chained and shackled inside one of Salé's underground matamores. In the distance, he could glimpse the sparkling Atlantic, but there was not a single European vessel riding at anchor. Most reputable foreign merchants had long ago abandoned their trade with Salé, and only those with reliable contacts in the town still dared to ply an illicit trade with the corsairs. Pellow knew that none of these merchants would risk his livelihood for the sake of helping him to escape.

His stay in Salé was rather more comfortable on this occasion than on his first visit. While Commander Triffoe's men prepared their encampment outside the city walls, 'us newly married people had the liberty to go into the town, were lodged there, and most sumptuously feasted by the emperor's order.' Their pleasure was marred only by the knowledge that yet more European captives – seized at sea by the Salé corsairs – were being held in the city's infamous dungeons.

Commander Triffoe ordered the men to strike camp at dawn. He was anxious about the next stage of the march, which would take them through the forested flood plains of the River Cherrat. This uninhabited woodland was a haunt of lion, leopard and wild boar, and the men were instructed to keep a close watch on the tangled undergrowth as they rode. The commander was leading the troops when he was startled by a crashing noise from one side. Before he could wheel his horse around, a huge boar struck with great force, ramming its tusks into the belly of his stallion and 'killing his horse under him'. Pellow flinched when he saw the size of the animal, which had 'very long tusks as keen as knives . . . [which] will rip up anything'. His men reached for their guns and fired at the boar, which 'instantly lost his life'. The men sighted many more during their ride through the forest '[and] killed some hundreds'. They looked at their prey with hungry eyes, hoping for a feast at the end of the day, but Commander Triffoe prohibited them from eating the meat. He reminded these reluctant converts to Islam that boars were unclean and that 'their flesh is by the Mahometan law forbidden.'

The men pushed south along the banks of the River Cherrat, pausing occasionally to fish. At one point, the banks narrowed sufficiently to allow the army to ford the river. On the following day, Pellow and his men finally reached Kasbah Temsna, 'where I, by the pasha's order, immediately entered with two hundred of my men'.

The kasbah occupied a commanding hillside position, with sweeping views across the surrounding countryside. The wooded slopes were dotted with oaks and junipers, while the valley below was watered by the springs and rills of the El-Arîcha River. The kasbah itself – which was to be Pellow's home for the next six years – is no longer standing. Its pink pisé walls crumbled to powder long ago, and all trace of the structure has been sluiced away by the winter rains. But it was constructed according to a template that varied little throughout Morocco. The exterior walls were studded with towers that provided a platform for heavy weaponry. The entrance, too, was protected by cannon. Inside, there was probably a row of low houses, and there would also have been a little mosque roofed with malachite-green tiles.

Pellow was quickly disabused of the hope that the kasbah would provide him and his men with a comfortable home. 'At my entrance to the castle,' he wrote, 'I found all things pretty much in disorder, there being almost a general want of everything.' Commander Triffoe took control of the situation, 'sending us in provisions and stores enough for our subsistence for six months'. Once he had installed the men in the kasbah, he departed for Marrakesh with his own troops. Pellow, who was still just sixteen years of age, now found himself in charge of 300 fellow renegades. It was a remarkable change in fortune for a slave who, just a few years earlier, had been tortured to within a whisker of his life.

Pellow quickly discovered that life in Temsna was far preferable to his existence in Meknes. There was no fear of harsh treatment at the hands of the sultan, nor was there any fighting to be done. 'I and my comrades . . . [had] nothing to do,' wrote Pellow, 'but to contrive ways and means to divert ourselves . . . living in an amicable manner and passing our time very pleasantly.' Far from the imperial capital and surrounded by dense forest, the men spent much of their time hunting 'vast plenty of game, as partridges, hares and jackals'. Every time their guns blasted, the sky would fill with birds, which were picked from the air by the sharpest shooters.

Pellow himself spent four days a week hunting, 'and with very good success, killing vast numbers of all kinds, coming home at nights laden, and seldom or never failing to refresh ourselves by a good supper.' Now that Commander Triffoe was not around, the men ate with relish the wild boar they had shot. 'At our return home at night,' wrote Pellow, 'we never failed of three or four wild porkers roasted whole.' He and his men were even happier when they managed to acquire wine from the local population. 'The inhabitants of the country round' – almost certainly Jews – 'bringing us in several skins a week, together with many other presents, on account of our destroying the wild beasts.' Pellow added that the pork and wine were 'two very presumptuous breaches of their law at Meknes' – and would have been punished by death – but here in the countryside they could do exactly as they pleased. Although escape was impossible, for the area was crawling with informers, there was no one to keep watch on them within the compound of the kasbah.

Pellow and his men always dreaded the day when they would be called upon to fight for the sultan, and the summons eventually came within three months of their arrival at Kasbah Temsna. 'I received a peremptory command from the pasha [Triffoe] to attend him with two hundred of my men,' wrote Pellow, '. . . and to leave my other hundred to secure my several garrisons.' This news, which was a cause of despondency among all of the men at the kasbah, must have come as a particularly heavy blow Pellow. He had just learned that his wife was pregnant with their first child. Now he knew that he would not be there to see her through her pregnancy. He must also have feared that he would never set eyes on his child, since almost every campaign against rebel forces resulted in a large number of casualties and deaths. With the greatest regret, Pellow bade farewell to his wife, selected the requisite number of men and set out for Marrakesh.

The news that greeted him was as grim as he had anticipated. Several tribes in the Atlas Mountains had sworn themselves to rebellion, and their opening salvo was a refusal to pay their customary annual tribute to Moulay Ismail. Such disobedience could not be left unpunished, and the sultan had ordered that they be destroyed by force of arms. Pellow and his company were instructed to bring the unpaid tribute to Meknes, along with the captured rebel chieftains.

Pellow was appalled at the thought that, after five years of captivity, he was no longer merely an instrument of Moulay Ismail's regime, but an enforcer of it. He was even more horrified at the thought of doing battle with the rebels. Several of the tribes lived in the High Atlas and were entrenched in their mountain fastnesses. Their kasbahs were surrounded by precipitous walls of rock and ice, and the warriors inside had spent much of their lives fighting in this inhospitable terrain. Although many of Pellow's fellow renegades came from a military background, they knew little of the lie of the land and could only hope that their superior weaponry – and Commander Triffoe's leadership – would provide them with the advantage they so sorely lacked.

'We rested seven days at Marrakesh,' wrote Pellow, 'being ordered on the eighth early to march out and join the army.' After fording the fast-flowing River Nffìs, the men headed for the impoverished village of Amîzmîz – at the foot of the mountains – where a small group of rebels was believed to be hiding. Their leader soon made contact with Commander Triffoe and begged for mercy, claiming that 'he had no hand in the rebellion, as he understood had been basely and maliciously rumoured of him.' He proffered four fine horses and 'a handsome purse of gold', as well as several exquisite turbans. Commander Triffoe picked over these gifts and was rather pleased with them. According to Pellow, '[he] had not the heart to refuse'. After reprovisioning his troops, the commander ordered the men to strike camp and head upwards towards the snowline.

'We marched on foot up the mountain,' wrote Pellow, '. . . which, being very woody, steep and craggy, our horses could have been of no service to us.' The men began to suffer from the freezing nights and damp mountain air, and wished themselves back in the comfort of Kasbah Temsna. 'This being the month of February, [it was] wet, very cold and the nights pretty long.' The men pushed on until they reached the kasbah of Yahyâ ben Bel'ayd, which surrendered after a short, sharp engagement. Their spirits were further lifted when they learned that many of the surrounding mountain tribes were offering to submit, and that just four mountaintop kasbahs remained in rebellion against the sultan.

These particular kasbahs were almost inaccessible, clinging like eyries to the icy crags 'lying on or very nigh the top of the mountain'. They were lost in swirling banks of freezing fog, and the surrounding scree was 'covered with snow and very difficult to get up'. The men wondered how they would scale the upper slopes and at the same time conserve enough energy to attack the 4,000 fighters hiding out on the mountaintop. For two weeks, the atrocious weather hampered their offensive against the rebels. But on the sixteenth day, the wind shifted and it became mild and damp, 'there falling a very great flood of rain . . . washing the snow down the mountain'. The troops wasted no time in striking camp and scaling the mountain, scrambling over loose scree and dirty patches of snow. As evening fell, the weary men reached the first of the kasbahs, 'but found it quite desolate, the inhabitants having all retired into the next town, at about half a mile's distance'. The men pillaged all they could and then torched the place. Then, they 'retired to some distance, where [we] were settled for the night in an open camp'.

Commander Triffoe woke early after a fitful rest. He sent an uncompromising message to the rebels, demanding immediate obeisance to the sultan. The reply he received was unambiguous: 'the inhabitants would not on any terms surrender, but were resolved to fight it out, even to the last man.' Pellow was extremely anguished by this news. He had no idea of the strength of the rebel forces, but knew that his own men were fatigued, cold and suffering from a lack of food. Worse still, the terrain in the High Atlas was extremely rough and devoid of any vegetation. His only hope was that Triffoe, who had hitherto proved himself a competent commander, would not place them in unnecessary danger.

Triffoe had indeed put much thought into how to attack the kasbah. He was aware that his troops would be exposed to musket fire as they advanced on the stronghold and ordered them to make thick shields out of brushwood. This enabled a small group of sappers to reach the outer walls of the bastion. 'About a dozen of our best miners and an engineer advanced with their pick-axes and other necessary implements,' wrote Pellow, '. . . and immediately fell to work to undermine them.' As they tunnelled into the rocky ground, Pellow and his men 'kept a continual fire [of muskets], so that the enemy did not so much as dare to peep at those places of the walls where our people were carrying on their mines'. For three whole days the sappers dug tunnels under the kasbah walls. Then, when they had managed to hack their way through to the foundations, the underground tunnels were packed with powder.

The resultant blast was so powerful that it not only caused the entire kasbah to shake but carved a massive breach in the walls, allowing Pellow and his men to stream into the fortress. The rebels were shocked by their sudden reversal of fortune, but fought back tenaciously for three hours, 'during which there was on both sides very bloody work'. As the two forces engaged in hand-to-hand combat, muskets were discarded and the fight continued with swords and knives. The tide of battle eventually turned, and Pellow and his men gained the upper hand. After much butchery, the rebel forces were finally crushed.

In the previous showdowns, Triffoe had ordered all the survivors to be taken alive as prisoners of war. This time, he declined to show such clemency. All the men were put to the sword, while the women and children were viewed as booty and carried back to Meknes. The most beautiful women would end up in the imperial harem, while the children would become servants of the regime. The kasbah itself was plundered, destroyed and then burned to the ground. By the evening, only a few charred stumps remained.

News of the expedition's success was quickly carried to Moulay Ismail, who declared his wish to view the captured spoils of war. In addition to a large store of silver coin, Pellow and his men had seized more than 200 horses, as well as some fine bridles and saddles. One of these – which the troops intended to present ceremoniously to the sultan – was of exceptionally fine workmanship, 'strengthened with plates of gold, and curiously inlaid with many very valuable jewels'. The men had also seized scimitars and daggers, powder horns and gunstocks. There was a large quantity of honey and dates, along with dozens of kegs of gunpowder. But all knew that the most welcome gift would be the 200 black slaves who had been taken during the campaign.

Commander Triffoe led his forces towards Meknes and instructed Pellow to remain outside the city while he reported to Moulay Ismail about the recent campaign. 'The next morning, about eight o'clock, the emperor ordered the pasha [Triffoe] to bring the several prisoners into the yard.' Pellow himself was asked to lead them to the palace, and he remained in the sultan's presence while the rebels were quizzed about their insurrection. 'The old tyrant, looking at them very furiously . . . told them in an angry tone that they were insolent traitors, and they should soon reap the fruits of their late rebellion.'

Moulay Ismail was never known to show clemency towards those who contravened his will, and this occasion was to be no exception. 'He ordered three of the most notorious of them to stand with their backs pretty nigh to the wall.' The executioner was then told to cut off their heads, 'which he instantly did at two strokes, two of them being cleanly severed at one'.

Pellow was intrigued to discover that the sultan's chief executioner was 'an Exeter man, whose surname I have forgot, though I very well remember his Christian one was Absalom'. Pellow managed to speak to him when the bloodshed was over 'and he told me' – with no apparent irony – '[that] he was by trade a butcher'.

Moulay Ismail taunted the other rebels with execution, but eventually decided to pardon them on the understanding that they were 'never more to return to their old respective places of abode, but to reside at those which should be by him allotted for them'. They had one last ordeal to endure before being conducted from the palace. So that they should forever be known as rebels of the sultan, they were 'branded with a hot iron in their foreheads'.

After dealing with the rebels, Moulay Ismail ordered Pellow to show him the trophies and spoils. As the sultan picked over the bridles and saddles, he muttered about the wealth of the rebellious chieftains. 'These dogs are certainly very rich,' he said, 'but what was this in comparison of what they had yet left behind.'

He warned Pellow and his men that the huge array of goods they had seized 'was no more than . . . a small part of what was before his own'. He added that if no more booty was forthcoming, he 'would send his messengers to fetch it, with their heads into the bargain'. With those words ringing in his ears, Pellow was conducted out of the sultan's presence.

Thomas Pellow and the other European renegades in Morocco operated in a shadowy world of servitude and slavery. They were rarely subjected to chain gangs and hard labour, yet they were made to work for the regime they despised. The Frenchman, Pidou de St Olon, concluded that although the sultan's renegades lived apart from the other captives, 'they are no less his slaves.' Escape was impossible and freedom remained a dream.

The exact number of renegades forced to serve under Moulay Ismail remains unknown. They rarely figure in the tallies of captives that were compiled by ambassadors and padres. Nor were they considered worthy of being included in negotiations conducted by their home governments. Despised for having forsaken their Christian faith, they were abandoned to their fate.

This was a foolish mistake on the part of Europe's ministers, for the sultan's renegades vastly outnumbered the captives being held in the slave pens and played a crucial, if unwilling, role in keeping Moulay Ismail in power. Without the services of these apostates – many of whom were desperate to escape – the sultan would have been hard pressed to contain the country's frequent rebellions. The French consul, Jean-Baptiste Estelle, noted some years earlier that Moulay Ismail's armoury of 40,000 muskets was in large part cast by renegades, and he added that 'soon he will have more since, in Fez, Christian slaves are casting 400 cannon barrels a month, very fine and of good quality'.

One of the most celebrated of these renegade gun-founders was an Irishman by the name of Carr. A contemporary of Pellow, Carr had been captured as a young lad and voluntarily converted to Islam. 'The temptation was very great,' wrote the Englishman, John Braithwaite, who was to meet Carr in the late 1720s. 'He was offered fine women, and all the riches and grandeur of this country, which if he had not accepted of, he foresaw nothing but slavery, misery and extreme want.' Moulay Ismail showed unusual respect for Carr on account of his skill at casting weaponry. '[He] used to call him brother, and gave him clothes off his back, and would hug and caress him very much, and offered him the greatest governments in the country.' He even made him a kaid and for a short time promoted him to the rank of governor, with control over 'the frontiers of Guinea'.

Carr was a duplicitous individual whose principal skill was self-preservation. 'A very handsome man,' wrote Braithwaite, '[and] very ingenious . . . to us he seemed much to lament his condition and declared himself as much a Christian as ever.' Years of service in Morocco had left him broken and wretched, and he had frequent recourse to the bottle. 'He drank with us very hard,' added Braithwaite, 'and declared to us if it was not that he locked himself up every now and then and took a hearty dose of wine, he could not have supported his spirits, when he came to think he was for ever lost to his country and friends.' Carr typified so many of the sultan's renegades: he was desperate to return home, but knew that the chance of this happening was extremely remote.

Few other apostates won the trust of Moulay Ismail. Those who did rise to positions of prominence were quickly corrupted by their new-found power and authority. A Spanish surgeon called Laureano turned against his former comrades after being made the sultan's personal attendant. He converted to Islam, changed his name to Sidi Achmet and became a most unsavoury individual. 'His physiognomy is very bad, his heart deceitful, his behaviour brutal and impious, and he is a great enemy to Christians,' wrote Father Busnot. The most hard-hearted renegades were put in charge of Christian slaves, whom they treated with great contempt. Guilt about their apostasy may have played a part in their brutal behaviour, but they may also have been affected by sights of extreme cruelty. According to one unnamed slave, the worst fate for any European captive was to be 'belied, back-biten and beaten by some of their own number who are called Christians'. These 'Christians' – he means apostates – had gained their positions through flattery and deception, informing on former comrades who were slacking at work. They knew that they would only retain their posts 'on proviso that they shall make the other slaves work so much the harder'. To this end, they became savage and sadistic, and 'surpass the very barbarians themselves in cruelty, beating their fellows unmercifully'.

Although their complicity won them many privileges, they never had as much freedom as their fellow renegades in Algiers. One British consul, Joseph Morgan, reported that 'nothing was more common to be seen in the streets of Algiers, than parties of renegades, sitting publicly on mats, costly carpets and cushions, playing cards and dice, thrumming guitars, and singing *a la christianesca*, inebriating like swine.' The local population would mutter to each other that 'these renegades are neither Christians, Musulmans nor Jews; they have no faith nor religion at all.'

In Morocco, such outlandish behaviour would have earned them death, torture or banishment to the sandy wastes of the desert. In 1698, Moulay Ismail exiled 3,000 unruly renegades to the Tafilalt, where they eked out a subsistence among the palm groves. One another occasion, he despatched 1,500 renegades to the Draa – a desert region adjoining the Tafilalt – where they were 'employed to erect a city here for themselves'. Flogged by their overseers and burned by the sun, these unwilling converts to Islam found themselves treated little better than their erstwhile comrades in the slave pens.

Moulay Ismail was dependent on his renegades to quash rebellions, yet he never trusted them in the way he did his infamous *bukhari* or black guard. This formidable fighting force provided the backbone to Moulay Ismail's rule; from its ranks came his personal bodyguards, his crack troops and his slave-drivers. The black guard was fiercely loyal and highly trained, and the troops never wavered in their devotion to their master. They originated from Guinea, where most had been seized in battle or bought as slaves in exchange for 'salt, iron-ware, little looking glasses and other peddling toys that came from Venice'. They were led in chains to Meknes, where they were trained to act with the blind loyalty that had once been the hallmark of the Turkish janissaries. Their name, bukhari, came from their oath of allegiance to Moulay Ismail, which they swore upon a copy of the *Sahih* of al-Bukhari, a ninth-century theologian.

Those who formed the sultan's personal bodyguard were very young – between twelve and fifteen years of age – and their mothers were generally housed in the harem. 'He chuses 'em such,' wrote Pidou de St Olon, 'because he will not trust the guard of his person to those of a proper age, for fear of some attempt against him.' Extremely haughty in their manner, these brutal young guards were dressed in the most costly clothes – finely cut kaftans in purples, indigo and scarlet – and wore exquisite silk stockings, making a splendid sight as they strutted and drilled in the parade grounds of the imperial palace. They wore scimitars by their sides and carried heavy muskets, which, according to one English slave, 'they must keep, upon pain of death, as bright as when it first came out of the gunsmiths' hands'. Unlike most of the sultan's subjects, they were never allowed headgear. 'Their heads were shaved and always exposed to the sun,' wrote Pellow, 'for he affected to breed them hard.'

Pellow witnessed these bodyguards in action and was stunned by their ruthless efficiency. 'They were so ready to murder and destroy,' he wrote, '. . . that the kaids trembled at the very sight of them.' Always carrying out the sultan's orders to the letter, they took especial pleasure in dealing with those sentenced to be executed. If the condemned man was not to be killed immediately, they battered and beat him until he squealed for mercy.

Pellow witnessed their treatment of one victim, who was almost torn to pieces by the time he reached the place of execution. 'By the fury of their looks, and their violent and savage manner . . . [they] made a scene very much resembling the picture of so many devils tormenting the damned.'

As well as providing Moulay Ismail with his personal bodyguard, the bukhari patrolled Meknes and helped to supervise the sultan's Christian slaves. They were strict taskmasters, accustomed to whip and flog the captives under their charge. Francis Brooks was one of the British slaves who frequently felt the lash of these guards. 'The poor Christians were grievously hurried and punished by those hellish rogues,' he wrote. '[They] had scarce time to take any nourishment or eat any of their bad bread . . . but with a great many threats, stripes and blows by the negroes, bidding them turn Moors.' The bukhari also helped to enforce the sultan's rule in the rebellious mountain areas. There were said to be 150,000 black troops stationed in various parts of Morocco – 25,000 in Meknes and a further 75,000 in the garrison town of Mahalla, south-east of Salé. The rest were posted to kasbahs on the frontiers of the country.

Their number was constantly replenished by the great breeding farms and nurseries that Moulay Ismail had established outside Meknes. He visited these nurseries each year and would take back all the ten-year-olds to Meknes. The girls were taught cooking, washing and housekeeping in the imperial household, while the boys were prepared for military training. In their first year they were apprenticed to a craftsman; in the second, they learned to ride mules. In the years that followed, they were instructed how to make pisé – the earth and lime mixture that was used to build the great palace of Meknes. They would then be made to do hard labour in order to improve their physique. 'They took off their clothes,' wrote Pellow, 'and, laying them all in a heap, every one took a basket and removed earth, stones or wood.' In their fifth and sixth years they learned horsemanship, and when they reached sixteen years of age, they were enrolled into the army.

Moulay Ismail treated these trainees barbarously, believing that harsh treatment would toughen them and render them immune to pity. 'He beat them in the cruellest manner imaginable,' wrote Pellow, 'to try if they were hard. Sometimes, you should see forty or fifty of them all sprawling in their blood, none of them daring to rise till he left the place where they were lying.' The most loyal and fanatical would be singled out by the sultan and be made kaids, while those in their charge were ordered to obey their every command. Pellow said that the power often went to their heads. 'It was wonderful to see the indolence, state and the gravity of these young rogues,' he wrote. 'They used the haughty phrases of command, and talked of cutting throats, strangling, dragging and so forth.'

Some of the bukhari became horsemen – 'the highest esteem imaginable' – and were appointed stewards to the country's greatest kaids. They were also employed as emissaries, 'to carry the emperor's letter of thanks to any officer who served him well, or to call him cuckold, spit in his face, give him a box on the ear, strangle, or cut off his head'.

On occasions, select members of the black guard were called upon to carry out political assassinations. Moulay Ismail used one of his bodyguards to kill the richest Jew in Morocco, Joseph Maimaran, whose vast fortune had helped him secure the throne. Maimaran made the mistake of reminding Moulay Ismail of his debt, and the sultan responded by having him murdered. 'The negro did as he was ordered,' wrote Francis Brooks, who said that Maimaran was followed while he was out riding. '[The assassin] spied his opportunity very diligently, so spurred his horse over him, rode upon him, and trode out his brains.'

Moulay Ismail's relations with Morocco's large Jewish community were always ambivalent. The majority he treated with contempt, but a handful of the wealthiest – descendants of Jews expelled from Spain – were accorded senior positions at court. One of them, Moses ben Hattar, became treasurer of the court and played a prominent role in keeping Moulay Ismail in power. Another who found great favour with the sultan was Joseph Maimaran's son, Abraham. He was appointed comptroller of the imperial household soon after his father's murder. An ugly man, but a skilful survivor, he amassed a vast fortune and was only too willing to lend money to the sultan. Father Busnot thought he had 'a very ill presence', but conceded that he had 'a great deal of wit and a long experience'.

Neither of these two courtiers showed any interest in helping the Christian slaves. Father Busnot said that Maimaran was the one member of the imperial household 'that might do most service to Christians, if his inclination were towards it'. But Maimaran hated Christians with almost as much passion as the sultan himself and had no desire to improve the lot of the European slaves. Nor did any of Morocco's other influential Jews. One used to boast that he had amassed as many Christian slaves as Moulay Ismail. When asked what he intended to do with them, he gave a wry grimace and said 'that he would sacrifice one of them every Friday night until they were all consumed'.

Even the wealthy Jews were not immune to the sultan's wrath. On one occasion, he summoned a group of them to his palace and began to harangue them in a most unpleasant fashion. 'You dogs,' he began, 'I have called you all hither that you may take the red cap and embrace my law.' He told them that 'you have amuzed me above these thirty years with the coming of your messias . . . [and] if you do not positively tell me the year and day when he will come, you shall no longer enjoy your goods or lives.'

Genuinely alarmed, the assembled Jews asked for eight days in which to consider their answer. Moulay Ismail granted them this request and sent them out of his presence. When they returned the following week, they coolly informed him that their messiah would appear in thirty years. Moulay Ismail scowled and said they had answered thus in the knowledge that he would be no longer alive. 'I will deceive you in my turn,' he said. 'I will live longer than shall be requisite to make out your imposture.' He would probably have had the Jews executed for impertinence had they not had the foresight to present him with a huge sack of gold coins.

While a handful of wealthy Jews were content to support Moulay Ismail in power – and were reasonably well treated – the majority were poor and downtrodden. They were confined to ghettoes, known as *mellahs*, or places of salt, on account of the fact that Jewish butchers were compelled to pickle the severed heads of rebels and traitors. All were forced to wear black cloaks and caps, and they were obliged to walk barefoot through the unsanitary streets of Meknes, Fez and Marrakesh. Many were treated little better than the sultan's slaves and were subject to constant violence and abuse. 'They cannot walk about the streets but the meanest boy will affront them and pelt them with stones,' wrote one, 'while they dare not, upon pain of death, vindicate themselves or make any resistance.'

One of the few checks on Moulay Ismail's rule came from a most unexpected quarter. The sultan's first wife, Lala Zidana, exercised considerable authority over him and was adept at imposing her will. She was, by all accounts, a veritable harridan, 'black, and of a monstrous height and bulk', wrote Father Busnot in 1714. She had beady eyes and an elephantine belly, and had once been a slave of the sultan's brother, who had sold her to Moulay Ismail for sixty ducats. Quite why he was so infatuated with her remains a mystery. There were many at court who believed her to be a witch who retained the affections of the sultan by means of spells and incantations. She ruled the harem with great ruthlessness and – in common with Madame de Pompadour at Versailles – she ensured that her lover was supplied with a stream of young virgins. But unlike her French counterpart, Zidana had neither grace nor charm. 'When she goes abroad,' wrote Simon Ockley, 'she wears a sword by her side, and a lance in her hand; and is as cruel and imperious as the king himself.'

Zidana held sway over Moulay Ismail with machiavellian adroitness. She ensured that her first-born son, Zidan, was named as the sultan's heir, and she retained tight control over the harem. Her chief rival for the sultan's affections could not have been more different – a wistful young girl who had been brought to the harem as a Christian slave. Either Georgian or English, this apostate virgin soon bore Moulay Ismail a son, Moulay Mohammed. Fearful that her own position was under threat, Zidana turned on the girl with chilling aplomb. She falsely informed the sultan that his young sweetheart had been unfaithful and bribed witnesses to testify against her. The sultan was so incensed that he had the girl summarily strangled.

Zidana oversaw the murder of countless other rivals, including that of Moulay Mohammed. She also had a hand in the grisly execution of one of the sultan's kaids, who was ordered to be sawn in two. Even the sawyers were revolted, for they were told to start sawing between the thighs, rather than at the head, as was customary. '[They] were all bloody,' wrote Father Busnot, '[and] stood sometimes void of sense and motion, and the teeth of their saw tore off pieces of flesh, that none could endure to look at.'

Zidana continued to wield enormous influence over Moulay Ismail and was one of the only members of his household who could conceivably have led a palace coup. Yet she remained resolutely loyal, preferring her role as the power behind the throne. So long as her son was the sultan's official heir, she was content to confine her machinations to the bejewelled walls of the harem.

Moulay Ismail proved extremely adept at controlling the

European renegades, the black guard and the wealthiest Jews. Any one of these groups could have threatened his rule, yet they were always denied the opportunity to challenge his excesses. Those suspected of plotting against the sultan were instantly despatched with the blow of a cudgel or the slice of a sword. 'His government is more than despotick,' wrote Father Busnot. 'He treats all that belong to his empire not as free subjects but as slaves.' The padre added that Moulay Ismail saw himself as the very embodiment of the law, who killed in order to demonstrate his ruthlessness. 'He strikes off heads only to show his dexterity, without any remorse; or obliges his subjects to cast themselves down precipices headlong to exert his absolute authority.'

Visitors to the court were surprised by the extent to which Moulay Ismail retained his grip on power. He rarely displayed any concerns about being overthrown, even when there was a real danger of widespread rebellion. Father Busnot's visit to the court coincided with a period of great turmoil, when a number of powerful warlords were threatening to overthrow the sultan. Yet Moulay Ismail appeared to have not a care in the world, 'giving audience to strangers; indulging himself in the pleasure of the seraglio [and] spending the rest of his time in forwarding his slaves' work'. The padre was convinced that he was about to witness the destruction of Moulay Ismail, unaware that the sultan's extensive network of informers were monitoring every aspect of the rebellion. 'All was looked to be lost,' he wrote, 'when, by the means of some secret springs working without arms, without councils, without any visible efforts, all those storms were laid, the mutineers crushed, the ringleaders delivered up to him, and put to the most dreadful punishments his revenge could invent.'

Moulay Ismail showed an increasing tendency to draw comparisons between himself and King Louis XIV of France, yet he dismissed all other European rulers with a contumelious sneer. He told Pidou de St Olon that 'the emperor of Germany was only the companion of his electors; that the king of Spain was less master of his dominions than his ministers; that the king of England depends on his parliament.'

There was a certain truth to this, and it helps to explain why Morocco's chroniclers saw Moulay Ismail in such a different light from their European counterparts. In Morocco, his autocratic ruthlessness was admired just as much as it was feared. The sultan had crushed numerous mutinies and rebellions, and had unified the country under his iron rule. According to the Moroccan chronicler, Mohammed al-Ifrani, this alone was a cause for celebration. 'The prince of believers, Moulay Ismail, only stopped fighting against his enemies when he had tamed the whole of the *Maghrib* [Morocco], and conquered all the plains and mountains.'

Moulay Ismail had also declared a holy war against the Christian enclaves in Morocco and, true to his word, had seized back most of these infidel citadels. His vast population of Christian slaves – so abhorrent to all European writers – was another source of Moroccan swagger. 'He takes a pride,' wrote Father Busnot, 'and sometimes boasts before the captives, that he commands all the nations of Europe in the persons of his slaves.' It was not long before the sultan's willingness to hold Europe to ransom was being openly fêted by the courtly poets of Meknes:

> O, Moulay Ismail, O sun of the world,
> O thou for whom all creation would not suffice as
> a ransom,
> Thou art nothing less than the sword of God,
> which God has drawn
> from its scabbard to set thee alone among the *khalifas* [Islamic governors],
> As for him who knows not how to obey thee, it is
> because God has made him blind and that his steps
> have wandered far from where they ought to be.

★

The manner in which the sultan corresponded with Europe's monarchs also delighted the court. He hectored King Louis XIV about Christianity and sent him a letter – a copy of the Prophet Mohammed's missive to the Roman emperor, Heraclius – urging the French monarch to convert to Islam. 'Become a Muslim,' it read, 'submit yourself to the religion of Mahomet, and you will be saved . . . [but] if you shrink from this, you are committing a great crime.'

A fervent follower of Koranic teaching, Moulay Ismail was careful to display his religious orthodoxy whenever he was seen in public. 'He causes the Koran to be always carried before him by his *talbe* [religious scholars] as the rule of all his actions,' wrote Father Busnot. 'Wheresoever he is, he often lifts up his hands to heaven, and that very often when they are imbru'd with human blood.' The sultan ordered the construction of prayer places throughout his palace and often preached in the mosques, 'after such a manner . . . that he outdoes all the talbe'. He constantly reminded his courtiers that he was descended from the prophet and that his every word and deed was sanctified by God.

Such fanatical devotion to Islam was greatly admired in Morocco, but it was the source of growing consternation in the Christian West. 'It curbs none of his passions and justifies all his enormities,' wrote Father Busnot, '. . . [and] sanctifies the cruelties he exercises towards the Christians and Moors.' In the eyes of Busnot and many other Europeans, Moulay Ismail had co-opted religion for his own, diabolical ends. Although it brought him great power and authority in Morocco, it was provoking a growing backlash against Islam in almost every nation in Europe.

8 Turning Turk

A close-knit community, Penryn was all too familiar with the perils of the sea. Many families in the town had sons working on pilchard skiffs in the English Channel, and a few of the more adventurous traders had undertaken daring voyages to the West Indies, the Spice Islands and the Americas. The hazards of such oceanic voyages were considerable, and tempests, hidden reefs and the Barbary pirates had taken a grim toll over the previous century. Whenever shipwreck or piracy claimed the lives of Penryn's mariners, the town's inhabitants gathered for prayers in the ancient church of St Gluvias. The church was also where they assembled to give thanks for more welcome news. When, in 1717, the Turkish army was defeated by Prince Eugene of Savoy, the whole village had assembled to rejoice. The parish bell-ringers performed their duties with such gusto that the congregation rewarded them with the sizeable gift of 2s 6d.

Elizabeth and Thomas Pellow had received no direct news from their son since his departure from Falmouth in 1715. Their parting words had been to warn him of the dangers of the Barbary corsairs. It was only after he had set sail that they learned the troubling news that Moulay Ismail had torn up his peace treaty with the late Queen Anne.

Although Pellow himself had been unable to despatch a letter to his family, rumours of his capture and survival had almost certainly reached Penryn. At least one letter written by Pellow's shipmate, Thomas Goodman, had made it back to England. This confirmed that the *Francis* had indeed been captured and that the crew had been taken to Meknes as slaves. It also reported that they were being forced to endure hard labour and that conditions in the slave pens were truly terrible.

The Pellows, a poor family, stood no chance of gathering a ransom for their son. No letters or appeals in their handwriting have survived – they were probably illiterate – and they had little opportunity to travel to London in order to petition directly the secretary of state. But they did know one person who was in a position to help. Valentine Enys, the owner of the *Francis*, was a wealthy and entrepreneurial merchant with trading links that stretched as far afield as the tropical West Indies and the frosty Baltic. He frequently despatched vessels to Madeira and the Mediterranean, and had built an immense fortune from trading in wines, timber and costly cloth – 'druggetts, serges, calimoneos [and] perpetuans'. He had further augmented his wealth by speculating in the Cornish tin mines, a business that had won him important friends and contacts among London's mercantile community.

Enys had good reason to help the Pellows in petitioning the government. The capture of the *Francis*'s crew had also led to the loss of his ship, and he stood to benefit if ministers entered into negotiations with the Moroccan sultan. But Enys was a tough-nosed businessman who had, on similar occasions in the past, been prepared to cut his losses. He had also displayed a callous disregard for the men who served on his ships. In 1704, one of his vessels had been seized by French privateers who, on discovering that the captain, Anthony Dewstoe, was a neighbour of Enys, had demanded the sizeable ransom of £65. Captain Dewstoe expected his friend to pay the money, for he was being held in terrible conditions in Brest prison. But Enys demurred, arguing that the ransom was too high. He even had the gall to justify his decision to Dewstoe himself. 'No one in the world,' he wrote, 'would ever ransom a ship for more than the worth.' Although Enys did eventually pay the ransom – thereby freeing the men – his attitude was scarcely encouraging for the Pellow family.

Elizabeth and Thomas soon found history repeating itself. Enys's correspondence reveals that he was not unduly troubled by the capture of a small ship like the *Francis.* Nor did he make any effort to raise the ransom money that might have secured the release of the crew. He had written off the *Francis* as a lost vessel and saw little point in devoting time and money to a cause that was doomed to fail. The Pellows nevertheless pinned all their hopes on Enys and continued to pray that he would petition government ministers on their behalf. When he died in 1719, they must have felt that they had lost their most influential interlocutor.

Although the families of the Meknes slaves ceased to have any direct news after 1717, they did receive snippets of information from Consul Anthony Hatfeild. For the first two years of his tenure, Hatfeild had been unable to discover anything of substance about the captives being held in the slave pens. But in the autumn of 1719, he at last obtained a list of those who were still alive, which provided him with exactly the information he had been seeking ever since his arrival in Tetouan. It confirmed that twenty-six British vessels had been captured over the previous five years, including two from New England and one from Newfoundland. It also listed the names of 188 men who were still being held in the Meknes slave pens. Many more had died, apostatised, or simply disappeared without trace.

Consul Hatfeild forwarded the document to London in the hope that it would encourage fresh efforts to win the release of the slaves. There is no record of a copy being sent to the West Country, but it seems inconceivable that news of its arrival was not swiftly conveyed to Devon and Cornwall. If so, the Pellow family was in for a nasty surprise. Next to Thomas's name were the two words most feared by every parent of a captured mariner: 'turn'd Moor'. They now knew that their only son had converted to Islam.

Their reaction to this news remains a matter for conjecture, but it must have caused them grave concern. The discovery that a son or husband had apostatised was always a shock, and the few letters that have survived from the period provide a fascinating glimpse into the fears and prayers of men and women like the Pellows. When the Algiers slave, Joseph Pitts, informed his father of his forced conversion to Islam, the old man had been deeply distressed. 'I confess,' he wrote, 'when I first heard it, I thought it would have overwhelmed my spirits'.

Old John Pitts was so appalled by the news that he beseeched Church ministers to help him through his sorrows. These ministers displayed rather more understanding about his son's plight, arguing that apostasy caused by torture earned him the right to forgiveness and pointing out that the Church itself had devised a service of repentance for the few renegades who managed to escape from Barbary. The Laudian rite, as it was called, began with a public humiliation of the individual, who was made to kneel at the entrance of his local church dressed 'in a white sheet and with a white wand in his hand'. For three weeks the penitent was forced to remain in this garb, during which time he was told to keep 'his countenance dejected'. Then, after striking himself in the chest and kissing the base of the font, he was allowed to receive absolution and the holy sacrament.

The elder Pitts was not convinced that any apostate deserved forgiveness – even his own son – although he begrudgingly wrote a letter, urging him to return to the Christian fold whenever possible. 'I can hardly write to thee for weeping,' he said, '. . . what more shall I say to thee . . . I will pawn the loss of my soul upon the salvation of thine, if thou dost but duly and daily repent.'

Such a sentiment was quite possibly echoed by Elizabeth and Thomas Pellow on learning that they, too, had lost a son to Islam. They knew that he no longer stood any chance of being redeemed by the government, since apostates were considered to have forfeited their British nationality. The Pellows may also have feared local reaction to the news. Their offspring's conversion was a source of shame – one that could have stigmatised them in the little community of Penryn. Yet it would not always have been thus. Just a few decades earlier – in the days of the Pellows' grandparents – a tale of apostasy and Islam was more likely to have been a source of mirth.

The laughter could be heard from the farthest end of the street. It crescendoed into a loud roar before fading into the noisy hubbub of the town. It was the spring of 1623, and the Phoenix playhouse in London was packed with grinning, toothless theatregoers. They had gathered to watch *The Renegado*, a ribald farce set among the souks and slave markets of Barbary. With its cast of eunuchs, viziers and lusty viceroys – and its bawdy jokes about circumcision – it represented a world that was both comical and remote. When one of the characters is asked whether he will convert to Islam, he joshes that he is too attached to his foreskin:

> . . . I should lose
> A collop [piece of flesh] of that part my Doll enjoined me
> To bring home as she left it; 'tis her venture,
> Nor dare I barter with that commodity
> Without her special warrant.

The Renegado played to packed houses and was performed alongside other farces set in Barbary, such as *A Christian Turned Turk*. But by the 1640s, the prurient humour seemed inappropriate. The repeated attacks on the West Country – and the horrors perpetrated by the slave dealers – meant that the world of Islam was no longer quite so amusing. Thousands of Britons had been forced into apostasy in Algiers, Tunis, Tripoli and Morocco, and the stock-in-trade gags about circumcision, castration and sodomy no longer seemed entertaining, especially when wives of the slaves learned that their owners 'do frequently bugger the said captives'.

The concerns of these women, and the widespread anxiety about the Islamic world, would eventually penetrate the highest levels of government. On 19 March 1648, a pious young colonel named Anthony Weldon brought alarming news to the Council of State. He informed their noble lordships that the Koran – long considered to be both blasphemous and seditious – had been translated into English for the first time. Even more disturbing was the fact that its translator, Alexander Ross, was intending to publish his translation.

The ministers of the crown were horrified that such a book might soon be available to the public at large and were particularly concerned that it would lead to a wave of apostasies. They immediately ordered the sergeant-at-arms 'to search for the press where the Turkish Alcoran is being printed, and to seize the same, and the papers'. The sergeant was also told 'to apprehend the printer and take him before the Council of State'.

The printer was quickly arrested, and all his copies of the translation were seized and placed under lock and key. All future publications were banned, and Ross himself was summoned to the Council of State 'to give an account for the printing of the Alcoran'.

The records of his clash with the censors have unfortunately been lost. But Ross later wrote an essay about why he had undertaken his translation and must have used similar arguments when dealing with the councillors of state. He said that his 'newly Englished' edition – entitled *The Alcoran of Mahomet* – had been produced 'for the satisfaction of all that desire to look into the

Turkish vanities'. He conceded that the publication was likely to cause a storm of controversy, but considered his *Alcoran* to be essential reading for all who wished to understand the motives of the fanatical slave traders of Barbary. '[In] viewing thine enemies in their full body,' he wrote, 'thou maist the better prepare to encounter and, I hope, overcome them.' The depredations of the Salé corsairs were uppermost in his mind. 'There have been continual wars, and will be still between us,' he wrote. 'It concerneth every Christian who makes conscience of his ways, to examine the cause and to look into the grounds of this war.'

The councillors claimed that Ross was encouraging apostasy, which he countered by arguing that the Koran had 'already been translated into almost all languages in Christendom . . . yet never gained any proselyte'. But he concurred that the book could be dangerous in the wrong hands and said its circulation needed to be strictly monitored. 'It is not for every man to meddle with apothecaries drugs,' he wrote, '[for] he may chance to meet with poyson as soon as an antidote.'

The Council of State agreed to a man that Ross's English translation was an unwelcome addition to the growing number of books about the Islamic world. Yet they were taken aback by the force of his argument. Ross had made a powerful case for the publication of his book and may also have pointed out to the councillors that their action in suppressing his Koran was probably unlawful. Just four months earlier, two separate Whitehall councils had voted for the toleration of all religions in England, 'not excepting Turkes, nor Papists, nor Jews'.

When the Council of State weighed up the arguments, they conceded that Ross had the law on his side. Offering neither explanation nor apology, they retracted their decision to ban the book and informed Ross that his *Alcoran* could be published in English after all. On 7 May 1649, the presses were set up once again. Soon after, the first edition of the English Koran was published.

Ross was correct in arguing that his translation of the Koran would not cause widespread apostasy. Instead, it provided the raw material for countless bilious sermons and diatribes against the Islamic world. His *Alcoran* was pillaged and bastardised, and whole sections of the book were cited as proof of the falsehood of Islam and the dangers of apostasy. One of the most successful of these anti-Islamic bigots was Humphrey Prideaux, a Cornish divine whose native village of Padstow had long been familiar with the terrors of the Salé corsairs. Prideaux's book, *The True Nature of Imposture, Fully Displayed in the Life of Mahomet*, did not pull its punches. It played on every popular fear about apostasy, intertwined with a robust defence of Christianity.

When Prideaux had first tried to get his manuscript accepted, in 1697, the publisher is said to have wished 'there were a little more humour in it'. But when he made a closer study of this heady cocktail of bigotry and bile, he realised he had a potential best-seller on his hands. On the eve of publication, Prideaux himself had a sudden fear that he might have overstepped the bounds of decency. In an introductory letter to his readers, he urged them to discount any notion that he had maliciously distorted the truth in order to set forth Islam 'in the foulest colours'. He assured them that his book was a fair and balanced account, born of many years of study. 'I have been careful to set down all my authorities in the margin,' he wrote, 'and at the end of the book have given an account of all the authors from whom I collected them.'

Prideaux need not have feared what the general public would make of his book; *The True Nature of Imposture* was a runaway success and was rapidly reprinted in numerous editions. The first print run sold out immediately, and a second edition quickly followed. This, too, sold out, and a third and fourth reprint soon followed. As tensions flared on the Barbary coast, Prideaux prepared a further four editions between 1712 and 1718; the book would be reprinted once more in 1723.

Fear of Islam was a subject of equally heated debate in the crown colonies of North America – especially New England, which had lost a number of merchants and mariners to the Barbary corsairs. One of Boston's Puritan ministers, Cotton Mather, was particularly taxed by the issue of apostasy. He conceded that the slaves were suffering terrible deprivations in Morocco, yet believed that physical hardship was no excuse for spiritual weakness, rather that it should help the slaves to strengthen their Christian faith.

In 1698 – the year after the publication of Prideaux's book – Mather wrote 'A Pastoral Letter to the English Captives in Africa'. His tone was uncompromising, and he had few words of comfort for these bruised and battered men. 'Who gave you to the African pyrats?' he asked sternly. 'It was the Lord, against who you had sinned.' He insisted that their own faithlessness had led to their capture and reminded them that there was very little their friends could do to win their release. 'You cannot now make your moans to your consorts, to your parents, to your tender-hearted relations . . . but you must make your moans to God in the Lord Jesus Christ.'

Mather assured the slaves that he was writing 'for your consolation'. Yet few were in any doubt as to the real reason for his letter. The minister had been shocked by individual tales of apostasy and even more appalled to discover that large numbers of men had converted to Islam. 'We must let you know,' he wrote, 'that we are very much concerned for your being preserved faithful unto the death in that Christian faith which you have hitherto professed.' He begged these wretched individuals that, 'whatsoever miseries you undergo, you may not, in a vain hope of deliverance from those miseries, renounce the Christian religion'.

Slavery and apostasy continued to interest Mather for many years, but age did not temper his views. In his sermon, 'The Glory of Goodness', he was scathing about those who had renounced their Christianity. 'The renegades, for the most part, were those who suffered the least share of adversity,' he wrote. 'The fellows enjoy'd more prosperity, and lived in gentlemen's houses with much of idleness and luxury and liberty; these for the most part were they that fell into the snare of the wicked.'

Few in colonial North America were interested in understanding the world of Islam, and even in Britain there was almost no desire to peer beneath the surface of the frightening world of Barbary. One lone voice attempted to counter the anti-Islamic rhetoric. Simon Ockley was a brilliant linguist who from an early age had been 'naturally inclin'd to ye study of ye oriental tongues'. A country parson at Swavesey, in Cambridgeshire, Ockley spent much of his time poring over Arabic manuscripts in the university libraries of Cambridge and Oxford. '[He] consulted divers of our Arabic mssts,' wrote the Oxford-based Thomas Hearne, 'in which language he is said by some judges to be ye best skill'd of any man in England.'

Ockley was fascinated by Islamic culture and horrified at the general level of English ignorance and prejudice on the subject. He described Prideaux's book as 'very imperfect' – a generous description – and argued that a deeper understanding of Islam was 'more necessary than the being acquainted with the history of any people whatsoever'.

Ockley did all he could to fill this gap in knowledge. He translated scores of works by Arabic theologians and philosophers, and then embarked on his monumental *History of the Saracens*, which was completed in 1718. In his preface, he took a sideswipe at all who contented themselves 'in despising the eastern nations, and looking upon them as brutes and barbarians'. Having chastised those who allowed prejudice to rule their thoughts, he explained, with charming simplicity, his love of Arabic. His book included the *Sentences of Ali*, a collection of maxims by the Prophet Mohammed's son-in-law, which Ockley believed to be both instructive and wise. 'The sentences are full and to the purpose,' he wrote. 'They breathe a spirit of devotion, strictness of life and express the greatest gravity.' After setting out his reasons why such theology was worth reading, he castigated all who persisted in damning the world of Islam. 'There is enough, even in this little handful, to vindicate . . . the poor injured Arabians from the imputation of that gross ignorance fastened upon them by modern novices.'

Ockley received scant reward for his hard work and was invariably short of money. He was crushingly shy – particularly when he found himself in distinguished company – and squandered his one chance of improving his lot when he was invited to a dinner party hosted by the Earl of Oxford. Finding himself seated alongside some of the greatest lords in the kingdom, Ockley was so paralysed by nerves that he managed to offend almost everyone present, including his patron. He later apologised in writing to the Earl of Oxford, bemoaning the fact that he was 'struck dumb and almost insensible' by the assembled company. 'It is not the talent of every well meaning man to converse with his superiors with due decorum,' he explained. But his apologies fell on deaf ears. The earl refused to have any further dealings with Ockley, and the principal apologist for Islam sank into penury. When he died in 1720, his wife and children were left utterly destitute.

Thomas Pellow remained in Meknes for some weeks following the execution of the rebel leaders from the Atlas Mountains. He had been deeply disturbed by his previous audience with Moulay Ismail, who had threatened to kill him unless he could produce more booty from the recent campaign. Pellow had left the palace chamber in fear of his life. But the sultan's threats were often mere bluster, and this occasion was no exception. With his fury slaked by the execution of the rebels, he expressed delight with the black slaves and richly embroidered bridles.

After a tense few days, Pellow and his men were ordered to return to Kasbah Temsna.

'On our approach to the walls of the castle, all the women, and several of the men, came forth to meet us.' Pellow said that this was 'a meeting both of a great deal of joy and lamentation'. Sixty of the women in his company found themselves widowed during the recent campaign, while the rest were thankful that their husbands were safe and well. Pellow writes very little in his account about his relationship with his wife. He records neither her name nor her age, and provides few clues about the months that they had spent together at Kasbah Temsna. It may be that he was embarrassed about being married to a Muslim girl, even though she was from an influential family at court. Yet the few anecdotes he does mention suggest that there was warmth – perhaps even love – between the two of them. He was certainly pleased to be reunited with his wife, whom he had last seen during the early stages of her pregnancy. 'I entered very merrily with my girl,' he wrote, 'insomuch that I had forgot, as knowing her to be with child before our departure, to ask her if it was a boy or a girl.' His wife, upset that he seemed to care so little, played a trick on him. She told him that she had given birth to a girl some six weeks previously, but added that she so despaired of him ever returning home that she had given the newborn away.

Pellow was horrified and 'very much enraged', until his wife let out a stifled chuckle. She told him she was joking and added that she hoped he would be more attentive in future. 'The cunning gypsy ordered the child to be brought forth,' wrote Pellow, who was now able to hold the baby for the first time. He was enchanted with his daughter – whose name he neglects to record – and 'not a little pleased with the joke, laughing and embracing the child very heartily'. Over the next few years, she would become a source of the greatest pleasure and happiness. Every time Pellow was sent on a military campaign, he would dream of the day when he would be reunited with his daughter. '[She] always used, at my coming home wounded, to clasp her little arms about my neck, hugging and bemoaning her poor father and telling me that I should no longer go to the wars.' On one occasion, she asked him about his family in Penryn and announced 'that she and her mother would go with me to England and live with her grandmother'.

Pellow and his men soon managed to relax after their arduous campaign in the High Atlas. 'Now are we again at liberty to divert ourselves,' wrote Pellow, 'spending the best part of our time in shooting and hunting in the woods.' They resumed their sport of pigsticking, and spent their evenings drinking and feasting on the day's catch. But just a few months after their return to Kasbah Temsna they were ordered to crush yet another rebellion. A tribe in the sandy wilds of southern Morocco had risen up against Moulay Ismail, 'killing sixteen of the emperor's blacks sent there with his credentials to receive and bring them to Meknes their accustomed tribute'. Knowing that this was tantamount to a declaration of war, they had set to building defences, 'fortifying the town with strong walls and putting into it great quantities of warlike stores and provisions'.

Moulay Ismail ordered one of his sons, Moulay ech-Cherif, to lead a 40,000-strong force against the rebels. This new campaign was to be very different from the one that Pellow and his men had fought in the Atlas Mountains. Now, they found themselves in a barren country where the midday heat was oppressive. They tried to build defensive positions in the wasteland around the rebel town of Guzlan, but discovered that this was virtually impossible, 'the sand sliding so fast from underneath us'. Worse still, their cannon made no impact on the sandy defences.

Half despairing of their predicament, they fired directly into Guzlan, with the idea of causing as much mayhem and carnage as possible. After several weeks of intense bombardment, the shot-battered rebels were at their wits' end, and were forced to make sorties in an attempt to silence or capture the sultan's cannon.

Their second sortie spelled near-disaster for Pellow. Straying too far from his battalion, he suddenly found himself outflanked and hopelessly exposed. Although dressed in a djellaba, like the rebel Moors, his fair skin singled him out as a European renegade. Within seconds, several of the enemy had him in their sights.

There was the crack of a musket and the acrid stench of gunpowder. A split second later, Pellow felt a searing pain in his leg and collapsed to the ground. He would certainly have been killed by the rebels had his companions not come to his rescue. He was carried back to the camp with 'a musket shot lodging in my right thigh'.

Pellow was fortunate that the army was accompanied by renegade physicians whose skills were far superior to those of the Moorish mountebanks and quack doctors. '[The shot] was soon taken out by a German surgeon,' he wrote, 'a man of great skill and diligence, and I was most carefully attended by him.' Yet it was forty days before he was strong enough to use his leg, by which time the rebel forces had been defeated. '[They] beat a parley,' wrote Pellow, 'humbly imploring the general that they might be spared with their lives.'

General Moulay ech-Cherif's response was ambiguous. Although delighted that the rebels promised to swear their 'most dutiful obedience' to Moulay Ismail, he refused to guarantee them clemency. Indeed, he barracked them for behaving in a 'most insolent and contemptuous manner', and told them that they could not expect 'to become their own choosers'.

The slaughter began as soon as they had laid down their weapons. Moulay ech-Cherif had no intention of allowing the rebels to escape with their lives and ordered every man in Guzlan to be killed and decapitated. His plan was to carry the rebel heads back to Meknes, where he would ceremoniously present them to Moulay Ismail. But the general had not counted upon the terrible heat of midsummer, which caused the heads to putrefy within hours of being cut off. 'They became so stinking to that degree,' wrote Pellow, 'that he was obliged to be contented with the ears, which were all cut off from their heads and put up with salt into barrels.' Pellow added that the decision to dispose of these grisly trophies came not a moment too soon. 'For, had we carried so many stinking heads so long a way, it must certainly have very much annoyed the whole army, and probably have bred an infection in it.'

The troops were given a ceremonious welcome when they entered the great gates of Meknes. '[Moulay Ismail] was highly contented with the ears,' wrote Pellow, who added that 'the sight of the heads would have given him a great deal of pleasure, yet, as they were stinking . . . he thought them far better left behind.' The sultan ordered the salt barrels to be opened and the ears removed, so that he could examine them more closely. His intention was to keep them in storage and send them as a grim warning to any chieftain suspected of rebellion, but they pleased him so much that he decided to keep them for himself. 'They were all at last strung on cords,' wrote Pellow, 'and hanged along the walls of the city.'

9 At the Court of Moulay Ismail

Consul Anthony Hatfeild was weary of Morocco. He was subject to daily abuse at the hands of Moulay Ismail's kaids and taunted for his inability to release the British slaves. Worse still, he had run out of money. Ministers in London expected him to subsist on a special tax called consulage, which he was allowed to levy on any English goods imported into Tetouan. This was generous in theory, but rather less so in practice. Few British ships dared to call at Tetouan, and it was not long before His Britannic Majesty's consul found himself with empty coffers.

Moulay Ismail's officials derided the fact that Hatfeild had scarcely enough cash to feed himself. When consuls of other nations were sent to live in Morocco, they did so with a splendour proportionate to their rank. Yet the British seemed content to send their most lowly officials and then leave them without the means to bribe local governors. The kaid of Tetouan displayed particular contempt towards Hatfeild, writing to Joseph Addison to inform him that the British consul had 'a crude character which was harmful, and did no good'.

Hatfeild responded with his own series of letters to London, to 'acquaint your honours with [the] hardshipp attending our house'. But King George I had never shown any interest in Morocco and certainly entertained no notion of despatching any money to Hatfeild. The consul was left bemoaning the daily ordeal of living in Tetouan. Passing the town prison one morning – the date is not recorded – he was horrified to see a man 'hanged by the heels, with irons upon his legs, pinchers upon his nose, his flesh cut with scissors, and two men perpetually drubbing him'. The assailants continued to torture the man until he lapsed into unconsciousness.

In spite of all the hardships, Consul Hatfeild continued to gather intelligence on the movements of the Salé corsairs. They had grown increasingly bold since his appointment in 1717 and were freely roaming the North Atlantic in search of European vessels. 'The Sallymen . . . roves where they please,' he wrote in one letter to London. Shortly after, he reported the capture of four ships, along with fifty mariners. The corsairs also seized an Irish vessel, whose passengers included a woman. 'They advize me from Meknes that the woman . . . had been tortured almost to death to make her turn [Muslim],' he wrote. 'She says she will not, but during her tortures she fainted, and then they said she had turn'd; she is in the seraglio, and so lost.'

Consul Hatfeild's despatches were read with a mixture of anxiety and despair by ministers in Whitehall. The situation had become so dire that a group of West Country merchants wrote to Parliament, demanding that something be done. 'A great many persons are in captivity in Salé,' they said, '. . . where they endure unexpressible calamities.' London's merchants, who were also facing ruin, lamented the fact that their lucrative trade with Newfoundland was under threat. There was even more disquieting news from Algiers. The newly appointed consul, Charles Hudson, had been harangued by the ruling dey, who bragged that he intended to enslave all British subjects serving on vessels at enmity with Algiers. Ministers realised that such a situation could not be allowed to continue and began preparations for a new mission to Meknes.

Joseph Addison had retired in the spring of 1718; his replacement as secretary of state was James Cragg, a skilled politician who was judged to be 'as fit a man for it [the job] as any in the kingdom'. Cragg vowed that this new mission would succeed, come what may, and that all the British and North American slaves in Morocco would be freed and reunited with their families.

The man chosen to lead the embassy was Commodore Charles Stewart, a sure-footed sea captain whose urbane charm was overlaid with a natural swagger. Stewart was only thirty-nine years old, yet he bore the scars of a turbulent career at sea. His first voyage, in 1697, had very nearly been his last. His vessel had been attacked by a French warship off Dover, and Stewart's hand had been shot to pieces, leaving him with an ungainly stump. Undeterred by this misfortune, he returned to sea and served with distinction in the Mediterranean. Now, after five years of service in the Irish Parliament, he found himself spearheading a mission to Moulay Ismail's court.

Stewart was the perfect choice of plenipotentiary to Morocco. He had verve and charisma, and was more than capable of adopting the airs and graces of a haughty ambassador. Yet he was also a master of flattery and adept at disarming his enemies with a flow of oily obsequies. In the world of the Moroccan imperial court, where sycophancy was the sine qua non for success, Stewart would prove himself a master among men.

His ship, the *Winchester*, left Portsmouth on a breezy September day in 1720. She made a magnificent sight as she edged out of the harbour and into the Solent. Her sails billowed with the wind and the pennants were streaming from the mizzen-mast. Although she was indistinguishable from most other warships heading into the Channel, her cargo revealed that hers was a mission of peace, not war. In the darkness of the hold, wrapped in hessian and wood chips, was a hodgepodge of costly playthings for Moulay Ismail. These included a fine musical clock with a delicate chime, faience platters, four glass candlesticks, three chandeliers, 'one large fruit basket' and an exquisitely crafted parasol. There was also a selection of preserved fruits and spices – including ginger, cloves and nutmegs – and a large stash of Chinese porcelain. Every gift had been selected with the greatest care; there was even a huge sugar-loaf, which, it was hoped, would bring pleasure to the sweet-toothed sultan.

Commodore Stewart arrived at Gibraltar in the third week of October and wasted no time in despatching a letter to Basha Hamet of Tetouan, who officiated over much of northern Morocco. 'I take the liberty to acquaint your excellency of my arrival in these parts,' wrote Stewart, 'with full powers to treat of a peace.' His tone was polite but firm. He made veiled threats about military action against Moulay Ismail, but promised that if the sultan agreed to a peace, 'I shall then very readily in person throw myself at His Imperial Majesty's feet.'

Basha Hamet's reply was as charming as it was surprising. He expressed his 'great inclination' to sign a truce with Stewart – although he did not give any reasons – and sent over a draft treaty within a few days. It decreed that British ships and mariners 'shall not be stopt, taken away, imbezzled or plundered', but came with the proviso that any binding treaty had to be signed in person by King George I. It took more than six months for this to be achieved, and it was not until the following May – almost eight months after leaving London – that Stewart finally stepped ashore at Tetouan with the signed treaty in hand. He was feeling more and more confident that the British slaves would at long last be freed.

His sense of optimism increased still further when he discovered that Basha Hamet had prepared a lavish welcome. 'We found a sufficient number of tents, pitched for our conveniency,' wrote John Windus, one of Stewart's entourage. 'Among them [was] a fine large one that the emperor had sent from Meknes.' Basha Hamet had also instructed his chefs to prepare a mouth-watering feast to welcome Commodore Stewart to Morocco. They arrived bearing 'couscous, fowls, and a sheep roasted whole, upon a great wooden spit as thick as a man's leg'.

The basha himself arrived in mid-afternoon, along with a troop of 500 horsemen and soldiers. The British were most impressed by Basha Hamet's imperious looks and manner. 'His countenance is grave and majestick,' wrote Windus, 'having a Roman nose, good eyes and a well turn'd face.' To the pale-faced newcomers his skin seemed 'a little swarthy', and Windus felt he was 'inclining to be fat', but this did not detract from his 'very manly appearance'.

Basha Hamet was one of Moulay Ismail's principal lieutenants and one of the few who could facilitate Stewart's journey to the imperial court. After formally welcoming the commodore to Barbary, he promised to do 'all that lay in his power to make the country agreeable to him'. With a crafty smile, he added 'that he liked the English better than any other Christian nation'. Stewart might have been forgiven for asking why, if this was true, the basha had been instrumental in seizing so many British slaves. But he was anxious to build a bond of trust and managed to hold his tongue. He uttered instead some courteous platitudes, and the basha responded in similar fashion.

After a few days of feasting, Basha Hamet suggested that they head to his Tetouan villa so that they could dine in his newly planted arbour. Both Stewart and Windus were keen to see a Moorish garden, and they were not disappointed. 'There were fine oranges, lemons, and small apricocks of a very good flavour,' wrote Windus. The walkways were covered in delicate trellis, which was used to support climbing flowers and shrubs. 'Great quantities of carnations coming in thro' the canework and at the windows, make the arbour very delightful.' Although the weather was extremely hot, it remained cool and pleasant in the garden. 'We dined under a locust tree,' wrote Windus, 'that afforded a pretty good shade.'

Commodore Stewart and his entourage of liveried servants

and musicians spent many weeks enjoying the basha's hospitality in Tetouan, and it was not until mid-June that they at long last set out for Meknes. The numerous delays had meant that they were now travelling in the heat of summer – the very worst time to be on the road. '[We] began to have very hot travelling . . .' wrote Windus, 'which daily increased.' The wealth of Tetouan quickly gave way to impoverished villages and makeshift camps, where half-starved nomads scratched for food. 'The inhabitants . . . seem to live very miserably . . . their houses consisting of nothing but sticks, with a rush or cloth covering.' To Windus, with the memories of Tetouan still fresh in his mind, these people seemed to live 'very nastily'.

The travelling party had soon left the sparkling Mediterranean far behind and found themselves crossing a plain 'as even as a bowling green'. The heat became insufferable, and everyone found it hard to breathe as they rode through the dry dust. 'This day was so exceeding hot and sultry,' wrote Windus, 'that all manner of metal was heated to such a degree by the air . . . that we could hardly touch it.'

Nonetheless, there was considerable excitement as the men reached the Roman ruins of Volubulis, just sixteen miles to the north-east of Meknes. Windus, who was particularly interested in this rambling site, jumped down from his horse in order to poke through the rubble, finding fragments of inscriptions and a large bust, but little else. Moulay Ismail had already ransacked the place in search of adornments for his palace and signs of his vandalism were all too evident.

A messenger was sent to Meknes in order to inform the sultan of the imminent arrival of Commodore Stewart and his party. Basha Hamet seemed nervous about Moulay Ismail's response and expressed his concern that he would be punished for some unknown misdemeanour. 'No man goes before him,' explained Windus, 'but with the utmost fear, and in doubt whether he shall return alive.' On this particular occasion, the news could not have been better. The messenger was warmly welcomed by Moulay Ismail, and his reception was held to presage good news for Commodore Stewart as well. There was a feeling of optimism among the British retinue when, on Sunday, 2 July, they slept under the stars for the last time. After nearly three exhausting weeks of travelling, they were about to enter the imperial capital of Meknes.

Basha Hamet awoke at dawn and urged them to strike camp with all possible haste, so that they would arrive early in the city and 'avoid the prodigious croud we should have met with had the day been farther advanced'. A hurried gallop across the Boufekrane valley brought the men to the outskirts of the city where, in the half-light of day, they were led by officials to temporary lodgings.

The basha, who was instantaneously summoned to a meeting with the sultan, discovered that Moulay Ismail had woken in a foul mood. He accused Basha Hamet of being careless in his dealings with the Spanish garrison of Ceuta, and began 'severely threatning him and telling him he was not fit to command'.

He called for a list of all the senior officers in the basha's entourage and then proceeded to punish them for real and imagined crimes. One of the men was 'tossed' by four members of the black guard, who ensured that his neck was broken as he hit the ground. Another of the officers, Larbe Shott, was accused of sleeping with Christian women. His fate was to be 'tyed between two boards and sawed in two, beginning at his head and going downwards till his body fell asunder'. Windus, who was told about the execution by horrified onlookers, added that the corpse would have been eaten by dogs 'if the emperor had not pardoned him; an extravagant custom to pardon a man after he is dead, but unless he does so, nobody dares bury the body'.

Windus also learned that Moulay Ismail was filled with remorse on the day after the execution. Shott had appeared to him in a dream and revealed that God would condemn him for his brutality. This caused the sultan so much concern 'that he sent to the place of his execution for some of the dust his blood was spilt on, with which he rubbed himself all over as an atonement for his crime'.

Commodore Stewart and his men spent two days in their lodgings, awaiting orders from the sultan. On 5 July, they were told that they were being moved to more luxurious accommodation. The following morning, they were informed that Moulay Ismail wished to see the British ambassador immediately and was sending a guard to conduct him to the palace.

This guard pitched up almost at once – a colourful band of retainers and courtiers, supplemented by Stewart's own guard of honour. 'The ambassador [had] his livery men on each side,' wrote Windus, 'and after him the gentlemen of his retinue.' They were preceded by 'our musick' – probably a troupe of trumpeters – and several Moorish sergeants on horseback. As Stewart set off for the palace, he was surprised to notice a small band of ragged, exhausted-looking men, bringing up the rear. With a start, he realised that they were some of the British captives who had been specially released from the slave pens in order to take part in the procession. His instinct must surely have been to greet these broken men, but the sultan's kaids would not countenance any delay in reaching the palace. Nor would they allow their progress to be hindered by the crowds of local townsfolk. When Stewart's path was blocked by curious onlookers, they 'laid on [them] unmercifully, sometimes knocking them down'.

The ambassador and his retinue dismounted as they reached the outer gate of the palace. They passed through 'three or four larger courtyards, [then] sat down under some piazzas for about half an hour'. The slaves were still at the rear of the group, but neither Stewart nor Windus was able to speak with them. Everyone expected the imminent arrival of the sultan, and the men were told not to leave their allotted positions.

When another half hour had passed there were at last signs of commotion on the far side of the courtyard. Some courtiers could be seen entering through the gateway, followed by several guardsmen. Seconds later, Moulay Ismail himself appeared. Stewart and his men squinted into the sunlight as they tried to get a better view of him. 'At a distance we saw him,' wrote Windus, 'with an umbrellow over his head, his guards behind him drawn up in the shape of a half moon, holding the butt end of their pieces with their right hands, and keeping them close to their bodies.' These bukhari, or soldiers of the fabled black guard, were a most impressive sight as they formed a protective phalanx around the sultan.

Commodore Stewart was not at all overawed; indeed, it confirmed in his own mind the need to stage his own display of pageantry. With a stentorian bark, he ordered his men to break into military step. 'We marched towards the emperor,' wrote Windus, 'our musick playing, till we came within about fourscore yards of him.' The British contingent had hoped to impress Moulay Ismail with their music and marching. Instead, they found themselves outperformed by the unpredictable sultan. As Stewart approached, Moulay Ismail leaped off his stallion and threw himself headlong into the dust. 'It was surprising to see the old monarch alight from his horse and prostrate himself upon the earth to pray,' wrote Windus, 'in which posture he continued some minutes without motion.' The sultan's face was so close to the ground 'that the dust remained upon his nose when we came up to him'.

Commodore Stewart was about to offer his greetings when Moulay Ismail sprang up, jumped back on to his horse and snatched his lance from the bodyguard. Then, when he had recovered his breath, he ceremoniously beckoned the ambassador forward. 'We fell into one rank,' wrote Windus, 'and, bowing as we approached the emperor, he nodded his head [and] said *bono* several times.'

Windus studied Moulay Ismail with care, fascinated to be standing face to face with this extraordinary individual. He estimated him to be eighty-seven years of age – he was in fact seventy-five – and noted that the ravages of age were at long last starting to show. 'He has lost all his teeth,' wrote Windus, 'and breaths short, as if his lungs were bad; coughs and spits pretty often.' The sultan's phlegm was never allowed to fall to the ground, 'men being always ready with handkerchiefs to receive it'.

His aquiline nose, which had once looked so noble, was now accentuated by hollow cheeks, while his lengthy beard was wispy and thin. 'His eyes seem to have been sparkling,' wrote Windus, 'but their vigour [is] decayed through age, and his cheeks are very much sunk in.' Yet the sultan still cut an impressive figure as he sat resplendent on a jet-black horse, surrounded by fawning retainers. 'His negroes continually fann and beat the flies from his horse with cloths,' wrote Windus, 'and the umbrellow is constantly kept twirling over his head.' The slave entrusted with holding this chintz parasol took great care to move in step with the sultan, so that no sunlight ever fell on his sacred skin. Such caution was borne of experience; previous slaves had been summarily executed for failing in their duties.

Windus's only disappointment was that the sultan paid so little attention to his dress. He wore similar clothes to his courtiers, the only distinguishing features being his bejewelled scimitar and richly caparisoned horse's saddle, decked with pompons and streamers. 'It was cover'd with gold, and handsomely set with large emeralds.'

Commodore Stewart betrayed no nerves in the presence of Moulay Ismail. He played the ambassadorial role with aplomb, murmuring obsequies whenever suitable yet remaining politely firm in purpose. '[He] delivered His Majesty's letter, tyed up in a silk handkerchief, into the emperor's hand.' Then, in a clear voice, he informed the sultan that he had been despatched by

His Britannic Majesty, King George I, 'to settle peace, friendship and a good understanding between the two crowns'. He added, with more than a hint of irony, that he 'hoped he would accept' the costly gifts that he had brought to the court.

It was Moulay Ismail's custom, on first meeting foreign ambassadors, to open proceedings with a long lecture on Islam. But on this occasion, he merely grinned at Stewart and told him that 'he should have every thing he came for, because he loved the English.' The commodore responded by challenging the sultan to release his British slaves, stressing that this alone would be 'a convincing proof of the great regard he had for the English nation'.

Stewart also tried to inform Moulay Ismail of the growing strength of the British navy, but the sultan was not in a listening mood. 'It was very difficult to get the emperor to have patience to hear what the ambassador had to say,' wrote Windus, 'being fond of speaking himself.' Stewart interjected on several occasions and requested that the sultan put his signature to the truce drawn up in Tetouan. Moulay Ismail answered that this was not necessary, since 'his word was as effectual as his writing'. But when Stewart persisted, he agreed to the request and followed it up by giving the ambassador 'a present of nine Christians'.

Commodore Stewart's audience with Moulay Ismail coincided with the arrival at court of Thomas Pellow, who may well have been summoned from Kasbah Temsna in order to act as interpreter. Pellow was by now about sixteen years of age and had not heard any news from his parents for more than six years. He knew that Stewart was the only person who could conceivably facilitate his freedom and was encouraged by the fact that the ambassador was a decent and trustworthy individual. 'I cannot . . . help saying,' he wrote, 'that he, in every point, behaved in so polite, most Christian-like and majestic a manner.' Yet Pellow was also aware that Stewart's overriding task was to free the captives from the slave pens. Only once this had been achieved could the ambassador address the issue of the hundreds of British renegades at large in Morocco.

Pellow lamented the fact that Stewart had not arrived 'on the same errand about four years before', which, he said, would have 'prevented many aching hearts'. He added that if the British government had acted with rather more speed, 'my poor uncle, with many other poor Christian slaves . . . had probably been still alive'.

Commodore Stewart hoped to enter into immediate discussions about the release of the surviving slaves, but Moulay Ismail was anxious that the ambassador be shown the glories of his imperial palace. Affairs of state precluded him from leading the tour, as was his custom, so he ordered his Jewish treasurer, Moses ben Hattar, to conduct Stewart and Windus through the courtyards and chambers of the palace.

The vastness of the place, and the exquisite beauty of its adornment, was to leave a lasting impression on both men. Windus was particularly excited by what he saw and left one of the finest descriptions of the great imperial palace at its apogee. He had never before seen such a monumental edifice, nor was he familiar with the intricate swirls of creamlike Moorish stucco, which had been hand-sculpted by slaves from Andalusia. Moses ben Hattar began by showing the men the adjuncts of the palace that stood close to the Dar Kbira. 'The arches were wrought with plaister fret-work in flowers, after the Arabian manner,' wrote Windus, 'and supported by neat stone pillars, the square exceeding large and spacious.' No less beautiful was the sparkling tessellated flooring of the great courtyards, 'chequered with small tiles of divers colours, about two inches square'. Windus felt that these geometrical *zellig* tiles, with their radiating patterns of stars and hexagons, imbued the rambling buildings with an overall sense of harmony and proportion. 'All the apartments, walks, magazines, passages and underneath the arches being chequered,' he wrote, '. . . [make] the prospect of the buildings, which are all of a great length, extremely magnificent, beautiful and neat.'

Moses ben Hattar led the men in a south-easterly direction, towards the monumental Dar el Makhzen. The entire place seemed strangely deserted; all that could be heard was the muffled echo of workers toiling away out of sight. The clash of a copper pan, the chink of a chisel – these were the only noises that betrayed the presence of people inside the palace.

Every building seemed bigger than the one before, and even the palace storehouses were grander than anything Windus had seen in London. 'We were led into a magazine near a quarter of a mile long, and not above thirty foot broad,' he wrote; 'in it there hung up great quantities of arms in cases and three rows of rails, which were covered with saddles.' Moses ben Hattar gleefully pointed to the gates of Larache – captured from the Spanish during the siege – along with 'a great deal of ironwork, some espadas [swords] and other Christian swords'.

Once Stewart and Windus had admired the weaponry, they were led through empty piazzas towards one of the several harems, which was out of bounds. Here, too, all was quiet. The spicy scent of cedarwood betrayed a newly constructed ceiling and the smell of smoke hinted at nearby kitchens.

'From thence, passing through some neat long walks, and passages of chequer-work, we came to another building, with a large garden in the middle, planted round with tall cypress trees.' This lush tangle of greenery had been designed to resemble the fabled hanging gardens of Babylon. It had been sunk sixty or seventy feet below ground level and had a terraced walkway, suspended over the trees and shrubs, which stretched for more than half a mile. 'The top of it [is] all the way thick-shaded with vines and other greens,' wrote Windus, 'supported with strong and well-made wooden work.' In the summer twilight hours, the languid fragrance of blossom hung heavy in the air.

The great palace quarters on the far side of the gardens were still under construction, and Windus was horrified to see teams of Christian slaves sweltering under the torrid July sun. '[We saw] the Christians upon the top of high walls,' he wrote, 'working and beating down the mortar with heavy pieces of wood, something like what our pavers used to beat down the stones, which they raise all together and keep time in their stroke.' Windus wanted to get closer, in order to witness with his own eyes the conditions in which the captives were held. But Moses ben Hattar felt that the two men had seen enough. He led them back to Moulay Ismail, who was examining a storage depot that was 'kept in order by twenty-eight English boys'.

Moulay Ismail was delighted to see Commodore Stewart: '[He] cryed out as before, *bono, bono*, and asked him how he liked his palace.' Stewart had been truly astonished by the scale and luxury of what he had seen 'and told him it was one of the noblest upon the face of the earth'. The sultan was gratified and thanked God for the ambassador's reaction. 'Then,' wrote Windus, 'some of the English boys, falling prostrate . . . [gave] him the usual salutation, *Allah ibarik phi amrik Sidi*, (i.e.) God bless thy power.' Moulay Ismail asked the slave boys to which nation they belonged. When they replied that they were English, 'he bid them go home with the ambassador and see him to bed.'

Stewart and Windus spent the evening hours discussing their eventful day. As they supped on food from the sultan's kitchens, which Windus found to be a little 'high seasoned', they compared notes. The sultan's palace was far larger than any building in Europe. Even Versailles, the greatest and most opulent of its contemporaries, was quite tiny in comparison to what they had been shown. Yet their tour had covered only a small part of the entire palace complex, and it was not until the following morning that they would they get an accurate idea of its scale.

They were first taken to see the imperial workhouses, where

European slaves cast and smelted the weaponry for Moulay Ismail's mighty army. The workhouses were 'full of men and boys at work', observed Windus. 'They were making saddles, stocks for guns, scabbards for cymiters and other things.' They seemed to have been given advance warning of Stewart's visit, for they began to work with extraordinary energy when the men entered the building. The visitors' ears were assaulted by a cacophony of noise, which rebounded from wall to wall. Blacksmiths were flattening hammered iron on huge anvils; others were pumping bellows and chopping firewood. The diligence of the men, and the quality of their work, impressed Windus. 'Upon sight of the ambassador, they all fell a working together, which made an agreeable sound, and shewed that industry was in great perfection in this emperor's palace.'

After admiring the workmanship of the slaves, Stewart and Windus were taken to the Dar el Makhzen palace – an agglomeration of buildings that covered a far greater area than the Dar Kbira. This part of the palace was crowded with retainers and ministers, all of whom were anxious to catch a glimpse of Commodore Stewart and his entourage. 'We went through divers large and neat buildings, now and then passing gates guarded by eunuchs, who beat away all but those who were to conduct us.' They crossed another sunken garden, 'very deep, having a great deal of clover in it, for the horses of the palace'. On the farthest side were yet more palaces, 'supported with neat piazzas [colonnades]', as well as ornamented steps winding down into the garden.

Stewart and Windus were completely confused as to their whereabouts. They guessed that they had been led back into the heart of the imperial palace, for the adornments became increasingly lavish and ostentatious. Snow-white stucco was scooped into swirling arabesques; spandrels and corbels were adorned with star-bursts and curlicues. The mosaics, too, became ever more complex – a geometric interplay that fooled the eye and dazzled the senses. 'We came to the most inward and beautiful part of the palace,' wrote Windus, 'which also has a garden in the middle, planted round with cypress and other trees.' This edifice must have cost a veritable fortune to construct, for 'all the pillars of this building, which is of a vast length, are of marble, and the arches and doors of the apartments very finely workt'. Windus was informed that the pillars were Roman and had been brought to Meknes from Salé but it is more likely that they had been pillaged from the ruined city of Volubulis, which the men had visited just a few days earlier.

Their tour had by now lasted for several hours, and their spirits were beginning to flag. It was scorching hot in the midday sun, and they were suffering from parched throats and blistered feet. They were therefore relieved when their guide suggested they rest for a while before continuing with their visit. 'One of the queens sent us a collation of dates, grapes, melons, almonds and raisons, figs and sweetmeats of their making,' wrote Windus, 'with an apology to the ambassador because there was nothing better, it being Ramdam.'

The men were more than satisfied with these platters of juicy fruit: '[It] was very welcome, for walking had made us dry, so we sat down under the piazzas, and were attended by the maids of the palace.' Windus was enchanted by these pretty women – slaves – whose filigree jewellery clinked and jingled as they served the figs and grapes. '[Their] jetty skins received the embellishment of shining bracelets and silver trinkets, which they wore in great plenty upon their legs and arms.' They also had chunky chains of gold slung around their necks, as well as 'monstrous large earrings and other African ornaments'.

Stewart and Windus rested for several hours and continued their visit only when the worst heat of the day had subsided. They were taken to inspect underground cisterns, treasuries and gunrooms, where the quantity and variety of weaponry was startling. 'In these magazines may be seen bills, battle-axes, and warlike instruments of all sorts; a great many blunderbusses of different sizes, with brass barrels, helmets in boxes and wrapped up in paper.' There were flintlocks and arquebuses, halberds and hatchets. Windus noted that many of these came from European arms manufacturers and must have been seized on the battlefield or sold to the sultan by unscrupulous dealers. 'After we had seen a much greater store of arms than any of us imagined this prince had,' he wrote, 'we were led into the inside of an apartment.' This was Moulay Ismail's private chamber, which housed his enormous bed. Having studied its dimensions, Windus reckoned it 'would hold about twenty people'.

The ambassadorial tour of the palace continued for much of the day. Each time the men thought they were ending their visit they would turn a corner and stumble across an entirely new collection of palaces. Windus found the koubbas, or domed sanctuaries, to be particularly beautiful. One ceiling was 'finely painted of a sky colour, with golden stars representing the heavens and a golden sun in the middle, of curious workmanship'. Another koubba was filled with gifts presented by European monarchs, 'among which were seven or eight coaches . . . and his choicest goods; in one of them were hung up the fine glass sconces that His Majesty, King George had sent by the ambassador'.

The men passed one 'massy' building whose unfinished façade lacked any adornment. This, Windus was told, was where Moulay Ismail intended to be laid to rest. 'In the inside, they say, there is a chain that is let down from the middle of the roof, by which he intends his coffin shall hang.'

There were many plots of vacant land inside the palace complex, as yet devoid of buildings. One of these open spaces was crawling with 'large ratts . . . [that] ran about so thick that the ground was almost covered with them'. On the far side of this space was a fragrant pomegranate garden, linked to the palace by a strong bridge. This was joined to a 'causeway' or alley – still inside the palace complex – that ran for three miles towards the stables.

John Windus tried to take stock of all he had seen. He calculated that the main living quarters of Moulay Ismail and his wives were 'about four miles in circumference' and stood on the highest ground. The external walls were built of mortar that was 'in every part very thick'. Windus reckoned that each section of wall – there were too many to count – was approximately one mile long and twenty-five feet thick, enclosing many 'oblong squares a great deal bigger than Lincoln's Inn Fields', some of which were entirely decorated in mosaic tiling. Several contained sunken gardens of astonishing depth and were planted with 'tall cypress trees, the tops of which, appearing above the rails, make a beautiful prospect of palace and garden'.

Beyond the private quarters of the palace lay the ongoing building works of the Madinat el-Riyad – home to Moulay Ismail's viziers and courtiers, as well as his black guard, horses and huge stockpiles of grain. Although Windus tried to work out the total area of ground enclosed by the palace, he found it impossible since entire sections were continually being remodelled or enlarged by the sultan. He nevertheless calculated that if the various buildings were lined up, one next to the other, they would 'by a moderate computation' stretch from Meknes to Fez – a distance of some forty miles.

His incredulity at the scale of the palace was tempered by the fact that it had been built entirely by Christian slave labour, aided by bands of Moroccan criminals. 'It is reported that 30,000 men and 10,000 mules were employed every day in the building of the palace,' wrote Windus. He added that such figures were 'not at all improbable, seeing that it is built of hardly anything else but lime, and every wall worked with excessive labour'.

After two days spent visiting the building works, Commodore Stewart felt it was time to try to free the British and colonial

American slaves. He had brought scores of presents with him and now began to distribute them to the sultan's courtiers. More than fifty palace retainers were to be presented with gifts, including 'the king's head cut-throat' and an English renegade named John Brown, who was one of the guards employed to oversee the Christian slaves. Stewart had even brought a gift for 'the man that carrys the umbrella over ye king' and another set of presents for 'the people that carry the king's spare cloaths'. All of these costly gifts were handed to the sultan, in the hope of speeding up the release of the slaves. But Moulay Ismail warned that little could be done until the end of Ramadan. It was a frustrating time for Stewart and Windus. They could achieve nothing without the sultan's help, yet Moulay Ismail spent the greater part of each day in prayer. 'This is,' sighed an exasperated John Windus, 'the most religious age that ever was in Barbary.'

Ramadan finally came to an end on 15 July and was celebrated with much festivity and pageantry. The sultan led public prayers to mark the beginning of the great feast, followed by colourful processions to which the British retinue was cordially invited. The principal parade was to take place outside the city walls, and it was suggested that Stewart and Windus should watch the unfolding extravaganza from the walls adjoining the Spanish infirmary, where 'the prior had built a handsome scaffold for us'.

At exactly ten o'clock, the procession could be heard approaching, 'great numbers of foot firing, and horse cavalcading, some with launces and others with firelocks'. The soldiers discharged their guns with a careless abandon that shocked Windus: 'They sometimes set their turbants on fire, and burnt their faces in a desperate manner.' As the pall of gun-smoke drifted from the parade ground, a burst of sunlight lit up the colourful proceedings. Stewart and Windus glimpsed 'eight or nine blacks in a row, carrying large colours, with great gilt balls on the top of their staves'. The brilliant costumes of these bukhari made a splendid sight, yet they were followed by an even more flamboyant troop of guards and kaids. First came one of the emperor's sons, flanked by a mounted sentry. There was a stately calash, led by six black women, and an imperial guardsman carrying 'a large red standard with an half moon in the middle'. Close behind was a most magnificent troop of foot-guards, 'cloathed all in leopard and tyger skins', along with 'a guard of young blacks with launces and fire-arms intermixed'. All were firing their guns into the air, filling the parade ground with the acrid stench of burning powder.

Finally, the sultan himself arrived in the square. He clutched a gun in his hand, 'his umbrellow kept all the way twirling over his head, and the negroes continually fanning and beating the flies from his horse'. As he neared Stewart and Windus, who were standing on the viewing platform, he lifted his gun and aimed the muzzle at a Moroccan spectator who was standing too close. Windus was horrified, but before the sultan could shoot the man, 'the guards seized him, hawling him away, perhaps to be executed for his presumption'.

Moulay Ismail was surrounded by his most loyal horsemen, who were decked 'in armour, some gilt all over, others only their helmets'. They were followed by a most impressive array of foot soldiers, carrying spears and standards, battleaxes and bills.

Windus was astonished at the spectacle unfolding before him; the pomp and pageantry was unlike anything he had ever seen in London. He was even more amazed when the sultan's horses came into view, 'with saddles of beaten gold set with emeralds and other stones, some of which were very large'. Bedizened with sequins, tinsel and pompons, they made a most colourful if gaudy spectacle.

The procession was by no means over, but as all of the dignitaries had already passed Commodore Stewart decided to depart.

The morning's ceremony had made him hungry, and he was looking forward to the hearty feast promised by the Spanish prior. He quickly found himself disappointed. 'The prior . . . did his best,' wrote Windus, 'but his cooks being Spanish, the victuals were sadly drest for our taste, and his wine very bad.' Once lunch was over, and the last of the pageantry came to a close, Stewart and Windus returned to their lodgings to await the summons of the sultan.

Moulay Ismail had been giving much thought to the matter of the British slaves. He knew that it would be hard to evade releasing them now that he had signed the treaty. He was also in need of the ransom money, which was on its way to Morocco. But when he declared to the court his intention of freeing them – and word of his decision reached the slave pens – he found resistance from a most unexpected quarter. Many of the other Christian captives in Meknes, particularly the Spanish, were 'not desirous that so many English should be carried away'. They feared that they would have to fill their places in the labour teams 'and have a double portion of work'.

Envy, too, played its part. The other slaves were 'grieved to see the king of Great Britain so careful in endeavouring to release his subjects out of slavery, whilst they lay neglected and without hopes of redemption'. They sent a letter to the sultan explaining their woes and – much to their surprise – learned that Moulay Ismail was in agreement. He had become increasingly concerned about losing several hundred masons and carpenters, and sent a message to Stewart, warning him to return to England immediately. His only concession was that the ambassador could take with him the nine slaves he had already been given. This extraordinary volte-face left Stewart reeling. He was disgusted by such treatment, particularly as his gifts were now in the sultan's hands. Yet such behaviour on the part of Moulay Ismail was by no means unusual. A master of caprice, and chimerical to boot, he enjoyed running rings around visitors to his court.

Stewart, wondering whether the sultan would ever release his British slaves, asked Moses ben Hattar for advice, and was told that his best hope was to ask one of the sultan's favourite wives, Queen Umulez Ettabba, to intercede on his behalf. Stewart did exactly that, writing a long letter of explanation to the queen. His exasperation at the turn of events is clear; he begged the queen to help and asked her to 'represent these things to the emperor, and use your interest [so] that I may be dispatched in what I have requested'.

The queen went straight to Moulay Ismail and appealed to him on Commodore Stewart's behalf. She found the sultan in quixotic mood; he expressed his total willingness to comply with the ambassador's demands and told her that 'never came [a] Christian of more judgement and goodness' to his court. His only concern was that he had no idea how many British captives were being held in the slave pens, since a large number had either apostatised or died.

In the third week of July, Commodore Stewart received word that the deadlock was about to be broken. 'The emperor ordered all the English captives to be drawn together in his palace,' wrote Windus, 'and at the same time sent for the ambassador.' There had been so many delays and setbacks that Stewart had begun to fear he would return to England empty-handed. Now, the tables had turned once again, and the commodore felt confident of success for the first time. 'We went with the musick playing as before,' wrote Windus, 'and found the emperor sitting under some piazzas.'

As Stewart approached the sultan, Moulay Ismail clambered on to his horse and said, 'Bono, bono.' He was as disingenuous as ever, but proved the very model of courtesy. He apologised to Stewart for any misunderstanding and assured him that there was no question of the British and American slaves remaining in Meknes. He pointed to a large group of wretched men, signalling that these were the only slaves to have survived their long and terrible ordeal. Then, 'waving his hand to the captives, he bad them go home along with the ambassador into their own country.'

Few of the men dared to believe what they were hearing. They had waited six years for this moment and had prayed they would be released before they died of disease or starvation. Some of their colleagues had been butchered by the sultan himself. Many more had been battered by his monstrous black guard. These hardy survivors had mourned too many deaths during their years of captivity. Captains, masters and mariners: all had succumbed to the rigours of hard labour; on Thomas Pellow's vessel, the *Francis*, four of the men had died. Only Lewis Davies, George Barnicoat and Thomas Goodman remained alive. The crews of the other vessels had experienced an even greater death toll. Many hundreds of British mariners had been captured over the past six years, yet a mere 293 remained alive.

Moulay Ismail's words had a peculiar effect on each and every one of the men assembled in the palace courtyard. Suddenly, spontaneously, 'they all fell prostrate, crying out "God bless thy power".' They lay in the dust for some minutes, each man wondering if he dared to believe that his captivity was really over. There had been too many false dawns; now, at long last, their hellish existence seemed to be at an end.

When the men finally picked themselves up from the ground, they were warmly embraced by Commodore Stewart, who was anxious to leave Meknes as soon as possible, before the sultan could change his mind. He bade farewell to Moulay Ismail and began to lead the newly freed captives towards the great gates of the palace. As he did so, Moulay Ismail called out 'that he loved the ambassador and all the English, because he knew they loved him and his house'. He added that 'there should not be an English man a slave in his empire, for he would set them all at liberty in what part soever they were.' Then, with a dramatic flourish, '[he] galloped away with a launce in his hand, his guards running close behind him'.

When Moulay Ismail was out of sight, Commodore Stewart greeted the men properly and checked on their condition. He had every reason to congratulate himself, for he had managed to liberate all of the British and colonial American captives being held in the Meknes slave pens. But he had failed to free any of the women in the harem – if they were still alive – nor had he released the captives being held elsewhere in Morocco. One other group had also escaped his attention. Not a single British renegade was set free, even though many of these slave-servants had apostatised against their will and were desperate to return to their homes and families.

Among them was Thomas Pellow, who had acted as interpreter and advisor to the commodore, and who was present at all times during Stewart's stay in Meknes. The exact details are frustratingly vague; Pellow 'passed it by in his journal' because he knew that Stewart was intending to write his own account of the mission. But he certainly advised the commodore on his 'entrance, behaviour, usage and return' and also played a pivotal role in winning the delivery of the slaves. His reward was to be abandoned to his fate – left to the whim of the dangerous and capricious sultan. Pellow was distraught, for he had hoped and prayed that he might be released. He now knew that if he was ever to be reunited with his family in Penryn, his only option was to escape.

10 Escape or Death

On 1 December 1721, an exciting rumour began to circulate through the streets and markets of London. A ship had been sighted, sailing up the Thames Estuary – the flagship of Commodore Charles Stewart – and it had on board hundreds of gaunt and emaciated men.

It did not take long for the prattlers of Grub Street to conclude that these must be the English slaves recently freed from Morocco. The *Daily News* was the first to print the scoop. One of their reporters was sent downstream to verify the facts and returned with confirmation that the vessel did indeed belong to Commodore Stewart. He added that the captives 'are to land on Monday next . . . and will the same day proceed in a body from the waterside through the city'.

The city authorities had already been alerted to their arrival and were planning a carefully choreographed celebration. There was to be a solemn church service, followed by a colourful pageant through the streets of the capital. The day set aside for the festivities was Monday, 4 December, and they were planned to continue for much of the morning. In the event, they lasted a great deal longer.

Commodore Stewart did his best to prepare the men for a homecoming that looked set to be noisy, crowded and quite possibly overwhelming. The returning slaves were instructed not to shave or wash, and to remain in the filthy djellabas they had worn since leaving Meknes: Stewart wanted them to look as miserable and downtrodden as possible. The return of the slaves provided an excellent opportunity for the king and his ministers to highlight their role – albeit minimal – in securing their release. The more abject and wretched the slaves, the more the citizens of London would have cause to congratulate their ruler.

It is impossible to know the men's feelings as they sailed past the flooded fields and marshes of the Thames Estuary. Most were illiterate and the few who could write were emotionally ill equipped to record their sense of excitement or anxiety. They were certainly desperate to return to their families, yet must have felt apprehensive – and perhaps frightened – at the prospect. Few had any idea whether their wives and children were still alive, or of how their homecoming, sickly and destitute, would be greeted. The men were also unaware that their release from captivity had become a cause célèbre in England and that a vast crowd was awaiting their arrival.

The sharp change in weather was the first sign that they were nearing home. The searing heat of Meknes had slowly given way to the piercing chill of the North Sea, and cobalt skies had been replaced by lead-grey clouds. Now, as they approached London, a biting wind sent the men shivering below decks. Commodore Stewart's vessel edged slowly through the mud-ochre waters of the Thames Estuary, mooring below London Bridge on the morning of 4 December.

London's authorities had planned for the men to be taken directly to St Paul's Cathedral, where a solemn thanksgiving service was to be held in their honour. But the throng of riverside spectators was so thick that it was decided to lead them on a long tour of the capital's streets and alleys, in order that they could be viewed by as many people as possible. Their route was to plunge them into some of London's most colourful quarters, where both physicians and quacks jostled for trade alongside booksellers, grocers and mountebanks.

The newspapers of the day provide a remarkable snapshot of unfolding events as the men were paraded through the city. In Fetter Lane, surgeon John Douglas was in the midst of a public operation in which he was demonstrating and explaining 'the new method of cutting the stone'. Using only a small knife and a large pair of tweezers on his patient, he claimed his technique to be 'the safest and most certain way of operating'. In nearby Abchurch Lane, the apothecary J. Moore was proudly displaying 'a very broad worm, three yards and a quarter long', which had emerged from the backside of a bricklayer's wife. She had been 'a long time violently bad with faintings, gripes and flushings', ignorant of what was causing her to feel so ill. Moore's black worm powder soon provided the answer. She consumed a few spoonfuls and the offending parasite was immediately expelled.

As the men approached the crowds of Cannon Street, they could see a certain Richard Hayes perched on a podium and expounding on a new method of learning writing and arithmetic. Others were giving instruction in 'the Italian and French tongues'. In Red Lyon Fields there was an auction of the worldly belongings of 'the decease'd Sergeant Hae' – including some fine chinaware – while in St Clement's Coffee House there was an impressive sale of antiquarian books. None of these diversions could compete with the spectacle of 293 sick and wretched slaves being paraded through the capital 'in their Moorish habits'. The crowds pressed forward in their desire to see these bewildered men, who found it increasingly difficult to push their way towards the distant edifice of St Paul's.

Sir Christopher Wren's cathedral was the greatest monument in the capital. The construction work had finished just eleven years earlier, and its white stone sparkled in the pale winter sunlight. With its architectural symmetry and baroque dome, St Paul's was a world away from the rambling mosques and palaces of Meknes. The freed captives were shuffled into the gloom of the great church, which was thronged with city burghers and merchants who had gathered to gawk at the men and join in the thanksgiving for their release. Many of the slaves had spent their time in captivity lamenting the fact that they were forbidden to worship together. Now, they had the dubious pleasure of a long, slow and interminably dull service that would last for much of the morning.

It had been co-ordinated by the Reverend William Berryman, chaplain to the Bishop of London, who could not resist the temptation to deliver an excruciating sermon on the subject of captivity. 'The happy occasion of our present meeting,' he began, '[is] to congratulate you, my brethren, upon your return from slavery under the yoke of infidels.' Berryman conceded that the former captives would undoubtedly wish to enjoy 'the liberty of your native country'. But he issued them with a stern warning of 'the duties from hence incumbent upon you'. Many of these were religious, and Berryman provided the men with plentiful examples from both the Old and New Testaments.

Finally, after a sermon that must have taken at least an hour to deliver, Berryman reminded the men of the enlightened government to which they were returning. With a smile, he informed them that they were 'restored to the enjoyment of English air and English liberty, free from the despotick rule of your imperious lords'.

The freed slaves must have hoped that the service at St Paul's would mark the end of the day's proceedings. Many originated from the West Country and were anxious to head back to the docks in order to search for a vessel bound for Devon or Cornwall. But it quickly became apparent that the celebrations were by no means over. During the course of the church service, huge crowds had assembled outside the cathedral, hoping to catch a glimpse of the redeemed slaves. Furthermore, King George I himself had expressed a desire to meet the men. According to the *Daily Post*, the men were instructed to make their way to St James's Palace, 'to return thanks to his majesty for interposing in their behalf'. But they soon found their paths blocked. 'By reason of the great multitudes of people that crowded to see them, they were forc'd to divide themselves into several companies and to take different ways hither.' The men were only reunited as a group when they at long last reached the palace.

The king's residence – which only a handful of the men had ever seen – was on a very different scale to the imperial palace of Meknes. It boasted few exterior adornments and its façade was old and crumbling. 'Tho the receptacle of all the pomp and glory of Great Britain,' wrote Daniel Defoe, '[it] is really mean.' Nor could the court match the extraordinary panoply of viziers and eunuchs who constantly attended on Moulay Ismail. A retiring individual, King George I shunned the pageantry of formal state occasions. Whenever he travelled, he took circuitous routes so as to avoid 'much embarrassment and a great crowd of people'. On one occasion, he told his courtiers to ensure 'that there be as little concourse of noisy attendants at his landing, or on the road to London, as possible'.

Such public reticence made his appearance before the slaves a cause for surprise. He emerged from the presence chamber, where most courtly business was conducted, and walked down to his beloved garden. When he had made himself comfortable and was ready to see them, the ex-captives were led into the grounds of the palace. 'Upon their arrival [at St James's], they were let into the garden behind the palace, where His Majesty and their Royal Highnesses view'd them.' King George I rarely spoke English in public – he was much more confident in French – which may explain why he declined to address the men. But he seemed genuinely moved by their wretchedness and poverty, '[and] order'd £500 for their relief'. Other members of his household followed suit, donating an additional £200 to the fund. The collection from St Paul's – which amounted to £100 – was also given to the men. ''Tis believed that a much greater sum would have been gather'd if many charitable gentlemen and citizens could have found access through the prodigious crowd,' lamented the *Daily Post*. 'However, it is still hoped that such well disposed persons will send in their respectable contributions.'

Over the next few days, the freed slaves were much in evidence in the capital, and colourful stories of their slavery began to appear in the newspapers. So, too, did accounts of Commodore Stewart's rescue mission. One tale, not mentioned elsewhere, suggests that at least one of the released slaves had not made it back to England. 'It's reported among the British captives lately redeemed,' reads the *London Journal*, 'that on the day of their departure from the region of their slavery, an English captive, with a Moor, were nailed thro' the head, for having committed a murder.'

The publicity that surrounded the men's return – and the accounts of their captivity – enabled them to raise funds with ease. In addition to the king's gift and the money collected at St Paul's, the East India Company 'bestowed a donation of 150 guineas on the redeemed British captives'. The Bishop of London also gave them money, as did several of the capital's noblemen, and it was not long before the total sum raised amounted to £1,400. 'They have been able to cloath themselves in the dress of their native country,' recorded the *London Journal* some four weeks after their return, 'and most of them are now employed in the king's or the merchants' service.' It added that several of the captains 'have the command of merchant's ships given them again, in recompense of their great sufferings during their captivity'.

Within a few weeks of their return to England, all of the former slaves had disappeared from the public gaze. The colonial American captives headed to the docks in order to seek a passage back across the Atlantic. Whether or not they made it home remains a mystery. Some of the Englishmen decided to chance their luck on the high seas. Others returned to their families and loved ones. After six years of captivity, and a burst of publicity on their return, all of the ex-slaves wished to rebuild their lives in private.

Thomas Pellow was dismayed that Commodore Stewart had not negotiated his freedom. He was heartily sick of this troubled land, notwithstanding his Moroccan wife and daughter, and longed more than ever to return to the little port of Penryn. He had even been in secret contact with the few English merchants who still traded with Salé, 'yet could not I, although I very heartily endeavoured it, meet with any opportunity . . . wherein I might in any probability make my escape'. These merchants had struck lucrative deals with the corsairs – to whom they were selling gunpowder – and had no wish to jeopardise it by helping an escapee. Pellow concluded that rather than 'make any foolish attempts that way, I thought [it] was far better to let alone'.

Fleeing from Moulay Ismail's Morocco was indeed a perilous undertaking. Informers were scattered throughout the countryside and the black guard kept a constant watch on the movements of slaves and renegades. The difficulties were compounded by the fact that Meknes lay some four or five days' march from the Atlantic. Worse still, many of the Christian enclaves had been captured by Moulay Ismail, leaving escapees with little option but to head for Ceuta or Mazagan.

There were favoured seasons and days for escape – times when the slaves of Meknes had a slightly better chance of slipping away undetected. Father Busnot had advised setting out around the time of the equinoxes, 'because then the Moors do not lie in the field, having neither corn nor fruit to guard; and the great heats being over'. Germain Mouette added that Friday was the 'properest' day to escape, since many of the slave-drivers, and the feared black guard, spent much of their time at the mosque. It went without saying that any escape had to be made under the cover of darkness. No slave or renegade was brazen or foolish enough to risk his life with an attempt during the day.

Since it was a long and gruelling march to the Atlantic coast, the escapee had to hoard scraps of food for several months prior to his flight. All who made a bid for freedom knew that it would be impossible to acquire any provisions en route, and many found themselves subsisting on wild flowers, grubs and unripe corn. Water posed a greater problem than food, for it was impossible to flee from Meknes with anything more than a gallon or two. Springs and waterholes were few and far between, and those with year-round water were used by the local population. Many slaves prayed for rain when they set off, but their prayers were rarely answered.

One other option available to escapees was to acquire the services of a *metadore*, or professional guide. For an agreed sum, the metadore would lead an escaping slave from the outskirts of Meknes to the gates of the nearest Spanish presidio. Familiar with the terrain and dressed as a travelling merchant, he was able to avoid many of the hazards that afflicted unaccompanied slaves. But the metadore's services were strictly limited. He refused to help the slaves break out of their lodgings, nor would he supply any food. All he promised was to deliver the escapee to the gates of the presidio with speed and in safety. '[They] commonly travel all night,' wrote Father Busnot, '. . . with abundance of alarms [signals] along the way, known only to their guides.' Daylight hours were spent in woods or caves, where the escapees tried to snatch some rest. Even so, it was a wearisome journey for men who had often suffered from years of fatigue and malnutrition. 'Nothing can be more uneasy than such travelling,' wrote Busnot, 'which is always in the dark, along by-ways, through desarts and over impracticable mountains, with little provision and in continual fear.'

There was a very real concern that the metadore would abandon or kill the slaves under his charge. If he felt there was the slightest risk of being discovered, he would disappear into the night in order to save his own skin. There was good reason for such caution. Metadores were despised by Moulay Ismail, who showed them no mercy if caught. Busnot learned of two metadores who were captured while assisting the escape of several Spanish slaves. The sultan beat the slaves, as was customary, but reserved his full fury for the metadores. '[He] condemned the Moors to have their hands nail'd to the new gate of the city,' wrote the padre, 'and there to be devour'd by wild beasts.' One of the men lived for three days, 'after which his dead body was expos'd to be devour'd by wild beasts'. The other managed to pull his hand off the nail, only to be stabbed to death.

Thomas Pellow was familiar with many stories of escape and knew that any attempt would carry enormous risks. He was also aware that he would be turning his back on a lifestyle that carried certain privileges, despite the inherent dangers. An even greater dilemma was the thought that he would never again see his wife or daughter. Yet he was so desperate to escape from Morocco that he decided the possibility of freedom – however remote – outweighed all other considerations.

As a renegade, he had several advantages over the European slaves still being held in Meknes. He spoke excellent Arabic – he could certainly pass himself off as a wandering merchant – and had the freedom to choose the best moment to make his break. Most escaping slaves did so in little groups, but Pellow felt he stood a greater chance of success if he went alone.

His most recent posting was in Agoory, which lay some twenty miles from Meknes. He decided to head for the Portuguese garrison at Mazagan, today's El Jadida, where ex-slaves and renegades had been welcomed in the past. Although he provided few details of his flight from Agoory – he even neglected to record the date – he experienced little difficulty in travelling undetected to the coast. It took him just three and a half days to reach the windswept salt-flats of the Atlantic seaboard; shortly afterwards, he sighted the distant walls and bastions of Mazagan. 'The fourth following night,' he wrote, 'I got without any accident, and to my most unspeakable joy . . . [to] within a hundred yards at the utmost of the castle walls.'

Pellow could scarcely believe that his flight from Agoory had been so easy. He had managed to escape detection by the sultan's network of spies and informers, and had faced none of the usual hardships during his hike across Morocco. Now, he found himself standing so close to the walls of Mazagan that he could make out the individual blocks of stone. He stood on the threshold of freedom; all that he needed to do was to clamber over the ramparts and surrender himself to Mazagan's Portuguese governor.

But his run of good fortune was soon to come to an abrupt end. As he stood in total darkness, trying to work out the best place to scale the city walls, he was 'laid hold on by four Moors, who had that night been upon the plunder in the gardens, but had been disturbed therein by the Portuguese sentinels'. Pellow did not see them until it was too late; 'the night being excessive dark and windy, they in a narrow passage between two garden walls ran right against me and laid first hold of me.' It was a critical situation, but not irredeemable. Pellow spoke their language and might have been able to fob them off with a hastily concocted story. But he made 'a very unhappy mistake'. Convinced that the men were Portuguese, he informed them that he was a Christian, intent on escape.

He immediately realised that he had made a terrible error. The Moors could scarcely believe their luck in surprising an escapee and tightened their grip on the hapless Pellow. 'I was carried by them in a little time back to their main guard, and confined in irons, and early the next morning conducted by a strong guard of them to Azzemour.' His guards showed him no mercy and taunted him about his impending execution. 'After being severely handled by them,' wrote Pellow, 'I was carried before Simmough Hammet Beorsmine [Si Mohammed ben Othman], their commanding officer.'

This officer was powerless to execute anyone without authorisation from the town's governor, who was currently visiting the sultan in Meknes. He therefore 'ordered the Moors to put me in prison till his return, when he told them I should be very severely punished'.

The men who had seized Pellow were puzzled by the officer's attitude. They insisted that he did not need the governor's approval to execute a captured escapee and reminded him that Pellow 'was a Christian, and about to make my escape to Christian-land'. Their words eventually had some effect. Although the officer refused to send Pellow immediately to the gallows, he assured the Moors that his days were numbered. 'It was at last agreed between the governor and them,' wrote Pellow, 'that I should be kept till their next market-day, when I should be put to death in the market place.' The officer reminded the men that there was a market in four days, 'and during that time the neighbourhood might be acquainted with it, and come and see the execution'.

Pellow was terrified by what he heard. He had witnessed the power of the mob on many occasions and now knew that he had little chance of cheating death. He had come so close to making his escape, 'and now am I, as any may suppose, under a most grievous agony'. He could only pray that his execution would be quick and painless.

Pellow was led away by a detachment of guards and 'for their better securing me, I was directly guarded away by a multitude of those bloodthirsty villains, and put into a very deep and dark dungeon.' Told that food was wasted on a prisoner awaiting execution, he was to be kept 'without any allowance from them besides bread and water'. He was therefore extremely surprised when one of the officer's retinue arrived on the first evening with a bowl of meat. He was even more perplexed when this servant slipped him a secret message – dictated by the officer – to the effect that 'I should not be under any apprehension of danger from the mob, for that he had truly considered my case . . . [and] would deliver me from their rage, even to the hazard of his own life.' The servant could give no clue as to why the officer had taken such an extraordinary decision, nor could Pellow be sure that it was true. Yet the same servant appeared twice every day and each time he came with food and a similar message.

As the Thursday market approached, Pellow grew increasingly nervous. 'When he [the servant] brought me my breakfast that same morning (to which I had but little stomach), he told me that I should not despair.' He assured Pellow that the officer intended to spare him the fury of the mob.

Although desperate to believe the man, Pellow felt that he was clutching at straws. 'It was but the promise of an infidel,' he wrote, 'and at second hand, which made it the more uncertain.' He was half sick with worry when 'at ten o'clock, these blood-thirsty villains came, hauled me out of my dungeon, and led me through the street to the marketplace.'

His sense of panic increased still further when he found himself 'attended by an insolent mob, still increasing as we went, so that by the time we got to the marketplace, which was sufficiently crowded by the barbarians, to feast their eyes with the blood of an innocent Christian, I was almost ready to expire'. Pellow's worst fears were confirmed when he saw that Si Mohammed, the officer who had promised to save him, was standing next to the town's executioner. 'I [could not] help,' he wrote, 'at the sight of a long murdering knife in the hand of the executioner, being stricken with a very great terror.' Although the officer had promised to intervene to halt the imminent execution, Pellow felt that '[it was] very much to be doubted if that power would be sufficient to save my life'.

As the clamour of the crowd increased, Pellow's life of captivity flashed before him. Believing that nothing could save him, he watched in terror as the executioner prepared to do his business. '[He] had now his knife ready in his right hand, and with his left hand had taken fast hold of my beard, the better to hold back to cut my throat.' Pellow winced at the anticipation of pain and closed his eyes to the roar of the mob. A second passed, and then another. But suddenly – and without warning – there was a discernible shift in tone. The crowd was no longer crying in exultation. Rather, they were shouting out in rage.

Pellow opened his eyes and was amazed by what he saw. Officer Mohammed was standing beside him and gesticulating wildly to the executioner. 'My guardian angel,' he wrote, 'stepped forth and took the knife out of his hand.' Pellow noted that he did so with not a moment to spare. 'Had not he done [so] that very instant, he would, no doubt . . . have soon taken from me the small remainder of life that was left in me.'

The officer's unexpected intervention caused fury among the assembled crowd, who had been cheated of the spectacle of a bloody execution. 'And now is there a very hot dispute between the mob,' wrote Pellow, 'whether I should die or not being the question.' But he had been dramatically reprieved by Officer Mohammed, whose supporters pitched up in the market place and demanded Pellow's immediate release.

Pellow could not fathom why the officer was championing his cause and would never fully understand the reason for his actions. But he seemed to have become a pawn in a long-running struggle for control over rival factions in the town – one that Officer Mohammed fully intended to win. In saving Pellow's life, against the wishes of the mob, he had demonstrated his authority over his rivals.

Pellow was not yet safe. He was sent back to the dungeon, with the crowd continuing to taunt him that the next market day really would be his last. But Officer Mohammed 'told [me] not to despair' and assured Pellow that he would be released as soon as the town's governor returned. Even so, it was two months before Pellow was finally set free and told to leave Azzemour. 'In open daylight, [he] delivered me from my nasty prison, and set me again at liberty to depart.'

Pellow set off towards his garrison at Agoory without further ado. Why he did not press ahead with his flight remains a mystery. In his account of the incident, he claims that he was not inclined to break the oath he had made with Officer Mohammed and his retinue. 'As I had promised them, upon my honour, to return again to Agoory,' he wrote, 'so I did.' He arrived back at the kasbah after an absence of four months, expecting to be punished with great severity. Yet his escape bid was never once mentioned by his fellow soldiers, nor by his commanding officer. 'What I was very much surprised at,' wrote Pellow, 'I never once heard the last syllable from the emperor concerning this my attempt to escape.' The only conceivable explanation was that Moulay Ismail had not been apprised of his flight.

Pellow's escape had very nearly cost him his life, and he was extremely fortunate not to have been executed. Lesser men might have abandoned all hope of fleeing from Morocco, but Pellow vowed to die in the attempt rather than spend the rest of his life in servitude. 'Notwithstanding my so late miraculous escape from the bloody knife at Azzemour,' he wrote, '. . . I was then thoroughly resolved to pursue it.'

But it was some years before he could make his second bid for freedom. The exact date is unclear; Pellow's disclosure that it was during a period of civil turmoil suggests that it may not have been until 1728 or 1729. More certain is the fact that he decided to team up with fellow English renegade William Hussey, 'a Devonshire man', whom he knew to be 'very trusty and honest'. He was nevertheless cautious when he first broached the subject with Hussey. 'Now, Will, said I, I desire you will answer me sincerely to a question I am about to ask you.' Pellow informed Hussey of his desire to escape and asked if he would be prepared to join him. Hussey leaped at the opportunity, confiding to Pellow that 'it was what his soul had for a long time longed after; and he was ready, even at the expense of the last drop of blood, to make the experiment.'

The men headed for Salé and began to scour the coastline for a suitable craft in which to make their escape. Pellow had abandoned his previous idea of seeking refuge in one of the Portuguese garrisons and also felt that there was little point in waiting for an English merchant ship to appear in port. Instead, his plan was to steal a boat and sail her to the British garrison in Gibraltar. 'And now are mine eyes busily employed in looking sharp out after the ships then in the harbour, and my thoughts . . . on what other help I might with safety procure me.'

On the first morning after their arrival in Salé, Pellow and Hussey were presented with an unexpected opportunity to escape. They spotted a small sloop at anchor in the harbour – one that looked perfectly suited to their purpose – and Pellow befriended two of her Moorish crew. He informed them that he could provide them with wine, if they were interested, and the delighted sailors immediately invited him to come aboard their boat. As Pellow was rowed across to the sloop, he told them that he 'was one of the emperor's soldiers [and] that under him I bore an office of some distinction'. He continued chatting to them as he boarded the vessel, but was all the while 'viewing the dimensions of the sloop, sails & co.' With mounting excitement, he realised that this was the perfect ship in which to make his escape. 'Now is my heart to that degree inflamed,' he wrote, 'that every drop of the blood in my veins is upon the ferment how I should manage this affair.'

When Pellow was back on shore, he told Hussey of his conviction that they could engineer their escape in this very sloop. 'I do not in the least doubt,' he said, 'by our prudent management, [this vessel] will answer both our expectations, even without our losing any blood about the matter.' There was just one hurdle to overcome. The sloop required a minimum of three crew members, and Pellow asked Hussey if he could think 'of a third person that might be trusted, for that two were not sufficient to work the vessel'.

Hussey did indeed have a suggestion. He had once served alongside an English renegade named William Johnston, 'a Kentish man' who was currently stationed in Salé. Johnston had been captured at sea during the same summer as Pellow, while on a voyage from Lisbon to Amsterdam, and had voluntarily converted to Islam – the only member of his crew to have apostatised. 'I cannot altogether answer for his fidelity,' warned Hussey, 'though I never heard anything to the contrary of his being an honest man.' The two men approached Johnston with considerable caution and were relieved to discover that he was 'very desirous to make his escape'. Without further ado, the three renegades began to work out a strategy.

They proposed to offer a keg of brandy to the two Moors charged with guarding the vessel and encourage them to drink deeply. When they were inebriated and unable to fight back, Pellow and his friends would seize the sloop and slip quietly out of the harbour. They would then head northwards towards Gibraltar, which they were confident of reaching within a few days.

They decided to put their plan into action without delay. When Pellow next spoke with the guards, he again befriended them, saying, 'If you will come tomorrow night at ten of the clock, I will meet you here and bring with me some more brandy, sugar and lemons.' The Moors were only too agreeable, and Pellow asked if they minded him bringing 'my comrades, as honest cocks as any in Barbary, and we will go on board together and heartily enjoy ourselves'.

The three Englishmen spent the day in nervous excitement. They were confident of success, for the guards had already revealed themselves to be drunkards. Yet they were also on edge – aware that they were certain to be executed if their mission failed.

'We got all our little matters in readiness,' recorded Pellow, 'as two pair of pistols, the brandy & co.' Although the men had no charts or navigational equipment, they were not unduly troubled. They knew they could hug Morocco's Atlantic coastline until they reached Cap Spartel – the entrance to the Mediterranean – then use the stars to guide them north-eastwards across the short but treacherous Straits of Gibraltar.

At ten o'clock that night, the three of them made their way down to the waterfront. Pellow was delighted to see the approach of the sloop's little rowing boat and prepared to lead his friends aboard. But suddenly – and quite without warning – William Johnston announced that he had had a change of heart. 'To my very great surprise,' wrote Pellow, '[he] told us he could not by any means go that night.'

Pellow and Hussey were completely taken aback. The rowing boat was about to reach the shore, and there was no time to argue or reason. Both men realised that they had no option but to abandon their escape attempt and feared that they would now be betrayed by Johnston. Thinking on their feet, they went down to the waterfront, leaving their erstwhile comrade in hiding. They told the Moors that 'as we had good reason to believe there were some people on the watch, we had deferred our going on board till the next night.' As both men still hoped to escape on the sloop and had no desire to arouse the suspicions of the Moorish guards, they told them that 'in point of good manners, we had brought them a couple of bottles of brandy, sugar and lemons.' The two Moors seemed happy enough, 'telling us, after a most pleasant manner, that they would go on board and drink our healths, and that we might depend on their coming again the next night'.

Once the Moors had departed, Pellow and Hussey turned on Johnston with a vengeance, telling him angrily that 'in an affair of that nature, to do as he had done was using both us and himself very ill.' Pellow added that he had wrecked a very real chance of escape. 'Had he gone about as heartily as he promised,' he said, 'we should in all likelihood have been then safely landed on some Christian shore, quite out of the power of the Moors.' What made the two men even more frustrated was the fact that the sloop was filled with guns, beeswax and copper 'to the value of five or six thousand pounds'. Such a cargo would have proved a huge bonus if and when the men reached Gibraltar.

Johnston was in no mood for compromise; indeed, he was equally furious with Pellow and Hussey. Having reappraised the idea of escape, he thought it to be a highly foolish undertaking. He had also spent much time reflecting on whether or not he really wanted to take flight. In England, he would have neither money nor prospects and would be returning to a life of abject destitution. Here in Morocco, he was provided with free meals and had a position of sorts as one of the sultan's foot soldiers. With haughty disdain, he told Pellow 'that he had again considered maturely of the affair . . . and found it to be quite different from what it had first appeared'. He said that he thought their plan was nothing more than 'a foolish whimsey come into our heads [and] impossible to be executed'. He then declared his intention of informing the governor of Salé if the two men persisted in their escape.

Pellow was appalled, for he knew that this would spell his immediate doom. He asked Johnston if he was speaking in earnest, and the renegade replied with some relish that he was. When Pellow heard this, he was unable to control his temper. '[I] could no longer forbear him,' he wrote, 'but directly drew my sword and gave him a very deep wound across his face.' It was unfortunate that he had not killed Johnston, 'for after my giving him this shrewd cut . . . he went directly to the governor'. Determined to have his revenge, Johnston proceeded to reveal every detail of the escape plot.

Salé's governor was stunned that these runaway slaves should attempt to escape from under his very nose and ordered Pellow to be brought to him directly. 'Looking at me very fiercely,' wrote Pellow, 'and turning up the white of his eyes sullenly, [he] told me that he never thought me to be so much a villain.' Declaring that Johnston deserved nothing but praise for informing on his erstwhile comrades, the governor informed Pellow that unless he could justify his actions – which he thought most unlikely – he would 'be punished in a way deserving of so notorious a crime'.

Pellow had given some thought as to how best to defend himself. He told the governor that Johnston was lying and said that he could prove it – but would only do so in the presence of Johnston himself. The governor, who relished the spectacle of two Englishmen arguing for their lives, ordered the renegade to be brought forth instantly.

Johnston spoke first, repeating the details of Pellow's intended escape. But when it was Pellow's turn to speak, he sang a very different tune. He said it was Johnston who had initiated the idea of escape and that he had, 'of a long time back, continually teazed me to join with him'. Pellow added fuel to the fire by telling the governor that Johnston had been so persistent in his desire to escape that his only option had been to gash him with his sword. '[For] his so wicked importunities,' he said, 'I gave him the cut.'

The governor listened with incredulity to Pellow's story, but his disbelief was tempered by Pellow's insistence that he had a witness who could confirm everything. The governor promptly summoned William Hussey, whom he proceeded to cross-examine.

Hussey immediately realised that his life – and Pellow's – were at stake. He proved a sterling alibi, informing the governor that if Pellow had not slashed Johnston, then 'he had fully designed to have given it himself.' When asked to explain further, Hussey delivered the *coup de grâce*. He said that 'for a long time back, I have not been at quiet on [account of] Johnston's frequent importuning me to join with him in escape.' He added that Johnston had repeatedly asserted that Pellow was also intending to escape – something he had found hard to believe. 'This, sir, I must confess very much surprised me,' he said, 'I having always found Pellow very easy under his present condition.'

The governor, having listened to Hussey's story with rapt attention, thought long and hard before he spoke. At length, he turned towards Johnston with beetled brow and told him 'that he could not imagine how he could invent such a damnable lie', adding that if Hussey had not given evidence in Pellow's defence, '[he] must in all likelihood have taken away the life of an innocent person'. He then ordered Johnston to be clapped in irons, and informed Pellow and Hussey that they were free to go.

The two men could scarcely believe that their hastily concocted tale had succeeded in convincing the governor of their innocence. Pellow, in particular, had once again proved himself to be a survivor – one whose quick wits and bold tongue had saved him from serious punishment. He remained furious with Johnston for having wrecked the very real chance he had of escaping from Morocco. Yet he felt guilty about the punishments that Johnston was certain to receive and begged the governor to pardon him. He also presented him with forty ducats, 'which I had been a long time before scraping together', and said that he hoped this would lead to Johnston's speedy release.

William Johnston's betrayal had a profound effect on Pellow. It served to remind him of the extraordinary dangers of trying to escape from Morocco and brought home the fact that he had twice gambled with his own life. He vowed to be more cautious in the future, and it was to be some years before he gathered the courage to make one final, and desperate, bid for freedom.

11 Blood Rivals

Two years had passed since Commodore Stewart's successful mission to Meknes, yet there was no sign that the sultan intended to release his other European slaves. The great palace works continued apace, and thousands of captives still toiled on the rambling walls and ramparts. The size of the slave population ebbed and flowed during this time. New ships were constantly being brought into Salé, along with their captive crews, keeping Moulay Ismail supplied with fresh slaves. But a large number of men being held in Meknes had chosen to apostatise, turning their backs on their erstwhile comrades. The slaves they left behind in the slave pens could only hope and pray that their own governments would send an emissary to negotiate with the sultan.

In 1723, it seemed to some of those slaves that their prayers were about to be answered. On a sparkling October morning in that year, a group of French padres could be seen splashing through the surf in Tetouan bay. Father Jean de la Faye and his brotherhood had landed in Morocco with costly presents and money in the hope of emulating the extraordinary success of Commodore Stewart. Full of optimism and in high spirits, they were buoyed by the belief that they would manage to buy back all of their countrymen in captivity.

The French had led a number of missions to Meknes in the early years of Moulay Ismail's reign, and on each occasion they had managed to free several hundred of their enslaved compatriots. But the sultan had grown increasingly prickly in recent years, and the padres had therefore channelled all their finances into freeing the slaves of Algiers, Tunis and Tripoli, where they stood a greater chance of success. Now, with news of the British triumph in everyone's minds, Father Jean and his comrades felt it was time to reopen negotiations with Moulay Ismail.

Their arrival in Tetouan was not greeted with quite the same enthusiasm as had been accorded to Commodore Stewart. Basha Hamet, the local governor, insisted on examining Father Jean's presents, then brusquely informed him that the crates of Chinese faience and gilded cloths were unsuitable. He was offended by the padre's manner and showed his displeasure by locking up several of his French slaves in the local prison. When Father Jean went to visit these men, he was horrified. 'The dampness, stench and amount of vermin in this prison would be capable of killing them in a very short time,' he wrote.

The padres decided to press on towards Meknes, even though they were short of food and supplies. 'Since our departure from Tetouan,' wrote Father Jean, 'we have not found a single drop of good water.' Although he and his men filled their casks from rivers and streams, 'the water stank, was murky, and full of worms and insects on account of there being no current.'

Most visiting dignitaries were accorded a modicum of respect when they arrived in the imperial capital. But Father de la Faye and his men were poorly treated from the outset and lodged in accommodation that was scarcely better than that in which the slaves were held. 'We only saw daylight through an opening which was in the ceiling of the reception room,' wrote Father Jean. He was unable to fathom the reason for the sultan's disregard. It may have been provoked by regret at having released his British captives, but may have been just another instance of the sultan's quixotic nature.

After a few nights in Meknes, the padres were surprised to

hear a knock at the door of their lodging. They were greeted by a handful of French captives who had bribed their guard into allowing them out of the slave pen. 'As soon as we set eyes on their miserable state,' wrote Father Jean, 'compassion changed our joy into pain.' He wept freely at the pitiful condition of the captives and wanted to spend the evening praying with them. But the men had to return to their quarters without delay, for they were fearful of being discovered. 'After a little speech to strengthen them, and encourage them to persevere, they left.' Later that night, Father Jean despatched a small purse of coins to the slaves, in order that they might bribe their guards to provide them with additional rations.

Several days passed before Father Jean and his men were granted permission to visit the French captives in the slave pens. They were appalled by the conditions and fought back tears as they listened to harrowing stories told by the slaves. The men complained that the hard labour was truly punishing: 'work which continues from dawn to dusk without stopping, through rain and the heat of the sun, without any respite'. Father Jean also learned that nationality made no difference to the way in which the slaves were treated. He spoke with Dutch, Portuguese, Genoese and Spanish slaves, and all told a similar story. He was also told that female captives were treated with even greater cruelty. One woman who had refused to convert to Islam had been tortured so badly that she had died of her injuries. 'The blacks burnt her breasts with candles; and with the utmost cruelty they had thrown melted lead in those areas of her body which, out of decency, cannot be named.'

After several days of waiting at court, Father Jean received word that the sultan was prepared to grant him an audience. This was the first piece of good news since his arrival in Morocco, and he made haste to prepare his presents: two huge looking-glasses, a damascened hunting rifle, gold brocade and three trunks of faience. He then headed to the imperial palace where

Moulay Ismail was waiting in anticipation of his gifts.

The sultan's great age – he was seventy-six – was at last beginning to show. His frame was withered, his head shook continually and his darting black eyes – which were always small – had sunk deep into his head. They accentuated his extraordinarily fleshy lips, 'on which he rests his tongue when he's not speaking, which means that he dribbles continuously'. Yet he still cut an imposing figure, surrounded by dozens of fawning attendants. 'We noticed that when the sultan wanted to spit,' wrote Father Jean, 'his favourite Moors approached to receive his spit in a tissue. One received it in his hands, and rubbed it in his face as if it was a precious ointment.'

The padres were quick to notice that Moulay Ismail was wearing yellow, his killing colour, 'which denoted that he was going to order some executions'. They did not have to wait long to witness the bloodshed. Four criminals were ushered into the courtyard and the sultan ordered them to have their throats slit. When they begged for mercy, he temporarily commuted their death sentence to a sound beating. They were given 300 blows of a cudgel and tossed three times. They were then trussed up and executed.

The padres, horrified by the spectacle, felt sick and faint. Their fragile condition was made worse by Moulay Ismail's insistence that they stand in the midday sun, which Father Jean found 'très piquant'. But he did not dare to complain and eventually succeeded in starting negotiations to release the slaves.

Father Jean was shocked to discover that there were only 130 French captives in the slave pen – a fraction of the number he had expected to find. Death and disease had claimed a large number, while many more had chosen apostasy as a means of release. The surviving few had been held in captivity for many years. Germain Cavelier, aged sixty-one, had spent four decades in slavery. Nicolas Fiolet had been a slave for thirty-eight years. Most of the others had spent at least two-thirds of their lives in the slave pens, but had never given up hope that one day they would be rescued.

Father Jean soon grasped that Moulay Ismail had little intention of releasing them for the money he had at his disposal, demanding instead a staggering 300 piastres for each captive and refusing to accept the costly presents as part of the payment. As the padres haggled over the price, they became increasingly frustrated with the recalcitrant old ruler. With mounting anger, they informed him that their only desire was 'a reasonable treaty, in the hope of retrieving, with our funds, a part of our slaves, if we couldn't have them all'.

But time was fast running out. Many of the men were at death's door, and the padres watched, helpless, as one of the captives, Bertrand Massion, collapsed from injuries he had received at the hands of the slave-drivers. 'He had suffered several times the martyrdom of being hit with a rope and stick,' wrote Father Jean. 'We saw his body full of a thousand weals which he had received.' He had also been slashed with a knife and 'endured the torment of an iron clamp around his head'. Massion was never to taste the freedom for which he had yearned so long. He died in the slave pen's little infirmary, after enduring more than thirty-five years as a captive.

Father Jean spent several more weeks in negotiation with Moulay Ismail, but he now realised that all his efforts were in vain. The sultan agreed to release fifteen of the oldest slaves in return for the presents, but was adamant in refusing to free the rest. With great reluctance and a heavy heart, Father Jean admitted defeat. On 11 November came the most difficult moment of all. 'We went to the *canot* [slave pen] to bid farewell to the slaves that remained in captivity,' he wrote. 'We exhorted them to stay steadfast in their faith, and encouraged them with the hope that other fathers would come back in more favourable times.'

Father Jean viewed his mission as a failure and blamed himself for the lack of success. Although he managed to persuade

Moulay Ismail to part with two more slaves, bringing the total to seventeen, it was not an achievement of which he was proud. 'Seventeen slaves did not satisfy our desire to release the irons from a greater number,' he wrote. The padres decided to press on to Algiers, where they felt more confident of success. But they met with unusual stubbornness from the ruling dey and managed to release just forty-seven slaves. It was a most disappointing result, yet Father Jean nevertheless decided to stage a noisy procession of the freed slaves when they arrived back in France. It was not quite the triumph that had greeted Commodore Stewart's return to London, but the sight of these dishevelled individuals was enough to move many to tears as they were paraded through the villages of northern France.

The erratic behaviour of Sultan Moulay Ismail dissuaded any Spanish padres from sending an embassy to Morocco, recognising that as they stood so little chance of buying back any captive Spaniards, the men would have to be abandoned to their fate. The redemptionist fathers decided instead to sail to Tunis and Algiers, where the slave population still numbered around 25,000. In three missions between 1722 and 1725, Father Garcia Navarra managed to release 1,078 slaves, although he was infuriated by the dey's insistence that he buy both Catholics and Protestants. When the Spanish padre curtly remarked that the latter were heretics and therefore undesirable, the dey exploded with rage. 'What I want, the Lord God wants,' he fumed, 'and the king of Spain had better want it too.'

One of Commodore Stewart's last actions before leaving Morocco had been to persuade Consul Hatfeild to remain at his post. Hatfeild was extremely reluctant, but fell victim to the commodore's considerable charm. For four more years he battled against destitution, but by the summer of 1726 he was in despair. His coffers were once again empty and no one in London seemed to care. When the Salé corsairs towed in yet more British

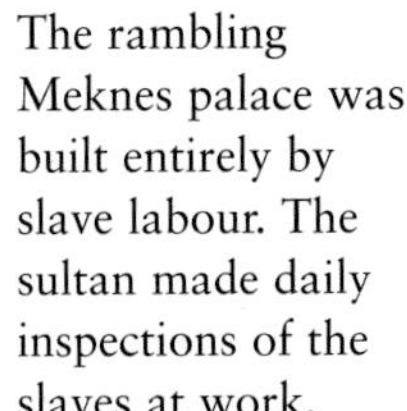

The rambling Meknes palace was built entirely by slave labour. The sultan made daily inspections of the slaves at work.

aug 2 1716 John Pellow Frunees of Falm: from Gallipeli wth Oyl for London
Tho: Goodman . Mate
Tho: Grimes . . . . 06 April 26 1716
Jno Donnall
Lewis Davis . . . . 06 augr 16 1717
Bryant Clark
George Berrycott
Tho: Pellow Boy Turnd Moore

Do Robt. Fowler George from Gallipeli wth oyl for Topsham . . . . . . 06 aug 22 1717
Steps: Morris Mate
Mathew Elliot . . . . 06 Apr 22 1717
Jno Green
Wm Loud
Tho Dean Boy

aug 3 1716 Richd Ferriss Southwark of London from Portsmo: wth Wheat for Leghorn 06 8ber 7 1716
Wm Drew . . 1 Mate

In 1719, a list of British slaves still alive in Morocco was sent to London. The eighth name on the list is 'Tho: Pellow, Boy, Turn'd Moor'.

Scores of alms collectors worked on behalf of the Barbary slaves; the post was included in a 1688 edition of *The Cryes of the City of London*.

Slaves were forced to wear heavy chains. One captive in Salé said his shackles weighed fifty pounds.

European padres made frequent attempts to buy back slaves. The sultan accepted their presents with alacrity, but only rarely released his captives.

King George I commanded a large navy, shown here encircling his portrait, but it proved ineffectual in tackling the Salé corsairs.

Secretary of State, Joseph Addison, tried to win the release of the British slaves in 1717. The mission failed when his emissary insulted the sultan.

Commodore Charles Stewart was urbane and charismatic; he proved skilled at dealing with Moulay Ismail. His right hand was shot off during a sea battle against the French.

Moulay Ismail treated foreign envoys with contempt. He gave long lectures on Islam and staged public executions for the edification of his visitors.

Freed slaves were treated to triumphant processions on their return home. Thousands of Londoners turned out to see the British captives released in 1721.

Escaping slaves faced many hazards: informers, the black guard and a lack of fresh water. Wild animals posed an additional danger; these two escapees are killing a sleeping lion.

Slaves escaping by boat were at the mercy of wind and weather. William Okeley and others (pictured) built a skiff and sailed to Majorca. Pellow also hoped to escape by boat.

Sir Edward Pellew bombarded Algiers with overwhelming force. The once-great city was reduced to rubble and the ruling dey sued for peace.

The dey of Algiers surrendered to Pellew and released all his captives. It marked the end of white slavery.

The crumbling walls of Meknes palace reveal the scale of the sultan's building project. They were severely damaged in the earthquake of 1755.

This long alley, flanked by palace walls, is where Moulay Ismail liked to ride in his chariot; it was drawn by his wives and eunuchs.

The sultan's monumental granary – the *heri* – now lies in ruins. It was said to be large enough to contain a year's harvest from the whole of Morocco.

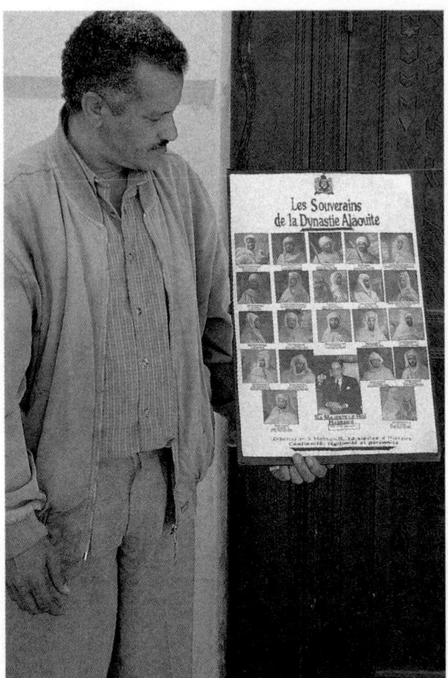

The guardian of Moulay Ismail's tomb shows how the present king of Morocco is descended from the same Alaouite dynasty.

You can buy almost anything in Salé's Souk el-Kebir. Three centuries ago the only item on sale – at a cost of £35 each –- was European slaves.

vessels and marched their captives in triumph towards Meknes, Hatfeild decided to quit. He could no longer face the indignity of diplomatic impotence.

His replacement was John Russell, who arrived in Morocco in the spring of 1727, intending to head directly to the court of Moulay Ismail. His meeting with the sultan, however, was destined never to happen. At the end of March, dark rumours began to circulate through the court – rumours that were soon confirmed as true.

Moulay Ismail had fallen sick several months earlier, and his closest courtiers quickly realised that he would not recover. He demanded that his physicians work harder to find a cure and grew increasingly frustrated when their elixirs and potions failed to restore him. 'His distemper towards his latter end became so nauseous that no-one could bear the room where he lay, notwithstanding all the art of perfumes.' So wrote John Braithwaite, who accompanied Consul Russell on his mission to Morocco. Moulay Ismail remained as virile as ever, despite his bodily decay, and summoned his wives and concubines to his bedside in order to relieve his suffering. 'For his recovery,' wrote the Frenchman Adrian de Manault, 'he demanded such disgusting acts that decency won't allow us to relate them.'

His end, when it came, was quite sudden. His ancient frame was already racked with disease when he contracted a 'mortification in the lower part of his belly'. This prevented him from moving, and the chief eunuch perceived that the end was imminent. On 22 March, 'at the hour the muezzin calls the faithful to midday prayer', the great Moulay Ismail finally expired. He was eighty years of age and had ruled Morocco for a remarkable fifty-five years.

None of the sultan's courtiers recorded his final mutterings, and it is impossible to know if he went to his death with a clear conscience. In the course of his reign, he had overseen the deaths of thousands of men and women, a number of whom had been butchered by his own hand. He had ordered countless courtiers to be dragged behind mules until they were dead and had slain dozens of his imperial guard. Several of his sons had been put to death, and he had maimed and mutilated many of his wives. At least two of his subjects had been sawn in two, and numerous kaids and officers had lost eyes and limbs. But Moulay Ismail had reserved his greatest contempt for his slaves, who had been butchered and tortured, mutilated and broken.

The survivors would doubtless have rejoiced at the news of the sultan's death, but it would be two months before word spread from the inner recesses of the palace. According to Thomas Pellow, who was at Kasbah Temsna at the time, the secrecy was 'for certain reasons of state'. John Braithwaite's account of the sultan's death provides much greater detail. He claimed that Moulay Ismail himself had demanded the deception in order to stop the orgy of pillage and violence that traditionally followed the death of a sultan. Imperial palaces were often looted and sacked, and rival usurpers raised armies to fight for the succession.

Moulay Ismail hoped to secure the throne for his chosen son, and the few courtiers present at his deathbed had been forced to swear that on no account was news of his passing to percolate through the palace. It was imperative for the court to continue functioning as normal, in order to retain the pretence that Moulay Ismail was still alive. The sultan's kaids – ignorant of his death – were greeted at the palace as if nothing had happened. Although they were denied an audience, their presents were accepted by the chief eunuch. Messengers came and went. Orders were proclaimed in the sultan's name. A full eight weeks passed without anyone except the courtly elite knowing anything about the sultan's death.

Moulay Ismail had originally nominated his son, Abdelmalek, as successor. But Abdelmalek's recalcitrance had infuriated him, and he offered the throne instead to another son, Ahmed ed-Dehebi. Ahmed was secretly informed of his father's death and hurried to Meknes in order to quietly take control of the reins of power. Abdelmalek remained ignorant of events, but he watched his brother's movements with increasing suspicion. Convinced that a courtly conspiracy was afoot, he forced his way into the palace in order to discover the truth. When he was evicted by his father's courtiers, he knew that something was seriously amiss.

The courtly inner circle now realised that the deception could no longer be maintained, especially as rumours were spreading throughout Meknes. 'The people who suspected something, having not seen the emperor for some time, began to murmur,' wrote Braithwaite. He added that large crowds began to gather outside the palace gates, 'in a very tumultuous manner, desiring to see their king'.

Knowing that it was time to proclaim Ahmed ed-Dehebi as sultan, the chief eunuch decided to do this in as dramatic a fashion as possible. He spread a rumour that Moulay Ismail was much recovered and would soon be paying a state visit to the nearby shrine of Moulay Idris. 'Accordingly, at the day appointed, a covered coach drove thither in which the king was supposed to be, attended by the whole court.' The route was thronged with onlookers who flung themselves into the dust as he passed. All believed that the great Moulay Ismail was alive and well, and they were eager to catch a glimpse of this veteran survivor when he reached the shrine. 'When the coach arrived,' wrote Braithwaite, 'the people began to be impatient to see their concealed emperor.' They yelled his name and urged him to step out of the carriage. For several minutes, the assembled courtiers lay prostrate on the ground. The bodyguards stood rigid. The crowds waited in suspense. Suddenly, the doors of the sultan's coach were flung open by a guard, and the hideous truth was revealed. Inside the carriage, Moulay Ismail's putrid corpse was propped up with silken cushions.

As the gasps faded away, the chief eunuch delivered an address to the crowd. He explained that his stratagem had been designed to assure the smooth succession of Ahmed ed-Dehebi and added that the new sultan was finally in control. Civil war had been averted, and Meknes was in safe hands. The corpse could now be buried in the mausoleum that Moulay Ismail himself had constructed.

News of the sultan's demise was proclaimed throughout the kingdom, reaching remote garrisons and kasbahs with remarkable speed. Thomas Pellow was still at Kasbah Temsna when he received a visit from one of Moulay Ismail's officers, Kaid el-Arbi ben Abbou ould ej-Jebli. Pellow, initially suspicious of the kaid's arrival, told him 'that in case he had anything to say to me, he should advance with a few [troops] only to the foot of the wall'. But the kaid assured him that he had nothing to fear. '[He] told me that the old emperor was actually dead, and that Ahmed ed-Dehebi was, by the general consent of the black army, proclaimed at Meknes.'

The new sultan consolidated his position with remarkable speed. He was formally presented with the keys to Meknes on the same day that Moulay Ismail's death was made public and entered the city a few hours later. His first act was to present the black army with 220,000 gold ducats – a gift that was greeted with great enthusiasm. They saluted their new sultan and, according to Pellow, threatened 'death and destruction to everyone who would not acknowledge him'. The sultan also took control of the treasury and began compiling an inventory of all the golden objects scattered throughout Meknes palace. He stripped his father's wives of all their jewellery and added it to his treasury. He even toyed with the idea of selling his white slaves, in the hope of augmenting his treasury coffers. To this end, he ordered two slaves from each European nation to return to their homelands 'to encourage the princes which ruled there to buy back those of their subjects which were enslaved'.

News of Moulay Ismail's death was greeted with much rejoicing in the imperial capital. 'The moment his death became known,' wrote Pellow, 'all the inhabitants of Meknes retired every one to their houses, abandoning all the public works on which Moulay Ismail had unprofitably kept them incessantly employed.' But the sultan's army of European slaves were not so fortunate. Ahmed ed-Dehebi soon decided against selling them back to their respective governments. He had inherited from his father a passion for building, and the captives now found themselves serving an equally megalomaniac master. 'He embellished his Moroccan palace in surprising fashion,' wrote Adrian de Manault. 'He covered the inside of the harem with gold leaf. The largest rooms were ornamented with marble basins, in which clear and transparent water ran, and in which a huge quantity of fish was placed.' The ceilings of these rooms were most extraordinary, covered with mirrored glass that reflected everything in the room below, 'so that you could watch the fish swimming'.

Sultan Ahmed ed-Dehebi had acted with great prudence in securing the throne, but it quickly became apparent that he lacked the streak of ruthlessness that had enabled his father to remain in power for so long. Pellow said that he maintained control only by constantly distributing gifts to his crack troops. '[He] was a man of a most generous, though very sottish nature,' he wrote, 'being almost ever drunk, giving the blacks a great deal of gold, and many other valuable presents, insomuch that their hearts were for the present entirely his.'

The new sultan was also a gourmet and dilettante, who devoted the greater part of each day to the pleasures of the table. 'He didn't find enough variety in the traditional Moorish cuisine,' wrote Adrian de Manault, 'so he tasted all the foreign stews that could excite his sensuality and awaken his appetite.' Selecting four slaves from the most diverse areas of Europe, he ordered them 'to prepare dishes according to the custom of their country'. It was not long before the new sultan had virtually abandoned affairs of state in favour of lengthy bouts of eating and drinking.

⋆

It was most unfortunate for John Russell that his arrival in Morocco coincided with the death of Moulay Ismail. Although Ahmed ed-Dehebi's accession had been engineered to avoid civil unrest, the countryside was soon swarming with brigands. Consul Russell stayed in Tetouan for six months, debating whether or not to travel to Meknes, before concluding that the potential benefits of doing so outweighed the risks. The Salé corsairs were threatening to seize yet more vessels, and it was imperative that the new sultan ratify the treaty that Moulay Ismail had signed six years earlier.

As Russell progressed towards Meknes, accompanied by attendants and porters, he was staggered by the number of European renegades he met en route, never realising that so many slaves had chosen to apostatise rather than endure the miseries of hard labour. Anxious to learn more about life in the sultan's service, he managed to speak with one of the British renegades, a man named Daws, when he arrived at Fez. 'He turned renegade about forty-six years ago,' wrote Braithwaite, '. . . and has had two wives in this country.' When Russell and Braithwaite asked why he had apostatised, Daws replied that '[it] was the late king's threatning to kill him'. He added that 'in those days there were no hopes of being redeemed.' Daws said that many of the English renegades were 'carpenters, caulkers [and] sail-makers' – men with skills that Britain, with her rapidly growing navy, so desperately needed.

The city of Fez was in rebellion against the new sultan and under a constant state of siege. Russell and Braithwaite were surprised to discover that numerous European renegades were serving in the ranks of the besiegers. 'I was accompanied from the camp by one Nugent,' wrote Braithwaite, 'an Irish renegado, and three English.' When he admired one of the heavy mortars, he was told that the gunner was a Frenchman. He was also taken to see an entire battalion of renegades – 600 of them – who came from right across Europe. '[They were] mostly Spaniards, some French, some Portuguese, and about thirty English and Dutch.' All had been forced to do hard labour in Meknes and had converted to Islam in order to escape their chains. 'As we returned home,' wrote Braithwaite, 'we were led into a yard where we saw several Christian carpenters making carriages for cannon, under the direction of an old Spanish renegado.' He was horrified by the pitiful physical condition of the European renegades. 'Those of them that I saw at Fez,' he wrote, 'were sad, drunken, profligate fellows, half naked and half starved.' He said that many more had been 'sent to garrison remote castles upon the confines of the country, where they are obliged to rob for their subsistence, until the country people knock them on the head'.

In the third week of November, Consul Russell and his entourage left Fez and headed towards Meknes. Russell had been assured that there were no British slaves in the imperial capital, but two captives managed to make contact with him soon after his arrival. Argalus Carter had been a slave for nine years and had served in the household of one of Moulay Ismail's sons, while William Pendergrass had been plucked from a Dutch ship three years earlier.

Russell was ushered to court on the day following his arrival. He and Braithwaite immediately realised that the order and discipline so skilfully imposed by Moulay Ismail was a thing of the past. 'We were kept waiting about an hour in this anti-apartment of the king's,' wrote Braithwaite, who was alarmed to see courtiers fighting among themselves. 'All [was] in such an uproar,' he wrote, '[that] one would have thought himself on the common side of a jail than in the palace of a great emperor.' At length, the Englishmen were informed that the sultan was ready to receive them. 'Behold . . . two great wooden gates were flung open, and we discovered his imperial beastliness sitting under a wooden canopy.'

Consul Russell behaved with extraordinary gravitas, presenting the sultan with his gifts and condoling with him on the death of his father. 'But it might as well have been let alone,' wrote Braithwaite, 'for his imperial highness was so drunk he could scarcely hold his head up.' He had to be helped to his feet by his eunuchs, who struggled to shuffle him across the room, while terrified courtiers crawled around on their hands and knees.

Russell and Braithwaite were disgusted by the depravity of the sultan. His skin was 'very much pitted with the small-pox' and he was 'very much bloated in the face'. His front teeth were missing, which gave him 'a very ugly figure', and his green silk turban was dishevelled and 'hung loose like a drunken man's'. Russell's audience was over before he had had a chance to mention the treaty. The sultan was carried away by his eunuchs, having uttered scarcely a word. His chief vizier was rather more effusive, clinging to Russell's shirt-tail and assuring him that his demands would be met. 'He protested how much he loved the English and promised mountains,' recalled Braithwaite. 'He compared the English to the apple of his eye, and made several other odd and extravagant compliments.'

Russell had hoped to get restitution for the English vessels seized in contravention of the peace treaty. Instead, he and Braithwaite found themselves visited by a steady stream of European renegades in search of money or help. One of them – an Irish woman called Mrs Shaw – recounted a woeful tale to the two men. She had been imprisoned in Moulay Ismail's harem, and the sultan, 'having an inclination to lie with her, forced her to turn Moor'. The ensuing sexual encounter was not a happy one, and the sultan gave her to a disreputable Spanish renegade who treated her with great brutality. 'The poor woman was almost naked and starved,' wrote Braithwaite; '. . . she had almost forgot her English, and was an object of great charity, having a poor child at her breast not above a fortnight old.' Russell, moved by her plight, said that she could visit him as often as she wished while he remained in Meknes.

On the day after Mrs Shaw's visit, Russell was told that a West Country renegade was waiting outside his lodgings. He invited him in and learned that his name was Thomas Pellow. 'Today we were visited by one Pellow,' wrote Braithwaite, 'a young fellow of a good family in Cornwall, but now turned Moor.' Pellow was now twenty-three years of age and had been out of England for twelve long years. Braithwaite already knew something of Pellow's story from the slaves he had spoken with in Meknes. 'The Christian captives gave this young man a wonderful character,' he wrote, 'saying he endured enough to have killed seven men before his master could make him turn.' All in the slave pens respected Pellow's bravado and resolution, and were no less impressed by his astonishing skills of survival.

Russell and Braithwaite were now able to hear the details of his capture and hardships directly from Pellow himself, who revelled in being able once more to speak in his native tongue. He talked of his adventures in the service of the late Moulay Ismail and bemoaned the fact that he had spent almost half his life in Morocco. With his sun-blackened skin and long beard, he must have struck the two newly arrived Englishmen as looking more Moroccan than English. 'Pellow, being taken very young, spoke the Arabick language as well as the Moors,' recalled Braithwaite. He was impressed with Pellow's eloquence and said that he spoke with great clarity about the events he had witnessed in the country, 'giving a very good account of it'. Pellow also told them of his military escapades and his desperate bid to escape from Morocco after being left behind by Commodore Stewart. 'He is at present a soldier,' wrote Braithwaite, 'as all the renegadoes are who have no particular trade or calling.' He added that Pellow had done far better for himself than most of the other former slaves, whose 'allowance of pay and corn is so small that they are in a starving condition, being obliged to rob and plunder for the greatest part of their subsistence'.

Pellow almost certainly introduced Russell and Braithwaite

to the sultan's chief weapons expert, the Irish renegade named Carr. This one-time slave had risen to a senior position in the courtly hierarchy and even had his own European slaves to attend to his needs. 'Mr Carr gave us a very elegant dinner after the English manner,' wrote Braithwaite. 'We sat upon chairs, and eat out of pewter, with knives, forks and table linen etc.' The men had not eaten a square meal since leaving Tetouan, and Carr's dinner party was most welcome. 'We had wine, punch and a consort of musick played by Christian captives.' As the slaves struck up a merry tune, Russell and Braithwaite allowed their glasses to be filled and refilled by the hospitable Mr Carr.

Consul Russell began to realise that his sojourn in Meknes was futile. Carr's entertainment had provided a welcome diversion, but there was no escaping the fact that he was wasting his time. Russell's woes multiplied when a tremendous rainstorm caused water to seep into his room. 'It rained into Mr Russell's bed,' wrote Braithwaite, 'and all over his chamber, so that there was scarce any walking in or out of it.' The next morning, shortly after Russell had left his chamber, the sodden ceiling came crashing down.

Russell hoped for one last audience with the sultan, but Ahmed ed-Dehebi was becoming increasingly temperamental. On 21 December, '[he] ordered the boy that looked after his pipes and tobacco to be flung down a precipice for stopping his pipe too hard'. Russell repeatedly requested a meeting with the sultan, but on every occasion he was refused. 'The truth is,' wrote Braithwaite, 'his majesty was drunk, and so he was likely to be the next day and the day after.' This was confirmed by the sultan's physician, a Spanish ex-slave, who said that the sultan's daily routine was a monotony of debauchery and hard drinking. 'He drank with his ministers until he fell down, and then the eunuchs carried him to bed, until he had slept off his last debauch.'

While Russell petitioned the courtiers for an audience,

Braithwaite took the opportunity to visit the slave pen. He said it was 'remarkable for nothing but filthy smell', even though conditions had improved somewhat in the months since Moulay Ismail's death. The slaves had a certain freedom of movement, and enterprising renegades had set up food stalls for the few who managed to beg or steal some money. Nevertheless, the daily routine remained hard for most captives, especially those from northern Europe. 'I do not know a more moving spectacle than that of the Dutch people,' wrote Braithwaite. 'These poor creatures had – ever since we came into the country – depended upon their liberty, and Mr Russell had always assured them of it.' Russell had genuinely hoped to negotiate their freedom, but his efforts had come to nothing. 'The women were inconsolable,' wrote Braithwaite, 'and the most part of them almost distracted with grief.'

On 10 January, more than five weeks since Consul Russell's first meeting with the sultan, he was met by a flustered courtier within the compound of the imperial palace. The courtier said that the sultan wished to see him immediately and warned that he would be appearing in the next few minutes. Russell scarcely had time to compose himself before the great gates swung open and Ahmed ed-Dehebi entered the courtyard, clutching a large gun and flanked by statuesque guards carrying gold-tipped pikes. He stopped before Russell, muttered 'buono Christiano' and asked to see the British king's letter. Having expressed his pleasure that his own name was written in gold calligraphy, he promised not to capture any more British mariners. Then he made a majestic exit, offering Russell 'a present of six captives' as he left.

The consul was both surprised and delighted. He and Braithwaite had achieved their goal of ratifying the 1721 treaty and were at long last free to escape from the horrors of Meknes. 'We were so rejoiced at the prospect of our liberty,' wrote Braithwaite, 'for we had looked upon ourselves but in a sort of captivity, that we made all the haste we could home.' They set out for Tetouan almost immediately, and the freed slaves followed a few days later. What neither man realised was that all their work was about to be rendered futile. A series of bloody revolutions was to sweep the sultan and his successor from power, and the ensuing chaos would have dire consequences for Thomas Pellow, the European slaves and the thousands of renegades in Morocco.

Thomas Pellow learned of the turmoil within a month or two of his meeting with Russell and Braithwaite. He had returned to Agoory when he was told that the black army had mutinied against the sultan and declared their support for his brother, Abdelmalek. 'They had surprised Moulay [Ahmed] ed-Dehebi in his own house,' wrote Pellow, 'keeping him there under a very strict guard.'

The catalyst for their action was a shocking event that occurred in the spring of 1728. The sultan's drunkenness had long scandalised his courtiers, who had done everything in their power to keep it concealed from the citizens of Meknes. But the townsfolk were soon given a graphic display of his debauchery. 'Going one Friday to the mosque to prayer, he was so drunk that when he prostrated himself, according to the custom of the Mahometans, he vomited up his wine.' The assembled crowd was appalled, and the sultan was forced to retire to his palace where he faced a barrage of invective from his wives. According to John Russell, who immediately sent a report of the incident to London, these formidable women 'reproached him with irreligion for defiling his body with strong liquor so nigh the ramadan'. They were so disgusted that they took to the streets, whipping up a storm of protest against their husband's scandalous behaviour.

The Moroccan populace did not need much convincing that the sultan was unfit to govern. The city of Fez, already in revolt, refused to recognise 'a prince immersed in the debaucheries of the table, and made stupid by wine'. Now, the people of Meknes followed suit. The sultan might yet have clung to power, but when the court's *ulama*, or religious councillors, turned against him, even Ahmed ed-Dehebi realised his days were numbered. He fled from Meknes in panic, and the throne was offered to his brother, Abdelmalek. According to the Arabic chronicle of Muhammad al-Qadiri, the new sultan was chosen for his 'resolve, mastery, excellent conduct and policy, great justice [and] love of learning'. He may indeed have had all these qualities, but he was also foolish and careless. His first error was to allow his brother to escape from Meknes. His second was to voice public criticism of the black army.

Thomas Pellow was extremely concerned about the consequences of serving under the new sultan, who intended to use his European renegades to punish all who opposed his rule. He was even more hesitant when he heard that the black army was wavering in its loyalty and looked set to throw its support behind Ahmed ed-Dehebi. When Pellow was brought news that the deposed sultan was in the vicinity and had assembled a huge number of troops to help him reclaim his throne, he 'went directly to him and marched with him to Meknes'.

The imperial city had been constructed in such a way that no invading army could ever hope to scale its walls. The only chance of capturing the place was to bombard the defenders into submission. Ahmed ed-Dehebi proceeded to do just that, ordering salvo after salvo to be fired into the heart of the city. Sultan Abdelmalek's forces put up stiff resistance, but came under increasingly heavy fire from the besieging forces. For forty-eight hours, the battle raged around the city gates. Eventually, Ahmed ed-Dehebi's soldiers – who included Thomas Pellow – managed to break through the defences and seize the kasbah at the heart of Meknes. All inside were summarily put to the sword. 'What was seen there,' wrote Adrian de Manault, 'was not so much the image of a war, but of a butchery.'

Once this initial slaughter was over, the victorious troops went on the rampage, looting, pillaging and attacking the undefended slave pens. 'There was no distinction between Muslim, Jew or Christian,' wrote de Manault. 'The fathers were killed or injured [and] sacred vases were profaned with indignity.' According to Muhammad al-Qadiri, there was 'widespread looting and rape, and other shameful acts occurred back in the kasbah'. The city's governor and the principal officers were accorded no mercy. '[They] were nailed by their hands and feet to one of the gates of the city,' wrote Pellow, 'in which miserable manner they lived three days.' The governor's hands and feet 'were so torn by the weight of his body, being a lusty man, that he fell down from the gate'. He was fortunate to be despatched by a whirr of scimitars.

It was a desperate time for the European slaves, who had neither guns nor swords with which to defend themselves against the black army. 'We believe we must comment here on the glory of the French,' wrote the Frenchman, Adrian de Manault. 'Amongst the Christians which were compelled during this disorder to change their religion, there was none of that nation which renounced the faith of Jesus Christ.' Once every area of the city had fallen under Ahmed ed-Dehebi's control, the surviving slaves were forced to cleanse the streets in preparation for the victorious leader's triumphant entry.

Ahmed ed-Dehebi had killed huge numbers of people in his battle for Meknes, but one key insurgent was not among them. 'As to Abdelmalek,' wrote Pellow, '[he] fled thence through a by-gate in the night time, as was rumoured, to Old Fez.' The rumour was true. He had indeed fled to Fez, where he was given a cautious welcome into the city. No one was in any doubt that the offer of sanctuary was tantamount to a declaration of war.

Thomas Pellow was one of the 60,000 troops sent to capture and kill Abdelmalek. 'Now I am one in the above number before

Old Fez,' he wrote, noting that the city's defenders were 'strongly fortified, resolutely resolved and well provided'. There was nevertheless a feeling of optimism among Ahmed ed-Dehebi's soldiers, for they made a formidable sight as they assembled on the hillsides outside the city's ancient walls. '[They] encircled Fez,' wrote al-Qadiri, 'as tightly as a ring on a finger.'

The battle began in earnest on 16 August 1728, when wave after wave of the black guard attempted to storm the city ramparts. The European renegades meanwhile set to work with their great guns. '[They] pounded it with cannonballs and bombs from all sides,' wrote al-Qadiri, '[and] the bombs caused much destruction.' Each shot caused the walls to shudder and crumble, but they failed to open any breach through which the crack troops could pour. Renegade sappers mined the walls and detonated explosives, but still failed to open a passage. 'Thanks to God's kindness,' wrote al-Qadiri, 'although the wall went up in the air from the blast, it returned to its original place without having suffered any damage.' The bombardment was so intense that the sultan's gun carriages began to fall to pieces. Ahmed ed-Dehebi was beside himself with frustration. It was imperative that the carriages were replaced with the utmost urgency, but he knew that the best craftsmen were in Salé, almost one hundred miles away. The sultan needed someone dependable for a mission that could quite possibly decide the outcome of the siege. He turned to Thomas Pellow, whom he had witnessed fighting alongside his forces at the battle for Meknes. Pellow and his men were ordered to head to Salé and commission 'the making of new carriages for our field pieces, the old ones being, through the so frequent shocks of such weighty and high metalled cannon . . . to that degree shaken as they were become in a manner unserviceable'.

Pellow set off to Salé as requested and oversaw the construction of the new gun carriages. He then had them dragged overland to Fez, 'where I was by Moulay [Ahmed] ed-Dehebi, most kindly received'. Pellow's service earned him praise and gratitude from the sultan. Instead of having to abandon his offensive against Fez, as he had feared, Ahmed ed-Dehebi was now able to redouble his attack. Once his cannon were remounted on the new gun carriages, his forces 'kept almost a continual battering upon the town'.

Yet still the defenders held out against the besieging forces, growing increasingly confident that the great walls would save them. Emboldened by the black army's lack of success at storming the city, they began infiltrating the sultan's camp and killing men in hand-to-hand combat. One of these sorties pushed deep into Pellow's battalion. His men first realised something was amiss when there was a flash of light and a resounding boom. Seconds later, they found themselves being fired on from all sides. 'It was my mishap,' wrote Pellow, '. . . to receive two musket shots within a few minutes' time of each other, one passing through my right thigh and the other through my left shoulder.' He also received a 'shrewd cut' to his left hand, which bled profusely. 'And now am I in a bloody condition,' he wrote later, '. . . being tapped in three several places, insomuch that from my excessive loss of blood from them all, I really thought that I could not have long survived it.'

Pellow was indeed in a serious condition. The wound to his hand was extremely deep, and he soon collapsed from the loss of blood. 'Now am I laid on a bier,' he later recalled, 'in order to be carried to an hospital.' As he lay in severe pain, the sultan himself rode past and, recognising Pellow, expressed regret that such a trusted comrade was so badly wounded. 'He said he was very sorry for me,' wrote Pellow, '. . . and ordered three surgeons to go along with me and to use the best of their skill for my recovery.' In reward for Pellow's earlier service, he presented him with fifty gold ducats and also ordered that 'I should have a quarter of fresh mutton brought in every day.'

Events in Fez were meanwhile reaching their denouement. As neither side saw any prospect of breaking the deadlock on the battlefield, in mid-December 1728, emissaries from each camp met to negotiate a possible truce. To everyone's surprise, their discussions bore fruit almost immediately. It was agreed that Morocco – which had remained united throughout Moulay Ismail's long reign – should now be divided in two. Abdelmalek would be installed as ruler of Fez, while Ahmed ed-Dehebi would reign as sultan in Meknes. It was also decided that the brothers should meet face to face, in order to seal a bond of trust between them.

Pellow, who had been nursed back to health by German renegade physicians, was witness to the extraordinary events that followed. As Abdelmalek was conducted towards his brother's tent, he was searched by the captain of the guards who found him concealing a poignard and a pistol with which he was clearly plotting to murder his brother. The weapons were confiscated and he was led sheepishly into Ahmed ed-Dehebi's presence. The sultan feigned insouciance and let his brother off with a mild rebuke. 'Instead of venting his wrath and vengeance upon him,' wrote Pellow, '[he] contented himself with making some reproaches, and those without sharpness.' But Ahmed ed-Dehebi was inwardly seething and was not content to leave the matter there. Abdelmalek was arrested and put in the custody of one of the sultan's most feared black guards. He was then taken to Meknes and kept prisoner until further notice. Six weeks later, he was visited by Ahmed ed-Dehebi's henchmen and strangled to death. 'And lest he might not be dead enough,' wrote Pellow, 'they gave him each a stab with their long murdering knives through his body.'

Sultan Ahmed ed-Dehebi had every reason to celebrate his triumph, for he was now the undisputed master of Morocco. His rebellious brother had been sent to an early grave and the city of Fez had surrendered unconditionally. But the sultan was not to enjoy the fruits of his victory for long. On 5 March 1729 – just four days after his brother's murder – he suddenly and dramatically dropped dead.

'His death was occasioned,' wrote Pellow, '. . . by his drinking a small bowl of milk at his entrance into Meknes from Fez.' This milk was rumoured to have been poisoned by the mother of Moulay Abdallah, yet another of Moulay Ismail's sons. If so, her stratagem proved entirely successful. On the day of the sultan's death, Moulay Abdallah was granted the throne.

In the midst of all the butchery and bloodshed, which had lasted for many months, the slaves in Meknes had been temporarily freed from hard labour. But Moulay Abdallah had no intention of discharging any of them. He had dreams of remodelling his late father's pleasure palace, repairing its war-battered ramparts and creating ever more lavish chambers. The Christian slaves were ordered back to the building works and Moulay Abdallah assumed personal control of the construction. 'He had them strengthen the walls of the seraglio with twenty-six bastions,' wrote de Manault, '. . . on which he installed several batteries of cannon.' The sultan was unhappy with the view from his principal harem, which overlooked the vast imperial quarters known as Madinat el-Riyad. This section of the palace contained the mansions of many of the greatest courtiers, as well as bazaars, baths and a college. It was held by many to be 'the pride and joy of Meknes', and much of it had been personally overseen by Moulay Ismail. Now, Sultan Abdallah had it razed to the ground, ordering his slaves to destroy it with picks and shovels. The sultan derived particular pleasure from watching them getting injured while engaged in the demolition. 'While the slaves were working,' wrote de Manault, '. . . one of his pleasures was to put a great number of them at the foot of the walls which were about to collapse, and watch them be buried alive under the rubble.'

Thomas Pellow was also witness to some of these atrocities. He was particularly concerned for the slaves being held at Boussacran, just outside Meknes, who were treated in 'a most grievous and cruel manner'. The sultan set them to work, 'digging a deep and wide ditch through a hard rock round his pleasure house, himself with his severe eye being their overseer'. It was back-breaking labour, and Abdallah compounded their woes by slashing their rations to the absolute minimum.

Pellow was soon troubled by far more terrible news. He was still recuperating from his wounds received at Fez when a messenger galloped up on horseback to inform him that 'though he never cared to be the bearer of ill news, yet he could not forbear telling me that my wife and daughter were both very lately dead, dying within three days, one of the other.'

Pellow was utterly distraught. He had been married for almost a decade, and the birth of his daughter had been an occasion of great pride. She had provided him with comfort from suffering and had helped him battle against the constant loneliness and homesickness. Now she was gone and it was almost too much to bear. '[I was] often reflecting on the loss of my wife and daughter,' he wrote, '. . . especially the child.'

She had delighted Pellow and he had often speculated as to whether he would one day take her back to Penryn. Now, her death had robbed him of that distant dream. His only consolation was the thought that amidst the slaughter and bloodshed that were a daily reality in Morocco, his wife and daughter were, perhaps, 'better off than they could have been in this troublesome world'.

12 Long Route Home

TURBULENT MONTHS FOLLOWED THE DEATH of Pellow's wife and daughter. The country was riven by warfare and brigandage, while tribal chieftains wrested great tracts of land from Sultan Moulay Abdallah's control. The citizens of Fez rose up again, refusing to accept the barbarous sultan as their ruler. He responded by ordering the black army to crush them once and for all.

Pellow had hoped to escape from Morocco during these troubled times, but he was forcibly drafted into the second battle for Fez. He found himself 'swimming through a fresh sea of blood, the scene opening in new and deeper colours'. The black army behaved with utter depravity during this new campaign, raping and torturing with undisguised glee. Pellow was horrified, witnessing 'nothing but death and horror . . . for the space of some seven months'. Eight hundred of his European comrades were slaughtered, and he was once again wounded. '[I had] two musket shots in my left shoulder and fleshy part of my buttock,' he wrote. When he had recovered, he was sent to fight against truculent tribes in the interior of the country. Even this did not mark the end of his woes. In the autumn of 1731, the sultan ordered Pellow to take part in a slave-gathering expedition to Guinea, on the west coast of Africa.

Pellow was deeply troubled by this news. '[It] really gave me some disquiet,' he wrote, '. . . as being work cut out for me for at least two years.' He was now twenty-seven years of age and had survived countless dangers in the sixteen years since he had left his native England. This new voyage was certain to be extremely dangerous, for it involved crossing the vastness of the Sahara desert, traversing wind-sculpted sands where water was rare or non-existent. Entire caravans had gone missing in previous years – their terrible fate only discovered when search parties stumbled across bleached bones in the sand. The slave-gathering itself was also a hazardous business as the tribes of Guinea were ferociously hostile to such expeditions. Pellow feared that he would meet his end in some violent skirmish in equatorial Africa.

Yet he retained a glimmer of hope that the expedition might facilitate his escape from Morocco. His caravan was heading for the River Senegal, a swamp-choked artery that discharged its waters into the Atlantic Ocean. French slave traders had been exploiting this river since the 1630s, and had built a little settlement on St Louis Island at the mouth of the river. Pellow knew that if he could reach this trading post and make contact with the French, he stood a very real chance of securing a passage home.

He had an even greater chance of success if he could press on towards the River Gambia, which lay some 150 miles to the south. There was a British slave-trading post on James Island, in the river estuary, which was permanently occupied. Pellow knew that the governor was almost certain to offer him refuge if he managed to reach it unscathed.

Such hopes seemed remote as he contemplated the long journey ahead. The expedition was being planned on a truly grand scale, for which more than 12,000 camels had been assembled. As the Sahara could only be traversed in the six months between autumn and spring, preparations were extremely rushed. As soon as the camel train was ready, the caravan set off for the deep south.

The first part of the route, from Meknes to Marrakesh, followed a well-trodden trail. The caravan made brief stops at several villages before halting outside the walls of Marrakesh. The merchants and camel drivers replenished their supplies and water casks, while waiting for newcomers to arrive. The caravan then set off in a south-westerly direction, reaching the coastal port of Santa Cruz within nine days. Hereafter, it swung inland, pausing briefly at the shrine of Sidi Ahmed ou Moûsa, a famous holy man.

The barren valleys that encircled the shrine presaged the beginnings of the desert. Berber villages gave way to nomadic encampments and there was a dramatic change in the landscape. 'The oasis of Oued Noun,' noted Pellow, 'is the last that way where the inhabitants live in houses.' A few days later, he sighted his first sand dune, marking the gateway to the Sahara. The caravan had picked up many more merchants and camels on the way and now consisted of no fewer than 30,000 men, with double that number of camels. Even by the standards of the time this was a vast undertaking, requiring a great deal of organisation. There was no safety in numbers on a long desert crossing. Indeed, a large caravan could quickly deplete the scant supplies of water that it hoped to find en route. There was also a great danger that stragglers would be picked off by lawless desert Bedouin.

The men set off southwards, aware that they were now about to enter the most arduous stage of the expedition. It was 500 desolate miles from Oued Noun to Chingit, the caravan's destination, and the landscape was one of scrub and sand. The dunes were constantly shifting, eradicating any recognisable feature, and there was no well-trodden trail. In such a bleak environment, where years could pass without rainfall, the waterholes were indeed few and far between. It took great skill and experience to locate the rare springs of palatable, if brackish, water.

Pellow was surprised to discover that the guide hired to lead the caravan was blind. He told Pellow that he used his nose to lead them from waterhole to waterhole, sniffing the sand to determine their exact position. Pellow was sceptical of the man's powers and grew seriously alarmed when six days passed without his finding any water. On the seventh day, Pellow and his companions paused to drink from their waterskins, but 'to our very great astonishment found them . . . quite empty, the excessive heat of the sun having exhaled the water through the pores of the leather'. They now had only their emergency rations, which would sustain them for just a few more days. Thereafter, they would be doomed to a thirsty death in the desert.

The men complained to their guide, who was unfazed by their anxiety, asking one of them to scoop up a handful of sand and hold it to his nose. 'After he had sniffed upon it for some short time, he pleasingly told [us] we should, before two days' end, reach other springs and have water enough.' The great caravan staggered on for another two days under the insufferable heat of the sun. 'In the morning of the second day . . . he [the guide] desired that another handful of the sand of that place might be taken up and held to his nose.'

The sceptics now decided to test the guide in order to see whether or not he had the skills that he claimed. One of them had retained a small bag of sand from two days previously and now presented this to the blind man. 'After he had snuffed on it for a much longer time than at first,' wrote Pellow, 'he told him that either the army was again marching back, or that he had most grossly and basely imposed on him.' When informed that it was sand from two days earlier, he was angry that the men had not trusted his abilities. He demanded that they scoop up some sand from where they were now standing and 'after just putting his nose to it, [he said] that we should, about four o'clock that afternoon, have water sufficient'. The caravan pressed onwards until they sighted a distant speck of green in the desert.

'At last,' wrote Pellow, 'we got up to these so very much longed after wells . . . [and] drank our fill.' Their arrival came in the nick of time, for the waterskins were completely dry.

This method of finding water intrigued Pellow and he quizzed his guide about his 'wonderful and surprising knowledge in smelling to the sand'. The man replied that he had traversed the desert thirty times and, 'finding his sight gradually declining, he had, by often making the experiment . . . attained to this so wonderful knowledge.' Such skills were, in fact, by no means unique to this particular guide. They had been in use for centuries among the nomadic tribes of the Sahara; the medieval Arab traveller, Ibn Batouta, and the sixteenth-century adventurer, Leo Africanus, both mention similar techniques.

The men rested for a few days at the waterhole before continuing on their way. Autumn was by now well advanced, yet the sun still beat down relentlessly on the great caravan. For days on end, the horizon brought no relief except for the flicker of silver mirages. But these long desert crossings always held unexpected surprises, and Pellow's was to prove no exception. 'One day, as I was riding . . . my camel happened with one of his feet to hit against something which sounded very hollow.' Pellow jumped down, intrigued to know what object lay beneath the sand. 'It is a human corpse,' explained his guide, 'which hath for some time lain buried in the sands, till through the excessive heat thereof, it is dried to a kecks [mummy].'

The men later discovered a second mummy, suggesting that they had stumbled upon the ghastly remains of a caravan that had perished in the desert. Pellow, appalled, 'with the point of my sword soon found [it], and digged it up in a little time.' The corpse looked as if it had lain there for centuries. 'It was as hard as a stock-fish,' he wrote, '[and] had all its limbs and flesh (though shrivelled) entire, all the teeth firm in the gums.' He put his nose to the skin, expecting it to stink, but was surprised to discover that it had no odour at all. 'As to its being in any way nauseous,' he wrote, 'a man might, without offence, have even carried it in his bosom.'

After five months spent crossing the desert, the caravan was finally nearing its goal. The presence of nomads was the first sign that they were approaching Chingit. Soon after, the merchants in the vanguard spotted a vast number of tents in the desert. They had at long last reached the remote but fertile oasis.

This settlement lay more than 1,500 miles from Meknes, yet it was firmly under the sultan's control. During his reign Moulay Ismail had despatched several military expeditions to the area, forcing the nomadic tribes to submit to his authority. Chingit was an important staging post – the point at which two of the great Saharan caravan routes converged. It also lay within easy reach of the River Senegal – erroneously known as the Wadnil or Upper Nile. Moulay Ismail had intended Chingit to become a marshalling depot – a place where African slaves could be assembled and branded before being marched northwards to Meknes.

The sultan was not alone in exploiting the River Senegal; the French had shipped large numbers of slaves from this part of Africa to their plantations in the Caribbean. According to one of France's commercial agents, Jean Barbot, the Senegalese were 'tall, upright, well-built, well-proportioned and loose-limbed' and were much prized for their fine features. 'Their noses are somewhat flattened, their lips are thick, their teeth as white as ivory and well set, [and] their hair either curled or long and lank.' The women had particularly enticed Barbot, just as they had Moulay Ismail, being 'well shaped, tall and loose limbed', and seeming 'lively and wanton and eager to be amused'. Barbot was gratified to discover that they spent much of their time completely naked and said that 'all of them have a warm temperament and enjoy sexual pleasures'.

The English, too, had long been exploiting this stretch of African coastline. The establishment of the Royal African

Company in 1672 had led to an explosion in the number of slave-gathering expeditions to Guinea. It had also encouraged English traders to sail farther south along the coastline of Africa, establishing forts and slave pens wherever there was the possibility of acquiring large numbers of captives. The exact tally of slaves being shipped across the Atlantic each year is impossible to calculate, but it is known that one short stretch of the Gold Coast had no fewer than forty-three slave stations. One of these, Cape Coast Castle, had dungeons that could accommodate more than 1,500 slaves at any given time.

The trade in black slaves had been given further impetus in 1713, when the Treaty of Utrecht conferred upon Britain the infamous Assiento licence. This permitted her slave dealers to supply 144,000 black Africans to Spanish America, in addition to the vast numbers that were already being sold into enforced labour on the cotton farms and plantations of North America and the Caribbean. There are numerous surviving accounts of the hellish nature of the long Atlantic crossing. Chained, half starved and still suffering from the enforced march from the interior of Africa to the coastal slave stations, the captives faced months of squalor in insufferably hot, claustrophobic and unsanitary conditions. For many, being bought by a Moroccan slave dealer would have been infinitely preferable to being sold into slavery in North America.

Neither the English nor the French slave dealers were particularly choosy about the slaves they bought or seized. Moulay Ismail had been rather more discerning, demanding infants and young children who could be brought up to be ruthless and loyal. These slave-soldiers had fought in scores of battles during the course of his reign, and many thousands had been killed in intertribal warfare. The successive sieges of Fez had further depleted the black army, leaving Sultan Moulay Abdallah in very real need of fresh recruits.

'We marched thrice to the Wadnil,' wrote Pellow, 'and all such as made any the least resistance we brought under subjection with the sword.' Having neither weapons nor armour, the tribesmen who lived on these riverbanks were powerless to resist and it was easy for the Moroccan soldiers to hold chieftains to ransom. '[They] were either obliged to bring in the tyrant's exorbitant demands,' wrote Pellow, 'or to suffer the severe plundering of the army.' He added that the merchants with whom he had travelled were utterly ruthless, 'stripping the poor negroes of all they had, killing many of them, and bringing off their children into the bargain'.

Pellow had a stroke of good fortune during his first trip to the river. It coincided with a French slave-gathering expedition, and he was delighted to see a French trading vessel riding at anchor in the middle of the river. Being 'about eight tons', wrote Pellow, 'and manned by twelve sailors', this was far larger than the flat-bottomed slave boats that the French were accustomed to send upstream, and it offered Pellow the tantalising possibility of a passage back to Europe. But his dream of being rescued was to prove extremely short-lived. As soon as the Moroccan soldiers spied the French vessel, they determined to ransack it.

Pellow was aghast as he watched them put their plan into action. 'The Moors swam off to [the vessel],' he wrote, 'boarded it and hauled to the shore.' They captured the twelve crew members who might have saved Pellow, then proceeded to gut the ship of her cargo. She was a veritable treasure trove – one section of her hold was laden with elephant tusks while another was crowded with black slaves. These were taken to Chingit, and the vessel was then set alight. The French on St Louis Island were being sent the unambiguous message that the blacks of Senegal were an exclusively Moroccan preserve.

Stationed at Chingit for much of the winter, Pellow was forced to undertake three voyages to the River Senegal, during which 'we got together a very great booty, as gold, ivory [and] blacks.' How many slaves were captured is not recorded, although

Pellow says they were 'to the value of some millions of English pounds sterling'. The haul was clearly sizeable – just as it had been in the days of Moulay Ismail – making a significant contribution to the black slave trade, in which an estimated 15 million Africans were sold into slavery.

When there were no more slaves to be had, the great caravan prepared to leave Chingit. There was a flurry of activity as camels were made ready and the slaves sorted into groups. The return journey was to be even more hazardous than the outward desert crossing; it was essential that such a large caravan keep up a brisk pace to avoid running out of supplies. There was a brief discussion among the leaders about what to do with the twelve French captives. It was decided to take them back to Meknes, for they were certain to please Sultan Moulay Abdallah. In the event, four died during the long traverse of the desert and only eight half-starved survivors made it to the imperial capital.

The sight of so many slaves on the move was a tempting sight for the desert Bedouin, and the caravan came under attack on several occasions. Pellow served in one of the armed groups charged with defending the camel train and received a head wound in one clash. But the decisive action of his men saw off the Bedouin; 'after this skirmish,' he wrote, 'we travelled on unmolested.'

After months on the move, the caravan finally stumbled towards Kasbah Tadla in the winter of 1732. This fortress, halfway between Marrakesh and Meknes, was at the time playing host to the sultan. '[We] found Moulay Abdallah waiting our coming,' wrote Pellow, 'diverting his time in plundering the country and murdering his subjects.'

The leaders of the caravan expected him to be delighted with their haul, for they had brought back large numbers of child slaves from Senegal. But they had seriously misjudged the sultan, who was heir to all the caprices of his late father and no less cruel. He inexplicably accused the leaders of neglecting their duty and ordered eighteen of them to be summarily executed. 'When the tyrant was glutted with blood,' wrote Pellow, 'we marched with him at our head to Meknes.' The child slaves were taken away for instruction; the French captives were incarcerated in the slave pens; and 'the caravan was separated and sent home to their respective habitations.'

Sultan Moulay Abdallah's ever-strengthening grip on power encouraged him to widen his offensive against his European enemies. Although he concluded treaties with both the English and the Dutch, his Salé corsairs frequently acted in breach of these agreements, and the sultan connived at their actions. In October 1732 the British ship, *Eagle*, was towed into Salé harbour. Her passengers and crew – which included seventy Portuguese – were sent as slaves to Meknes. Other ships were also taken and the number of British captives in Morocco was soon well into three figures again.

The British government once again despatched an emissary, John Leonard Sollicoffre, to the sultan's court. He was accompanied by a Jewish interpreter from London, Salom Namias. The two men found Moulay Abdallah in ill humour and in no mood to negotiate over the freeing of his slaves. When Namias persisted in calling for their release, the sultan grew angry. 'Take away Mr Jew,' he said to his guards, 'and burn him directly.' Namias begged for his life, but the sultan reiterated his command that he should be burned. '[This] they instantly did,' wrote Pellow, 'laying him flat on his belly, heaping in a most cruel manner the wood upon him alive, and in a little time he, with grievous shrieks, and no doubt in very great agonies, expired.'

Sollicoffre's mission proved a failure – and a costly one at that. He spent more than £1,300 on his voyage to the court, but did not succeed in releasing a single slave. Worse still, the sultan's show of defiance encouraged Salé's corsairs to redouble their attacks. They seized four more British vessels – along with many from other European nations – and sent their crews to Meknes. When Pellow met one batch of British captives on their arrival in the city, he asked whether any of the men came from Cornwall. 'They told me, yes, there was one coming up named George Davies, of Flushing.' Pellow immediately recognised Davies and greeted him warmly. But Davies saw nothing familiar in Pellow's sun-blackened features and asked who he was. '"Why", said I, "you and I were once schoolfellows together at the church town of Milar."' Davies looked at him again and realised it was indeed Thomas Pellow, 'who I have of a long time heard was in his childhood carried with his uncle into Barbary'. Pellow confirmed that this was undoubtedly true and told Davies that 'I was very glad to see him again, though very sorry it should be in that part of the world under such unhappy circumstances.'

The capture of George Davies and his men aroused such protest in London that Sollicoffre was sent straight back to Morocco, where he managed to secure another meeting with Sultan Moulay Abdallah. On this occasion, he found the sultan in a more obliging mood, promising to release all 136 slaves – at a price of 350 crowns per head – although refusing to free any of the Spanish and Portuguese men captured aboard British ships. Sollicoffre handed over the money before the sultan could change his mind and hurried the released captives aboard his vessel.

He was quietly pleased that he had successfully completed his mission, but soon found that not everyone in Britain shared his sense of achievement. 'His Majesty was very glad to hear that you had procured the release of the English captives,' wrote the Duke of Newcastle in a letter to Sollicoffre, '. . . but was greatly displeased with your having agreed to pay so extravagant a price for them.'

Sollicoffre was accused of 'great misconduct' in paying the

ransom and found himself returning home in disgrace. Distraught at the criticism and sick with fever, he died a few months later.

On a moonless spring night in 1737, Thomas Pellow crept out of his Meknes barracks. Darting through shadows and keeping close to the city walls, he slipped out through the gates of the imperial capital. It was approaching midnight and the city was sound asleep. Pellow was making his escape.

He was now thirty-three years of age and had been in captivity for more than two decades. His wife and daughter had died almost nine years earlier, and the peaceful time he had spent at Kasbah Temsna was little more than a distant memory. Fearful of being sent on yet another dangerous campaign, Pellow decided that now – or never – was the time to make his break for freedom.

Although he left Meknes under the cover of darkness, he had no intention of travelling by night. Nor did he have any fear of being unmasked as a renegade. He spoke fluent Arabic, and his tanned skin and long beard enabled him to pass himself off as a wandering Arab merchant. He felt he was less likely to arouse suspicion if he travelled across Morocco in broad daylight.

He made rapid progress to the Atlantic coast, but the depredations of the corsairs had caused all European merchant ships to flee in panic. With weary reluctance, Pellow decided to push south towards the little port of Santa Cruz. He joined the entourage of a holy man who was roaming across Morocco, hoping that he would be safer travelling with a large group. But the unarmed and defenceless pilgrims were easy prey for the brigands that infested the roads. They were attacked on the very morning that Pellow met them – 'plundered and stripped' of their goods – and left virtually naked by the wayside. Pellow himself was robbed of the few possessions he was carrying, as well as most of his clothes. 'I was with Christian patience obliged to bear,' he wrote, 'and to travel on in this condition full three days in very cold weather.'

As he climbed the cragged slopes of the Anti-Atlas – the first stage of his route towards Santa Cruz – he met two Spanish renegades. They earned a living of sorts as itinerant quack doctors and took pity on his miserable condition. '[They] were to me very kind,' wrote Pellow, 'and true friends in necessity, giving me a piece of an old blanket, filling my belly with such as they had, [and] giving me friendly advice.' They told Pellow that it was relatively easy to earn a living in the remote mountain areas by posing as a physician. Many simple folk believed that Christians had healing powers, probably because Christ himself had healed the sick, and a number of renegades were doing good business among the superstitious Berbers of the High Atlas. The Spaniards provided Pellow with 'several of their medicines, and an old lancet and burning iron, to set up for myself'.

Pellow realised that crossing the Atlas Mountains in the guise of a travelling physician would enable him to conceal the true purpose of his voyage. It would also give him the opportunity to earn money and buy supplies. Beginning to feel more optimistic about his chances of success, he headed into more rugged terrain where he hoped to start practising his new profession.

He soon found the opportunity. As he passed through one nomadic settlement, he was approached by a woman who begged for help. She told him that her husband was in a poor condition and feared that he was approaching death. When Pellow examined the man, he saw that he was indeed in a desperate plight, '[for] his distemper was then gone very far and his condition very dangerous'. He said he would attempt to save the man's life by bleeding him, a common practice. If that had no effect, he would brand his skin with a burning iron.

Pellow had been given brief instructions on how to handle his tools, but this was the first time he had actually used them.

He bound the man's arm tightly with hemp cord, as the Spaniards had suggested, then reached for his instruments. He was aghast when he saw the state of the scalpel, which was 'very blunt and extremely rusty', and was 'at a very great loss how to perform [the operation]'.

Pellow's patient was already in pain, for the hemp cord had cut off the circulation in his arm, and urged him to perform the operation without further ado. 'In or near the vein,' wrote Pellow, '[I] gave him a very hearty prick.' But his hand slipped as he pushed in the knife and he was obliged to try a second time. 'I twice repeated it,' he wrote, 'and though I pricked him much deeper than at first, yet could I not for my life make him bleed.' The patient was squealing in agony and no longer able to keep still. Pellow therefore decided to burn the man and heated the branding iron until it was red hot. There was a terrible hiss of singeing as he applied it to the man's head, and the grisly stench of burning flesh. 'I made him to twist and cry out in a most piteous manner,' wrote Pellow, who proceeded to chastise the man for being 'a very faint hearted soldier'.

The patient was unconvinced by Pellow's treatment, but his wife was most grateful and begged him to dine with the family. Famished, Pellow graciously accepted. 'After I had filled my belly with couscous, and for my doctorship received six blankeels . . . I left them to their prophet Mohammed and their country doctors.' Alarmed at how badly he had wounded his patient, he had no intention of remaining in the neighbourhood.

As Pellow pushed on over the High Atlas, he proved increasingly successful at earning a living. He was usually given food by his patients, although their offerings were not always appetising. On one occasion he was handed a bowl of buttermilk and 'jerrodes' – locusts – which plagued the mountain villages every six or seven years. Pellow balked at eating such revolting-looking creatures. They were large – 'at least two inches long' – and as plump as a man's thumb. But hunger overcame his scruples and he popped a couple into his mouth. To his surprise, they tasted delicious. 'They are really good eating,' he wrote, 'and in taste most like shrimps.' He noted that the best way to cook them was to soften them first in salted water, boil them and then store them in vats of salt.

After more than six months on the road, Pellow glimpsed the Atlantic Ocean for a second time. With renewed optimism about escaping from Morocco, he decided to travel northwards along the coast until he sighted a European merchant vessel. He was pleased to discover several ships at anchor in the harbour of Santa Cruz, 'yet could I not meet with any so Christian-like commander as on any terms to carry me with him'.

Pellow was even more frustrated when he reached the port of Safi. There were two merchant vessels at anchor, one of which belonged to Joshua Bawden, a distant cousin through marriage. But Safi was in civil turmoil when he arrived and Pellow had to remain in hiding. 'Though I met him twice,' he wrote, 'and my blood boiled in my veins at the sight of him, yet did we not speak on either side.' Frantic at having come so close to escape, Pellow fell into a deep depression. 'I was more down in the mouth now than I had been from my first setting out from Meknes,' he wrote, 'reflecting on the many hardships and dangers I had thitherto undergone, and still no manner of appearance of an alteration.' With a heavy heart, he accepted that his only option was to press northwards to the port of Willadia.

He grew increasingly alarmed as he made his way along the coastal path. The countryside was awash with bandits and he was threatened and assaulted on several occasions. The situation deteriorated still further as he made his way over Mount el-Hedid. The locals were suspicious and hostile, and Pellow – who had neither musket nor pistol to defend himself – felt more and more vulnerable.

After a hard day's climb, he came to a mountainside house

that appeared to be abandoned. 'Being excessive weary and very drowsy,' he wrote, 'I laid me down in the sun and soon fell into a sound sleep.' He had not been sleeping for long when the owner of the house returned from the mountain. The man was friendly, but cautioned Pellow of the extreme dangers of travelling unarmed. Pellow admitted his fear and said that on the previous day he had met with 'a vast number of armed men, and . . . very narrowly escaped with my life'. The man urged him to proceed with care, warning that the path ahead was infested with cut-throats. 'They are a pack of the vilest villains in Barbary,' he said, 'and generally murder all they meet with.'

Pellow rested at the man's house overnight, and was given buttermilk and couscous for breakfast. Thanking his host heartily, he set off early before the sun grew too hot. With hopes of rejoining the coast within the next two days, he prayed that he would have a trouble-free hike over the remote and uninhabited mountain.

It was about ten o'clock in the morning when Pellow first knew that he was being tracked. Five 'footpads' were shadowing him and trying to determine whether or not he was carrying any weapons. Pellow suddenly felt afraid. It was a lonely and desolate place and there was no one to whom he could turn for help. He pressed on upwards with a growing sense of panic, increasing his pace and hoping to outflank his assailants. But when he looked around, he was alarmed to discover that they were almost upon him.

Seeing a small stone building higher up, he made this his goal. He walked faster and faster, then broke into a run, but the bandits were rapidly closing in on him. When Pellow glanced up the slope, he was horrified to discover that one of the men had outstripped him and now stood some distance in front. 'I was soon overtaken by a very speedy messenger,' recorded Pellow. With a real feeling of terror, he realised that he was trapped.

The attack was not long in coming. The man up ahead raised his musket and primed it for action. Carefully, deliberately, he pointed the muzzle directly at Pellow. His quarry was an easy target. Silhouetted against the sky and lacking any cover on the bleak mountainside, Pellow had nowhere to hide.

The musket flashed; the shot rang out. '[It passed] between my legs,' wrote Pellow, 'and grazing about half an inch within the flesh.' The wound bled profusely, drenching Pellow's clothing in thick blood. He limped on, desperate to escape his attackers, but the shot-wound 'slackened my pace to that degree that they were soon up with me'.

Pellow could go no farther. His leg wound was far more serious than he had first thought and was soon weltering in blood. As he slumped to the ground, dizzied by his injury, the pack of assailants launched themselves at him. They punched and kicked him until he no longer moved. Then, they stripped him of his possessions and left him in a coagulating pool of blood.

It is impossible to know what thoughts went through Pellow's mind as his pulse slackened. For years he had dreamed of returning to England, where his family and friends were fast becoming a distant memory. Now, as he lay close to death, he perhaps remembered his childhood in Cornwall and wondered sadly whether he would ever again see the little ports of Falmouth and Penryn.

In the spring of 1738, at the time of Pellow's brutal attack, an Irish sea-dog was sailing along the Moroccan coastline. Captain Toobin had a rich cargo of goods, which he was hoping to sell in one of the prosperous Atlantic ports. But he was finding his task both difficult and dangerous. He had to keep a sharp eye on the Salé corsairs, who were a constant threat, and had 'met with a great deal of trouble by way of the Moorish merchants'. Reluctant nevertheless to abandon his mission, he steered his vessel towards the little port of Willadia. It was while he lay at anchor, next to a Genoese brig, that he learned that help was at hand from a most unexpected quarter. A young Englishman – bruised, wounded and limping – had just arrived in town. He spoke fluent Arabic and was keen to help Captain Toobin.

The fact that Pellow had survived his attack was quite remarkable. He had come within a whisker of death on the slopes of Mount el-Hedid and was extremely fortunate to have escaped with his life. His assailants were still beating him when they were surprised by a larger group of bandits. Both groups scattered, abandoning Pellow on the mountainside. As evening fell and the temperature plummeted, his blood coagulated, staunching the flow from his wounds.

He was roused from his semiconscious state by the realisation that he was no longer under attack. Although badly injured and terribly weak, he noticed that the building he had been trying to reach was in fact extremely close. 'Making a bad shift . . . [I] got with much pain to the house,' he wrote, 'where I got me some herbs and staunched the blood, of which I had really lost a great deal.' The owner soon returned and was so horrified by Pellow's injuries that he took pity on him. 'Here I got a lodging for that night,' wrote Pellow, 'and some cous-cous for my supper' and, 'notwithstanding my wound, slept very well'.

Pellow woke early to find that he had recovered some of his strength. Having no wish to spend another night on the mountain, he decided to continue on his way. '[I] went limping on,' he wrote, hoping to be off the mountain by the end of the afternoon. He managed to reach the River Tensift, where he found a community of Jews, 'from whom I had some remedies for my wound, and a good supper, and a very civil entertainment for the night'. One of the men re-dressed his wound on the following morning and gave him breakfast before he set off en route to Willadia.

He made good progress during the day and had a most pleasant dream that night. 'Methought I happened to meet with a commander of a vessel, and who, though I had never seen him before, yet did he in a most Christianlike and courteous manner, offer . . . to carry me off with him at all hazards.' Pellow awoke early, more determined than ever to reach his goal.

Reaching Willadia at noon, he was overjoyed to discover two European merchant vessels in the harbour. The ship closest to the shore had sailed from Genoa and was laden with corn. Unlike the crews of most European vessels trading with Morocco, the men aboard were only too happy to make contact with an Arabic-speaking renegade. 'I went directly on board and was courteously received by them,' wrote Pellow. The men told him that 'they had been at a very great loss . . . for a linguist, asking me if I had dined and if I would eat any mullets.'

While the fish was frying in the skillet, Pellow quizzed the men about the second vessel in the bay. He was told that it belonged to Captain Toobin of Dublin, 'a very jolly, well-discoursed man', who was also in need of a translator. Pellow soon had a chance to meet the Irish captain, which gave him the surprise of his life. 'Before we had finished [dinner],' recalled Pellow, 'Captain Toobin came on board, and the moment I saw him I was thoroughly persuaded with myself that he was actually the same that I had so lately seen in my dream.' The two men had an instant rapport, and Captain Toobin invited Pellow aboard his ship. 'After drinking a cheering cup of wine,' wrote Pellow, 'he asked me how long I had been in Barbary.' Pellow explained the woeful story of his twenty-three years of captivity and his troubles in the service of the sultan.

When Toobin asked why he had not been successful in his previous attempts to escape, Pellow explained the extreme dangers of making a bid for freedom. 'I told him I had often endeavoured it, even to the very great hazard of my life.' He added that he had met English captains on several occasions, but that they had been too timorous to take him aboard. Toobin was appalled that Pellow's own countrymen could be so callous and vowed to take Pellow away with him. 'I tell you for your comfort,' he said, 'that you have met with a Christian at last, and here's my hand.' Pellow, scarcely able to believe his ears, asked Toobin if he really meant what he said. The Irish captain looked him straight in the eye and told him not to despair, 'for I am fully determined to carry you with me, even to the hazard of my life'.

Pellow was overcome with emotion and fought to hide his tears. Captain Toobin, too, was touched by the moment. 'He spoke with so much sincerity of heart,' wrote Pellow, 'and tender feeling of my sad case, that he could not forbear weeping.' He added that this 'raised my joy to that degree at his so tender behaviour that I could not forbear to keep him company'.

On 10 July 1738, Captain Toobin weighed anchor and put to sea. As Pellow was in danger of being unmasked right to the last, Toobin ordered him to remain below decks. 'For God's sake, Tom, take care you don't let any of the Moors see your face.' There was further panic when the ship drifted towards the dangerous port of Mamora, and the crew spent the night on deck in readiness for any attack. 'We got our arms upon deck,' wrote Pellow, '. . . putting into every one of them a new flint and charging it with three musket shot.' But the wind shifted during the night, enabling them to head back out to sea. 'Before sunrising, [we] were carried to seaward about five leagues,' wrote Pellow, 'and then we did not much fear any of their boats coming after us.' Captain Toobin was heading for Gibraltar, where he hoped to acquire fresh supplies from the British garrison.

Eleven days passed before the men at long last caught sight of Cap Spartel, which marked the mouth of the Straits of Gibraltar. Pellow, in ebullient form, spent 'most of that night in merry talk'. As the sun rose on 21 July, he caught sight of the Rock of Gibraltar itself. Just a few hours later, the vessel anchored in the bay and Pellow prepared to set foot on land controlled by his own countrymen for the first time in twenty-three years. It was another deeply emotional moment – and one that Pellow had awaited for two-thirds of his life. He feared that he was dreaming, 'and I had really a debate with myself if I was well awake'. But the sight of the garrison fort and the British soldiers marching and drilling reminded him that he had left Morocco far behind.

Captain Toobin went ashore before Pellow, in order to clear his arrival with Gibraltar's governor, Joseph Sabine: 'He told him that he had a poor Christian slave aboard his vessel that was taken by the infidels and carried into Barbary in the twelfth year of his age.' Toobin added that Pellow had 'undergone a great deal of hardship' and was in desperate need of assistance. The governor expressed his sympathies and granted Pellow immediate permission to land.

'It is impossible for me to describe the excessive joy I felt during all the time of our rowing to the shore,' wrote Pellow, 'though all may suppose it, after my so long and grievous servitude amongst the barbarians to be more than ordinary.' He had one final obstacle to overcome before he actually stepped ashore. The governor's permission had not been conveyed to the sentinels who guarded the harbour, and they refused to allow Pellow to land, telling him that their orders were to stop any Moor from setting foot in Gibraltar. '"Moor", said I, "you are very much mistaken in that, for I am as good a Christian, though I am dressed in Moorish garb, as any of you all."' They refused to believe Pellow, and it was not until the governor had contacted the harbour guard that Pellow was finally permitted to land. Only now did Pellow realise that his years of hell were finally at an end. 'I fell on my knees,' he wrote, 'and after the best and sincerest manner I could, offered up my most humble and hearty thanks to God for my deliverance.'

Pellow became an object of great curiosity within minutes

of stepping ashore. Word spread like wildfire through the garrison, and soldiers and sentries began emerging from the barracks in order to meet him. The sergeant of the guard was the first to quiz him, '[then] returned his hearty congratulations for my deliverance'. Next to appear was Mr Cunningham, the minister, 'and with him several of the head officers of the garrison'. One of these, John Beaver, was initially suspicious of Pellow and decided to test whether or not he was telling the truth. He asked if he had met Tom Osborne of Fowey during his captivity, a mariner with whom Beaver was personally acquainted. Pellow said that he had indeed met Osborne in Meknes and explained how the Cornish lad had been seized from Captain Richard Sampson's ship, the *Desire*, in 1715. 'To which Mr Beaver answered that all I had said was undoubtedly true, for that he knew Tom Osborne very well, and that he had heard him several times after his releasement and return to talk about me.'

Pellow, overwhelmed by the kind-heartedness of everyone he met, felt the need to offer thanks for his redemption. 'I went to church,' he wrote, 'and returned thanks to Almighty God before the congregation for my deliverance.' The congregation was deeply moved by Pellow's story, and the 'worthy gentlemen' among them decided to arrange for a collection. But before they could do so, the *Euphrates*, bound for London, sailed into harbour.

Captain Toobin went down to the waterfront in order to meet the commander, Captain Peacock, and ask him whether he would carry Pellow back to England, explaining that he had 'undergone so long and grievous a captivity in Barbary, and was so fortunately escaped thither'. The captain expressed his willingness to take Pellow, but warned that he was heading directly for London and was therefore unable to stop at any West Country ports. He was also intending to sail that very night and required Pellow to board the ship without delay. Pellow did not hesitate, even though it meant missing out on the church collection that was being raised in his name.

The *Euphrates* sailed that evening, but ran into a squall almost immediately. 'We met with very high and contrary winds,' wrote Pellow, 'and, according to the season of the year, a very high and troubled sea.' It was a dreadful voyage, and Pellow found it insufferably claustrophobic below decks. 'For my better breathing, I generally took up at night with the boat on the booms, where I lay me down to my rest covered over with an old sail.'

After twenty-four days at sea, the lookout sighted land on the horizon. To Pellow's unspeakable joy, it was the craggy coast of Cornwall. His neighbourhood of Falmouth could be sighted for a short while, but it soon receded into the thick sea mist. There was a moment of panic when one of the crew fell overboard, but he was plucked safely from the water and the *Euphrates* pressed on towards London. After thirty-one days at sea, she sailed up the Thames Estuary and docked at the quayside of Deptford.

Pellow had never before visited London and was daunted by the thought. He remained on board the ship for several days, considering how to organise a passage back to Cornwall. The rest of the crew went ashore and began circulating Pellow's story, gossiping in taverns about how they had returned from Gibraltar with a one-time English slave. Their tales soon reached the ears of a girl whose brother remained enslaved in Meknes. The sister of William Johnston – who had wrecked Pellow's second escape bid – appeared on board the *Euphrates* in order to learn if he had ever met Johnston. Pellow gave her a withering look. 'Yes, yes, to my sorrow,' he said, 'for had I not, it would in all likelihood have prevented me of many years' grievous captivity.' He recounted the story of Johnston's betrayal and told the girl that he wished he had cut off her brother's head. When she started to weep, Pellow felt guilty at having upset her and said he was sure that Johnston would escape before long.

After a week aboard the *Euphrates*, Pellow plucked up the courage to step ashore and, 'going directly to church, returned public thanks to God for my safe arrival in Old England'. He was entertained by Captain Peacock's steward, a Cornishman named William James, and was greeted by various other dignitaries in Deptford.

Pellow was desperate to get home to Penryn. He knew no one in London, and his only desire was to be reunited with his family. He asked William James for help in arranging a passage to Cornwall; James suggested that he go to Beels' Wharf, close to London Bridge, where Cornish tin vessels were accustomed to dock. Pellow headed there straight away and found three ships in the process of discharging their cargo. Their captains were drinking in the King's Head in Pudding Lane, where Pellow struck up a conversation with Captain Francis of Penzance, the commander of the little ship *Truro*. '[He] readily offered me a passage in his vessel,' wrote Pellow, '. . . which I most heartily thanked him for.' She was due to sail within ten days, giving Pellow time to get acquainted with the capital.

It was while he was wandering through the streets that he met the nephew of a visiting Moroccan ambassador, a man named Abdelkader Peres. Pellow was well acquainted with this nephew and was pleased to see him – 'much more,' he wrote, 'than ever I was to see him in Barbary'. The nephew took him to his uncle's ambassadorial lodgings, where Pellow was 'by the old man very kindly received'. Abdelkader Peres was quite charming and 'told me that he was very glad I was delivered out of an unhappy country'. He confessed to having no particular desire to return to Morocco, where yet another power struggle was under way, and asked Pellow to stay for supper. 'And after I had dined there that day on my favourite dish, couscous, and some English dishes, I returned to my lodgings in Pudding Lane.'

Pellow was resting when a messenger arrived to inform him

that his extraordinary story had just been published in one of the capital's newspapers. Pellow was surprised and asked to be shown the article. It told of his daring escape from Morocco, 'where he had been a slave twenty-five years, being taken by the Moors in the tenth year of his age'. Almost every detail in the report was wrong, and Pellow noted wryly that it was filled with 'Mr Newswriter's truths'. He met the author of the article soon after and scolded him for being 'very much to blame, for that I had given him no such licence, neither could I without asserting a very great falsity'.

The return of slaves from North Africa always generated tremendous public interest and the publication of such an article would certainly have led to calls for Pellow to be paraded through the capital. But he was fortunate to be spared the dubious honour of a public thanksgiving. Learning that Captain Francis was ready to sail with the next tide, he hastened aboard with his few belongings. He had escaped the crowds and now looked forward to the final leg of his long voyage home. 'The first tide we got to Gravesend, and the next to the Nore, and the third over the Flats and into the Downs.' As they entered the English Channel, they were fortunate to meet with a stiff easterly that blew them rapidly towards Plymouth. Finally, on 15 October 1738, at four o'clock in the afternoon, the *Truro* docked at Falmouth Pier, 'whence, being to Penryn, the place of my nativity, no more than two miles I got to the town in the evening'.

As Pellow neared his birthplace and family home, he was astonished by what he saw. In the half-light of dusk, he could see hundreds of people walking slowly towards him. The entire population of Penryn had turned out to greet a son they had long ago given up as lost. 'I was so crowded by the inhabitants,' wrote Pellow, 'that I could not pass through them without a great deal of difficulty.' His arrival in Penryn brought back memories of his arrival in Meknes in the summer of 1716, 'though this, I must own, was of a different and far more pleasing nature to me than my first entrance into Meknes'. Now, he was fêted by the crowd, who were overjoyed to have him home. 'Everyone, instead of boxing me and pulling my hair, [was] saluting me and, after a most courteous manner, bidding me welcome home.' Many of the villagers were anxious to know whether or not he recognised them, 'which indeed I did not, for I was so very young at my departure'.

Finally, at the top end of town, Pellow came face to face with his mother and father, who were by now probably in their late fifties. They did not know their son at first. He was so altered by his years in Barbary, and looked so different from the boy they had last seen in 1715, that they scarcely believed he was their own flesh and blood. Pellow was no less puzzled when he set eyes on his parents, who seemed to be complete strangers. 'And had we happened to meet at any other place without being pre-advised . . . we should no doubt have passed each other, unless my great beard might have induced them to inquire further after me.'

The three of them embraced and wept and embraced again. As they made their way back to the family home, Pellow began to tell them the extraordinary odyssey of his life. He spoke of his seizure and captivity, of his years in the service of the sultan. He told them of beatings and slave-drivers, of violent sieges and terrible wounds. He told them, too, of the countless men and women who had lost their lives in slavery.

His story would be repeated many times in Penryn. It would eventually reach the ears of a local hack, who immediately realised the potential of such a remarkable tale. He helped Pellow put pen to paper, and within two years of his return, *The History of the Long Captivity and Adventures of Thomas Pellow* appeared on the bookstands. It provided its readers with a fascinating insight into the horrors of white slavery in Sultan Moulay Ismail's Morocco.

Pellow's parents must also have had a story to tell. They had suffered years of anguish and grief, praying that they would one day be reunited with their only son. But their woes and tribulations are nowhere recorded, and not a single family letter has survived.

There are gaps, too, in Pellow's own account. He makes no mention of his sisters – who had perhaps gone to an early grave – nor does he speak further of his unwilling conversion to Islam. Instead, he chooses to dwell upon the miracle that had enabled him to endure and survive for so many terrible years. 'Nothing,' he wrote, 'but the Almighty protection of a great, good, all-seeing, most sufficient, and gracious God could have carried me through it.'

After twenty-three years of slavery, Pellow had returned to the fold.

Epilogue

THOMAS PELLOW'S RETURN TO ENGLAND did not mark the end of the white slave trade. A steady stream of Europeans and Americans continued to be captured – usually at sea – and held in wretched conditions in Algiers, Tunis and the great slave pens of Meknes. One of the most infamous incidents involving British mariners occurred in 1746, when the ship, *Inspector*, was wrecked in Tangier bay. All eighty-seven survivors were taken into captivity.

'Large iron chains were lock'd around our necks,' wrote Thomas Troughton, one of the ship's crew, 'and twenty of us were link'd together in one chain.' It was five long years before Troughton and his surviving comrades were bought back by the British government. Their fellow slaves were not so fortunate; the ruling sultan steadfastly refused to release his French, Spanish, Portuguese, Italian and Dutch captives.

But in 1757, the vacant Moroccan throne was seized by Sidi Mohammed, a shrewd and capable individual who was more open to foreign influences than his predecessors. He was 'endowed with penetration and judgement', according to the French consul, Louis de Chenier, and enjoyed conversing with European guests at his court. His enlightened opinions raised many eyebrows among his advisors, especially when he declared that Morocco's shattered finances would be better repaired by international trade than by piracy and slavery. His intention was to encourage vessels from every nation 'to trade with and enter his ports, being desirous of peace with the whole world'. To this end, he declared war on the corsairs of Salé and Rabat, who had opposed his accession to the throne. They were attacked by his imperial guard and quickly brought to heel. The governor of Salé was brutally stoned to death, and the inhabitants of Rabat were 'made to feel the resentment of the prince'.

The sultan followed his victory with a flurry of diplomatic activity. He proposed treaties with all the nations that for so long had been the victims of attack. In 1757, he signed a peace treaty with Denmark. Two years later, the British and Dutch also concluded a truce. Sweden followed suit in 1763, and the Republic of Venice added her name to a treaty soon after. Almost every European nation would eventually sign accords with the Moroccan sultan: France and Spain in 1767; Portugal in 1773; Tuscany, Genoa and the Habsburg Empire a few years later. In 1786, the newly independent United States of America also agreed a truce.

The once-great corsair fleet of Salé fell into disrepair during these long years of peace. After two decades of virtual inaction, many of the ships were rotting hulks, no longer seaworthy. European observers reported that the harbour contained no more than fifteen frigates, a few xebecs and some thirty galleys. It was a far cry from the days of old, and ships such as these were no match for the great navies of Britain and France. Yet old habits die hard, and Salé's corsairs continued to cherish vainglorious dreams of renewing their holy war against Christendom. They recalled the time when their mighty fleet, working in tandem with the still-powerful corsairs of Algiers and Tunis, had wreaked havoc on European shipping. In those days, the white slave auctions had reaped far greater dividends than the more peaceful business of international trade.

Sultan Mohammed died in 1790; his successor, Moulay Sulaiman II, displayed rather more sympathy towards his Salé corsairs – even though he ratified the treaties signed by his father. The new sultan went so far as to despatch his much-reduced fleet back to sea in the early years of the nineteenth century, with orders to attack European merchant ships that were trading with his enemies. There were fears that this was the prelude to full-scale hostilities against Christendom.

But the corsairs of Salé, and their fellow slave traders elsewhere in Barbary, were about to discover that they had finally met their match. In the summer of 1816 – exactly one hundred years after Thomas Pellow became one of Moulay Ismail's slaves in Meknes – they were dealt a devastating blow from which they would never recover. In what was to prove a most extraordinary deus ex machina in the story of white slavery, the Pellow family of Cornwall was about to take its terrible revenge.

The call to arms against Barbary was led by the eccentric British admiral, Sir Sidney Smith. He was passionate about the issue of white slavery and had established a movement devoted to ending the trade for ever. It was called the Society of Knights Liberators of the White Slaves of Africa and it rapidly drew influential members from across Europe. When at the end of the Napoleonic Wars crowned heads and ministers gathered to discuss peace at the Congress of Vienna, which began in 1814, Smith and his knights elected to join them. They organised discussions on the fringes of the congress and petitioned for a military showdown with the lawless rulers of North Africa. 'This shameful slavery is not only revolting to humanity,' thundered Smith, 'but it fetters commerce in the most disastrous manner.'

Sir Sidney and his knights drew attention to a trade that had ensnared at least one million Europeans and Americans over the previous three centuries. The largest concentration of white slaves had always been in Algiers. The city had a continuous population of about 25,000 captives between the years 1550 and 1730, and there were occasions when that number had almost doubled. During the same period, some 7,500 men, women and children had been held in Tunis and Tripoli. The number of slaves in Moulay Ismail's imperial capital was more difficult to ascertain, even though the conditions in which they were held were better documented than elsewhere in North Africa. The 5,000 captives reported by European padres were contested by Ahmed ez-Zayyani, who claimed that the real figure was at least five times higher.

Although North Africa's slave population had fallen to 3,000 by the time of the Congress of Vienna, Sir Sidney knew that this was a recent development. He was also aware that snapshot statistics told only part of the story. The number of slaves shipped to North Africa each year was always dependent on the rate at which they died, apostatised or gained their freedom. Dysentery, the plague and forced labour killed thousands, requiring the corsairs to put to sea in search of replacement captives. The ransoming of slaves also played its part in sustaining the flow. For two centuries, perhaps three, there had been an influx to Barbary of almost 5,000 white slaves each year.

The most powerful European leaders read Smith's petition with interest, but did nothing more than pass a resolution that condemned all forms of slavery. Smith was initially disheartened, but soon discovered that his plea for military action had made a deep impression on the rulers of southern Europe, who continued to suffer considerable losses at the hands of the corsairs. They supported his battle-cry and pointed an approving finger at America, whose government had taken bullish action against North Africa. It had sent a fleet to Algiers just a few months earlier and successfully forced the authorities to release all their American slaves. With this mission uppermost in their minds, the southern European rulers began taunting Britain's foreign secretary, Lord Castlereagh, for his lack of enthusiasm for an attack on Barbary. They accused him of deliberately turning a blind eye to the ravages of the corsairs, since Britain stood to benefit whenever her trading rivals were attacked.

Lord Castlereagh was stung by these criticisms. He had been

forceful in advocating the abolition of the black slave trade; now, he vowed to end the trade in white slaves as well. In the summer of 1816, he persuaded the British government to despatch a large fleet to the Mediterranean. Its goal was to compel the rulers of Barbary to stop seizing and selling European captives. There was to be no debate, no payment of bribes and absolutely no concession. 'If force must be resorted to,' read the British government's lofty statement of intent, 'we have the consolation of knowing that we fight in the sacred cause of humanity.'

There was never any doubt as to who would command this great squadron. In public life he was known as Lord Exmouth, the Vice Admiral of the Mediterranean fleet. But among his friends and family in his native Cornwall he was more familiar as Sir Edward Pellew – a collateral descendant of the same West Country family as Thomas Pellow. The orthography of the Pellow name had changed in the intervening decades, and Sir Edward had acquired a wealth and status that placed him in a very different social stratum to the humble Pellows of Penryn. But he remained deeply attached to his Cornish roots and had chosen to settle his family in Falmouth, less than two miles from Penryn. He was certainly familiar with Thomas Pellow's story and had a passionate interest in the white slaves of Barbary. When invited by Sir Sidney Smith to join the Society of Knights Liberators, Pellew had leaped at the opportunity. 'I am greatly obliged to you, my dear Sir Sidney, for thinking of me among your knights,' he wrote. 'I shall give it all the support I can.'

Sir Edward Pellew was the right man to tackle the slave traders of Barbary. Bullish and resolute, he was prepared to use overwhelming force to achieve his goal. He had set his sights on Algiers, the most troublesome city in North Africa, fully aware that the defeat of the city's corsairs would send an unmistakable signal to Tunis, Tripoli and Morocco. Pellew wanted nothing less than the total capitulation of every corsair and slave trader in North Africa.

His formidable fleet arrived off Algiers at the end of August 1816. He anchored his flagship, the *Queen Charlotte*, in the bay of Algiers and sent an uncompromising message to the ruling dey, Omar Bashaw. Omar was given one hour to capitulate unconditionally, release his slaves and renounce for ever the trade in captured Europeans. When the dey failed to answer, Pellew declared war.

His fleet made a most impressive sight as it manoeuvred into battle positions. He had eighteen men-of-war – some armed with more than 100 big guns – and his forces were bolstered by a squadron of six Dutch vessels. But his optimism about the battle ahead was tempered by the knowledge that Omar Bashaw was a shrewd military tactician, who had strengthened the city defences in anticipation of attack and had called upon the services of thousands of war-hardened fighters.

Each commander was aware that he was playing for the very highest stakes. If Pellew won the battle, the white slave trade would finally be brought to an end. But if he lost, the prestige of the Barbary corsairs would be hugely enhanced. The 3,000 slaves still being held in North Africa would be condemned to perpetual captivity, and European merchant vessels would once again be in danger of attack.

The battle began with a single shot fired from a land battery close to the shoreline. Whether or not it was fired accidentally will never be known, but it wrung a terrible response from the furious Pellew. He had already informed his various captains of the signal for action. Now, standing proudly on the deck of his flagship, he raised his hat high above his head, held it still for a moment, then swung it down towards the deck. As he did so, there was a thunderous roar as all the ships of his fleet opened fire. His own ship, the *Queen Charlotte*, heeled to port as her twenty-four-pounders blasted their first broadside at the city defences. In the maintop and foretop, the twelve-pounders also let rip, each gun unleashing 300 musket balls at the defending corsairs. As the townspeople of Algiers dived for cover, the other ships of Pellew's fleet discharged broadside after broadside, sending hundreds of cannon-balls crashing into forts, batteries and armed houses. The American consul, William Shaler, left a graphic account of the destruction wrought by Pellew's big guns. 'The cannonade endures with a fury which can only be comprehended from practical experience,' he wrote. 'Shells and rockets fly over and by my house like hail.'

The dey's forces put up a stiff resistance, firing an increasing number of cannonades at Pellew's fleet. The commander of the *Impregnable* reported that he had lost 150 killed or wounded, while the *Glasgow* was hit by dozens of rounds. Even more alarming was the accuracy of Omar's snipers and sharpshooters. A group of them were hiding in the mole-head battery, from where they were able to pick out the finely uniformed officers on the decks of the British ships. Several had their sights on Pellew, aware that his death would be a devastating blow to the attacking forces. Two musket shots passed clean through Pellew's clothing but – miraculously – left him uninjured. A third smashed the telescope he was clutching under his left arm. As the heat of battle intensified, a large splinter of wood was embedded in his jaw and a spent shot struck his leg.

Omar's forces grew increasingly confident as the day wore on. They were wreaking havoc on Pellew's fleet, shattering timbers with their heavy shot and disabling rigging and sails. 'Legs, arms, blood, brains and mangled bodies were strewn about in all directions,' wrote Lieutenant John Whinyates. 'You could scarcely keep your feet from the slipperiness of the decks, wet with blood.' Yet Pellew refused to withdraw to safety, for he believed it was his sacred duty to fight to the death. 'The battle was fairly at issue between a handful of Britons in the noble cause of Christianity,' he wrote, 'and a horde of fanatics.'

As dusk descended over Algiers, the tide of battle slowly began to turn. By ten o'clock, the British forces had rained down more than 50,000 cannon-balls on Algiers, reducing the main town batteries to rubble. Pellew could now turn his attention to the great corsair fleet in the harbour. He unleashed fire-bombs and shells into the tightly packed vessels, with devastating effect. 'All the ships in the port . . . were in flames,' he wrote, 'which extended rapidly over the whole arsenal, storehouses and gunboats, exhibiting a spectacle of awful grandeur and interest no pen can describe.' By one o'clock in the morning, everything in the marina was on fire, and the fireball was rapidly fanning out towards the city.

When dawn broke the next morning, Consul Shaler rubbed his eyes in disbelief when he saw the extent of the destruction. Much of the city lay in ruins, including his own consulate, and entire quarters of Algiers had ceased to exist. 'The city has suffered incredibly,' he wrote. 'There is hardly a house without some damage, and many are ruined.' The harbour presented an even more awesome sight. 'The bay was full of the hulks of their navy,' wrote Pellew's interpreter, Abraham Salamé, 'smoking in every direction.' He added that 'the most shocking and dreadful sight was the number of dead bodies which were floating on the water.' More than 2,000 Algerines had been killed – many of them corsairs – and an even greater number were fatally injured. The British, by contrast, had suffered 141 dead and 74 wounded.

Pellew was anxious to restart hostilities at first light, but he soon found that there was no need for further action. The dey of Algiers made a brief survey of his once-glorious capital and realised that he could no longer continue the fight. He surrendered unconditionally – a humiliating blow to his pride – and agreed to all of the British commander's demands. These included the release of all the remaining slaves in Algiers, and the abolition – for ever – of Christian slavery.

The 1,642 slaves being held in Algiers could scarcely believe that their ordeal was finally at an end. During the battle they had been chained together and moved to an underground cavern on the hillside above the city. When they learned of Pellew's victory – and discovered that their guards had fled – they tore free from their shackles and burst out of their temporary prison. 'We rushed out of the cave,' wrote the French slave, Pierre-Joseph Dumont, 'and dragging our chains, pushed forward through brambles and thickets, regardless of the blood streaming from our faces and bodies. We simply did not feel our wounds any longer.'

Abraham Salamé was shocked at the condition of the newly liberated slaves. 'When I arrived on shore, it was the most pitiful sight to see all those poor creatures, in what a horrible state they were.' But for the slaves themselves, this was the moment they had dreamed of for many years. They cheered, they sang with joy and then – with one exultant cry – they shouted, 'Long live the English admiral.'

Pellew himself was immensely proud of his role in destroying Algiers, and even more gratified when he was brought the news that Tunis, Tripoli and Morocco had also renounced slavery. The great slave auctions were to be closed in perpetuity, and all of the remaining captives were freed without further ado. 'To have been one of the humble instruments in the hands of Divine Providence,' wrote Pellew, '. . . and destroying forever the insufferable and horrid system of Christian slavery, can never cease to be a source of delight and heartfelt comfort.' Pellew's name was fêted across Europe, and many of the nations that had suffered from the white slave trade showed their gratitude for his triumphant victory, making him a knight of the Spanish Order of King Charles III and a knight of the Neapolitan Order of St Ferdinand. The Netherlands also gave him an honorary knighthood, as did the island of Sardinia. The Pope was so delighted by the news that he presented Pellew with a rare and extremely valuable cameo.

When Pellew finally returned home to his native Cornwall,

he was given a hero's welcome. For the first time in centuries, the local fishermen and traders could put to sea without any risk of being captured and held as slaves. Ministers in London were no less grateful, showering Pellew with honours. He was elevated to a new rank in the peerage and rewarded with a fabulous addition to his coat of arms. Henceforth, the heraldic shield of the Pellews was emblazoned with a Christian slave clutching a crucifix and breaking free from his fetters. It was a fitting symbol for a family that had a deep personal experience of the horrors of the white slave trade.

Salé, September 2002. A salty squall is shearing off the sea and the wind is wet with spray. On the exposed Atlantic strand, it stings the eyes and batters the ears. But in the lee of the gale – sheltered by a casemate in the shore-side ramparts – the air feels as clammy as a sponge.

At the mouth of the Bou Regreg river, froth-laced breakers are heaved on to the sandy bar. Two skiffs are struggling through the foam. The waters of the estuary are turbulent and treacherous, and many a Salé mariner has been sluiced beneath the waves while within sight of the welcoming lights of home. It was here that Captain Ali Hakem and Admiral el-Mediouni lost their ships. This, too, was where Thomas Pellow flailed in the surf before being plucked from the sea by his captors.

I clamber up from the oozy banks of the estuary and enter the walled city of Salé through the Bab Mrisa, one of the eight defensive gates that puncture the thick stone ramparts. Three centuries ago, this was the path trodden by wretched European slaves – men, women and children whose steps were slowed by the weight of their iron chains and shackles. Black slave-drivers hauled them to the place of auction, which was held each week in the Souk el-Kebir.

I retrace their footsteps to doom, jostling through the crowded alleys that weave towards the market place. Everyone in Salé seems to be heading in the same direction, and the city's heart is a dense mass of pushing, bellowing, elbowing, yelling humanity. Babies are squeezed tight to their mothers' breasts; a donkey is shoved through the crowds. A press of bodies surges us forward; we tighten into a bottleneck. There is the graveolent stench of a butcher's stall, the whiff of cumin and the tang of crushed mint. In the midst of this stifling chaos, where elbows are used like oars, traders are peddling their wares. A plump silvery mackerel is plucked from a basket; a water-seller jingles his bell.

The European slaves were punched, pushed and harassed through these narrow alleys. A final kick propelled them into the Souk el-Kebir, where all of the city's tortuous alleys conjoin. The market place is not much changed from how it looked in the seventeenth century. A few sad trees provide shade from the midday sun; a fountain seeps water on to the flagstones. You can buy anything in the Souk el-Kebir – plastic colanders, a spit-roasted chicken, a spray of chintz carnations. Three hundred years ago, the only item on sale – at a cost of about £35 each – was white slaves.

Thomas Pellow and his comrades were to meet an even worse fate than the captives who were auctioned in Salé. Transported to the half-finished palaces of Meknes, they found themselves constructing their epitaph in pisé, a necropolis so vast that neither earthquake nor warfare has managed to expunge it from the landscape. There is something awesome about this panoply of ruined pleasure palaces. The sultan conceived his imperial capital on a scale that still has the power to leave a lasting, haunting impression.

For Morocco's bards and chroniclers, this was the crowning triumph of Moulay Ismail's reign; they wrote paeans in praise of the city's magnitude and resplendence. 'We have visited all the ruins of the Orient and Occident,' wrote one, 'but we have never seen its equal.' The same chronicler added: 'Our sultan has not restricted himself to constructing one palace, nor ten, nor twenty. There are more monuments in Meknes than there are in the rest of the world put together.'

As dusk slips into the ruined alleys and thoroughfares, I stray into the deserted outer reaches of this imperial folly – long-abandoned chambers that once formed the domed mansions of the sultan's eunuchs and viziers. This was where the black guard strutted haughtily through the North African sunlight; this was where they beat and flogged the European slaves under their charge.

These crumbling walls cost the lives of countless thousands of captives – men, women and children from across Christendom. No one will ever know the exact number who died here, nor how many of their corpses were immured in the great pisé battlements. They have vanished for ever, burned to ghosts by the quicklime.

Sultan Moulay Ismail knew that dead men tell no tales. What he failed to foresee was that Thomas Pellow would survive twenty-three extraordinary years of slavery and adventure – and make it home alive.

Notes and Sources

White Gold has been drawn largely from unpublished letters and journals, as well as from contemporary published accounts written by European ambassadors, padres and the slaves themselves. The Arabic sources include seventeenth- and eighteenth-century chronicles, works by Moroccan historians, and letters written by Moroccan courtiers as well as by Sultan Moulay Ismail. All the Arabic sources have been consulted in French or English translations.

A full reference for each title will be cited when it is first mentioned. The place of publication is London unless otherwise stated. I have not sought to give page references for the many hundreds of quotations that appear in *White Gold*. Only those considered to be particularly illuminating – or hard to find – have been given precise references. A useful list of accounts written by slaves, along with those by other travellers and adventurers, can be found in Robert Playfair and Robert Brown, *A Bibliography of Morocco from the Earliest Times to the End of 1891*, 1892.

The manuscript original of Thomas Pellow's account is no longer extant, nor are any of the letters or notes that Pellow may have written during his twenty-three years in Morocco. Lieutenant-Colonel Thomas James, who served in the Royal Regiment of Artillery, claimed in his 1771 book, *The History of the Herculean Straits*, 2 vols., to have seen a manuscript written by Pellow. This is the only reference to the existence of such a manuscript.

Pellow's work was first published in 1740 under the prolix title *The History of the Long Captivity and Adventures of Thomas Pellow, in South Barbary. Giving an Account of his being taken by two Sallee Rovers, and carry'd a Slave to Mequinez, at Eleven Years of Age: His various Adventures in that Country for the Space of Twenty-three years: Escape, and Return Home. In Which is introduced, a particular Account of the Manners and Customs of the Moors; the astonishing Tyranny and Cruelty of their Emperors, and a Relation of all those great Revolutions and Bloody Wars which happen'd in the Kingdom of Fez and Morocco, between the years 1720 and 1736. Together with a Description of the Cities, Towns, and Public Buildings in those Kingdoms; Miseries of the Christian Slaves; and many other Curious Particulars. Written by Himself.*

I consulted this work alongside two more recent editions. The first was published in 1890 under the title *The Adventures of Thomas Pellow, of Penryn, Mariner.* It was edited by Robert Brown, whose excellent notes did much to verify the authenticity of Pellow's narrative. All quotations cited in *White Gold* are taken from this edition. A more recent publication is Magali Morsy's splendid *La Relation de Thomas Pellow*, published by Editions Recherche sur les Civilisations, Paris, 1983. This has an excellent introduction and detailed footnotes. It also lists the paragraphs that Pellow's editor plagiarised or adapted from other works.

None of the other documents concerning Thomas Pellow's shipmates has been published. Most of them – including letters and petitions – are held in The National Archives (PRO) in Kew. Full references are given below.

Prologue, pp. 1–8

pp. 1–3: The sultan's love of pomp, ceremony and courtly protocol is documented by many European ambassadors to the court. Their numerous reports and journals are detailed in the notes below. The most perceptive English-language account is John Windus, *Journey to Mequinez*, 1725. Windus, who accompanied Commodore Charles

Stewart's 1720–1 mission to Meknes, was fortunate enough to see the sultan's extraordinary chariot while taking a tour of the palace.

pp. 3–8: See my notes to chapters five and nine for more details about seventeenth- and eighteenth-century descriptions of Meknes palace. When I visited Meknes in 1992, my 'guide' was the French padre, Dominique Busnot, whose excellent book was published in English in 1715 under the title, *The History of the Reign of Mulay Ismael, the present king of Morocco*, London. His work, *Histoire du règne de Moulay Ismail*, Rouen, was originally published in French in 1714.

1: A New and Deadly Foe, pp. 9–29

pp. 9–11: The account of the 1625 attack on the West Country has been drawn largely from letters, notes and memoranda to be found in the various Calendars of State Papers. See particularly the *Domestic Series, 1625–6*, John Bruce (ed.), 1858. Page 83 contains a report by the mayor of Plymouth of the attack on Looe, and lists numbers of people and ships captured; see also p. 89.

Further reference to these attacks can be found in Allen B. Hinds (ed.), *Calendar of State Papers, Venice, 1625–6*, 1913; see p. 149 and note. This volume also contains a report by Zuane Pesaro, Venetian ambassador to England, which details how the corsairs 'plundered the country, carried off a large number of slaves, did immeasurable damage and committed cruelties causing such terror that seven large districts have sent their outcry to the court, an unheard of event'.

James Bagg's letter to the Lord High Admiral, which details the destruction wrought by the corsairs, is published in Henri de Castries' monumental work, *Les Sources Inédites de l'Histoire du Maroc*, 16 vols., Paris, 1905–48. See the first series, vol. 2, 1925, item CLXXII, p. 583. Francis Stuart's report to the Duke of Buckingham is also published in this volume, item CLXXIV, pp. 586f.

pp. 11–16: The most interesting sixteenth-century account of Salé and Rabat is to be found in Leo Africanus, *The History and Description* *of Africa*, Robert Brown (ed.), 3 vols., 1896. The description of Salé is in vol. 2, pp. 407ff. See also the long note on Salé's slow decline, pp. 574–80.

The best and most comprehensive account of the rise of the Salé corsairs is to be found in Roger Coindreau, *Les Corsaires de Salé*, Paris, 1948. This provides background to the Hornacheros and details their most audacious attacks on European targets. It also gives information about their ships, their unusual flags and their tactics at sea.

There is also much of interest about the Salé corsairs to be found in Budget Meakin's classic, *The Moorish Empire*, 1899. More recently, the success of the Sallee Rovers has been examined by Peter Earle in his excellent book, *The Pirate Wars*, 2003; and in Stephen Clissold, *The Barbary Slaves*, 1977; see especially chapter 9.

For more information about the Islamic fervour of the Barbary corsairs, see Daniel J. Vitkus (ed.), *Piracy, Slavery and Redemption: Barbary Captivity Narratives from Early Modern England*, New York, 2001. Nabil Matar's excellent introduction sheds a particularly revealing light on the motives of the corsairs; see pp. 11–12.

For more information on England's failure to deal with the crisis, and Sir Francis Cottingham's comments, see Stanley Lane-Poole, *The Barbary Corsairs*, 1890, p. 229. For other contemporary observations on the growth of Barbary piracy, see William Lithgow, *Rare Adventures*, 1928, pp. 114ff.; and John Smith, *The True Travels*, published most recently in *The Complete Works of Captain John Smith* (3 vols.), Chapel Hill, 1986. See especially chapter 28. Vincent de Paul's personal testimony of slavery in Tunis sheds light on the horrors of the slave market. See Graham Petrie, *Tunis, Kairouan and Carthage*, 1908, pp. 91–5.

The extraordinarily bold expeditions of Murad Rais are detailed in Coindreau, *Les Corsaires de Salé*, especially pp. 66–8. See also Clissold, *The Barbary Slaves*, pp. 31ff., for general information about the depredations of the corsairs.

The French padre, Pierre Dan, was in Algiers when Murad Rais returned from Baltimore, and he witnessed the sale of the Irish slaves.

See his *Histoire de la Barbarie et de ses Corsaires*, Paris, 1637, especially Book 3, pp. 277f. See also Book 2, pp. 178ff.

John Ward is one of the most fascinating renegade pirates to settle in North Africa. His story is outlined in Samuel C. Chew, *The Crescent and the Rose: Islam and England during the Renaissance*, New York, 1937, pp. 347–62. There are many contemporary pamphlets and documents about his misdeeds. The best and most comprehensive is Andrew Barker, *A True and Certain Report*, 1609. See also anon., *Newes from Sea of two notorious pyrats*, 1609. There is an account of Ward's character in Horatio F. Brown (ed.), *Calendar of State Papers, Venetian, 1607–10*, 1904, pp. 140ff. Ward's infamy was such that ballads were written about him. See A. E. H. Swain (ed.), *Anglia*, 1898, vol. 20, pp. 180ff. See also the Naval Records Society's publication, C. H. Firth (ed.), *Naval Songs and Ballads*, 1908. This reprints *The Famous Sea-Fight Between Captain Ward and the Rainbow*, with its memorable couplet supposedly uttered by Ward:

> Go tell the King of England, go tell him from me,
> If he reign king of the land, I will reign king at sea.

For more information about Salé's corsairs declaring the city a republic, see *The Travels of the Sieur Mouette in the Kingdoms of Fez and Morocco during his eleven years' captivity in those parts* by Germain Mouette. The date of the first English edition is unclear; it is a translation of his *Relation de la captivité du Sr. Mouette dans les Royaumes de Fez et de Maroc*, Paris, 1683. I consulted the version published in Captain John Stevens, *A New Collection of Voyages and Travels*, 1710 (2 vols.). Mouette's account is in vol. 2. All future page references refer to this book. See also the opening pages of Roland Frejus, *The Relation of the Voyage made into Mauritania . . . [in] 1666*, 1671. This is a translation of his *Relation d'un voyage fait dans la Mauritanie . . . en l'année 1666*, Paris, 1670.

pp. 16–22: Robert Adams' letter is in the Public Record Office (PRO), SP 71/12, f. 107.

John Harrison led a most interesting life. He fought in Ireland, was a groom to Prince Henry and served as a sheriff of the Somers Islands (Bermuda). He was also the author of five books. For more information, see the *Dictionary of National Biography*, vol. 25, 1891.

Harrison's various missions to Morocco are outlined in P. G. Rogers, *A History of Anglo-Moroccan Relations to 1900*, 1977, pp. 24–30.

All the surviving documents concerning this mission – including King Charles I's letter to the Moroccan sultan and various petitions by the wives of enslaved mariners – are printed in de Castries, *Les Sources Inédites*. See the first series, vols. 2 and 3. For more information about the cruelty of the Moroccan sultan, see John Harrison, *The Tragicall Life and Death of Muley Abdala Melek, the late king of Barbarie*, 1633.

pp. 22–9: William Rainsborough's commission for his 1637 voyage is published in de Castries, *Les Sources Inédites*, first series, vol. 3, p. 276. His account of the battle is in the same volume, pp. 309ff. For a more comprehensive account of the expedition and battle, see John Dunton, *A True Journal of the Sallee Fleet*, published in vol. 2 of the *Harleian Collection of Voyages*, 2 vols., 1745.

For more on Edmund Cason's 1646 mission to Algiers, see Sir Godfrey Fisher, *Barbary Legend*, Oxford, 1957, pp. 210ff. Cason's mission is also detailed in R. L. Playfair, *The Scourge of Christendom*, 1884. See chapter 5, pp. 63f. Thomas Sweet's letter to his family is quoted in Vitkus (ed.), *Piracy, Slavery and Redemption*.

The best and most detailed account of the corsairs' attacks on Spain is to be found in Ellen Friedman, *Spanish Captives in North Africa in the Early Modern Age*, Wisconsin, 1983. For more information about attacks on shipping from colonial North America, see Charles Summer's excellent short book, *White Slavery in the Barbary States*, Boston, 1847.

2: Sultan of Slaves, pp. 30–50

pp. 30–8: For general information on Moulay Ismail's rise to power, see Wilfred Blunt's biography, *Black Sunrise: The Life and Times of Mulai Ismail, Emperor of Morocco, 1646–1727*, 1951. See also Simon Ockley, *An account of South-West Barbary; containing what is most remarkable in the territories of the King of Fez and Morocco*, 1713, especially pp. 83–8. Another excellent source is Francis Brooks, *Barbarian Cruelty. Being a true history of the distressed condition of the Christian captives under the tyranny of Mully Ishmael, Emperor of Morocco*, 1693; see especially pp. 62–3. For more information about Moulay Ismail's late brother, Moulay al-Rashid, see Frejus, *The Relation*. See also Germain Mouette, *Histoire des Conquestes de Moulay Archy . . . et de Moulay Ismail*, Paris, 1683. Both Mouette, *The Travels of Sieur Mouette*, and Ockley, *South-West Barbary*, provide descriptions of the barren wastelands of the Tafilalt.

Jean Ladire's harrowing story is recounted by Dominique Busnot in his *History*.

The short account of Morocco in the sixteenth century is taken largely from Africanus, *The History and Description of Africa*. The Spanish ambassador's 1579 description of al-Badi is published in de Castries, *Les Sources Inédites*, first series, vol. 2, item XI, under the title *Relation d'une Ambassade au Maroc*.

pp. 38–50: The best history of the English garrison in Tangier is E. M. G. Routh, *Tangier: England's Lost Atlantic Outpost, 1661–1684*, 1912. J. M. Smithers, *The Tangier Campaign: The Birth of the British Army*, 2003, examines the long siege. See also Rogers, *Anglo-Moroccan Relations*; and Linda Colley, *Captives: Britain, Empire and the World*, 2002. For more on daily life in Tangier, and comments about Colonel Percy Kirke, see Edwin Chappell (ed.), *The Tangier Papers of Samuel Pepys*, 1935, especially pp. 48, 90, and 102. Kirke's mission to Meknes is described in an anonymous pamphlet entitled *The Last Account from Fez, in a letter from one of the Embassy, etc.*, 1683. See also Routh, *Tangier*, pp. 201–8.

The best account of Kaid Muhammad ben Haddu Ottur's stay in London is found in William Bray (ed.), *Memoirs illustrative of the life and writings of John Evelyn*, 2 vols., 1818; see especially vol. 1, pp. 505ff.

The English slave, Thomas Phelps, would eventually make it home to England. He wrote an account of his experiences, which was published in 1685 under the title, *A true Account of the Captivity of T Phelps at Machaness in Barbary, and of his strange escape.*

For full details of the English abandonment of Tangier, see Routh, *Tangier*. The best brief account of the negotiations that followed the withdrawal of troops is in Rogers, *Anglo-Moroccan Relations*.

3: Seized at Sea, pp. 51–72

pp. 51–7: The only account of Thomas Pellow's early life, and of the *Francis*'s departure from Falmouth, is to be found in Pellow's *Adventures*. For more information about Penryn, and the seafaring families that lived in the village, see June Palmer, *Penryn in the Eighteenth Century*, privately published in 1991. See also Daniel Defoe, *A Tour thro' the Whole Island of Great Britain*, 3 vols., 1724–7. For Peter Mundy's comments, see John Keast (ed.), *The Travels of Peter Mundy, 1597–1667*, 1984.

Much of the information about the capture of British and colonial American vessels in the period 1715–20 has been drawn from documents held in the PRO. The most relevant file, SP71/16, contains a wealth of information, including correspondence, petitions and consuls' reports.

For more information about the ships used by the Barbary corsairs, see Lane-Poole, *The Barbary Corsairs*, and Coindreau, *Les Corsaires de Salé*. On the preparations undertaken before putting to sea, see Dan, *Histoire de la Barbarie*. Dan also has much to say about the violence of their attacks. 'It is a terrifying thing to see the frenzy they work themselves into when they attack the ships,' he wrote. 'They appear on the upper deck, sleeves rolled up, their scimitar in hand, bawling all together in a most terrifying fashion.'

pp. 57–64: Joseph Pitts' account of his capture and subsequent years as a slave is one of the most interesting and perceptive accounts of slavery in North Africa. It was published in 1704 under the title *A True and Faithful Account of the Religion and Manners of the Mohammetans, with an Account of the Author's Being Taken Captive.*

Abraham Browne's fascinating account of his capture is little known. It was printed in Stephen T. Riley (ed.), *Seafaring in Colonial Massachusetts*, published by the Colonial Society of Massachusetts, Boston, in 1980. Captain Bellemy's grisly death is recounted in Brooks, *Barbarian Cruelty*.

Whether or not Delgarno was commander of the mystery ship sighted off Salé remains unclear. His flagship, the *Hind*, was undergoing repairs in Gibraltar after military action off Cape Cantin. See Morsy, *La Relation de Thomas Pellow*, p. 71, n. 13.

pp. 64–72: The best contemporary description of Salé is in Mouette, *The Travels of the Sieur Mouette*. See also Captain John Braithwaite, *The History of the Revolutions in the Empire of Morocco*, 1729, pp. 343ff.

The arrival in Salé was always a harrowing experience for new slaves. The French ambassador, Pidou de St Olon, witnessed the arrival of one batch and saw them suffer 'curses and hootings of the whole town, and particularly of the young fry, some of which follow them merely to bellow out a volley of abusive words, or throw stones at them'. His excellent book was published in English in 1695 under the title *The Present State of the Empire of Morocco*. It is a translation of his *Estat Présent de L'Empire de Maroc*, Paris, 1694.

The best general account of the treatment of slaves in Barbary is in Clissold, *The Barbary Slaves*. See also Christopher Lloyd, *English Corsairs on the Barbary Coast*, 1981. For more on slavery in Tripoli, see Seton Dearden, *A Nest of Corsairs*, 1905. The English slave, George Elliot, wrote a most interesting account of his life as a slave. His book, *A true narrative of the life of Mr G. E. who was taken and sold for a slave*, was published in 1780; see pp. 11–16. See also Adam Elliot, *A Narrative of my travails, captivity, and escape from Salle in the kingdom of Fez*, 1682. The best description of the Salé matamores, and the conditions in which slaves were held, is in Mouette, *The Travels of the Sieur Mouette*.

Virtually every account written by a former slave includes a description of the slave market and auction. One of the most interesting testimonies is to be found in William Okeley, *Ebenezer: or, A Monument of Great Mercy, Appearing in the Miraculous Deliverence of William Okeley*, 1675. This rare book was reprinted in Vitkus (ed.), *Piracy, Slavery and Redemption*; see pp. 150ff. Pitts' *A True and Faithful Account* also contains an interesting description of the Algiers market.

Pellow and his men were fortunate that their march to Meknes was undertaken without too much hardship. John Whitehead was one of many slaves who, in 1693, had endured great torment. 'After the fatigue of our journey, every day, sleeping in the night abroad under unwholesome dews that fell, and sometimes rain, made us all sick; some of an ague and feaver, and some of a feaver alone.' Whitehead wrote a fascinating testimony of his life as a slave. Entitled 'John Whitehead: His Relation of Barbary', the manuscript has never been published. The original is in the British Library, MS Sloane, 90.

4: Pellow's Torments, pp. 73–90

pp. 75–85: There are numerous descriptions of Moulay Ismail, as well as many accounts of his character, dress and appearance. Two Moroccan histories have proved particularly useful in assessing his long reign. *Le Maroc de 1631 à 1812* is an edited translation of Aboul-Kasem ben Ahmed ez-Zayyani, *Ettordjeman elmoarib an douel elmachriq ou 'lmaghrib*. The French translation is by Octave Houdas and is published by the Ecole des Langues Orientales Vivantes, series 3, vol. 18, Paris, 1886. The other account is Ahmad ben Khalid al-Nasari, *Kitab al-istiqsa li-akhbar duwal al-Maghrib al-Aqsa*. This was published in French under the title, *Chronique de la Dynastie Alaouie du Maroc*, Eugène Fumey (trans.). It is in vols. 9 and 10 of the *Archives Marocaines, Publication de la Mission Scientifique du Maroc*, Paris, 1906–7.

Some of the most perceptive and interesting contemporary descriptions are to be found in Busnot, *History*, and Brooks, *Barbarian Cruelty*. Whitehead, 'His Relation of Barbary', provides ample further evidence of the sultan's cruelty, while St Olon, *The Present State*, gives an account of the sultan's reception of foreign embassies. Other fascinating accounts about Moulay Ismail are contained in Jean-Baptiste Estelle's various memoirs; see de Castries, *Les Sources Inédites*, second series, vol. 3. For a modern analysis of his character, see Blunt, *Black Sunrise*. See also Defontin-Maxange, *Le Grand Ismail, empereur du Maroc*, Paris, 1928. For a penetrating analysis of the sultan's rule, see Henri de Castries, *Moulay Ismail et Jacques II*, Paris, 1903.

Another of the sultan's peculiarities was the way in which his skin changed colour according to his humour and temperament. He was a 'moletto by his colour', wrote Francis Brooks, 'but when he is in a passion, he looks . . . as black as an infernal imp'. Jean-Baptiste Estelle recorded that the sultan became 'unbelievably black' when he was angry. Busnot, too, was surprised by this strange phenomenon. When happy, the sultan was 'whiter than ordinary'. But when he was annoyed, 'he turns black and his eyes are blood red.'

The Koubbat el-Khayyatin can be visited to this day. A maze of tunnels lead deep into the earth, where they connect with storerooms and yet more tunnels. The inner recesses have been closed since the 1950s, when a couple of French holidaymakers descended deep into the labyrinth and were never seen again.

The punishment of slaves receives wide coverage in all of the narratives written by escaped captives. Okeley, Mouette, George Elliot and Brooks all wrote about the bastinado, as did Dominique Busnot.

Forcible conversion was widespread in Barbary, but there were many captives who decided to 'turn Turk' in order to escape the horrors of the slave pen. Pitts recounts his own experience of being forcibly converted in his *A True and Faithful Account*. There is also an excellent account in Dan, *Histoire de la Barbarie*. An even earlier description is to be found in *A True Relation of the Travels and Most*

Miserable Captivity of William Davis, Barber-Surgeon of London, circa 1597. This fascinating narrative was published in Stevens, *A New Collection of Voyages*. See also Mouette, *The Travels of Sieur Mouette*, pp. 100ff.

pp. 85–90: Much of this section has been drawn from documents in de Castries, *Les Sources Inédites*, series 2, vol. 2. Documents relating to the capture of Mamora are in this volume. See especially Germain Mouette, *Histoire des Conquestes*, which is also reprinted in this volume. Documents about the Larache campaign are in vol. 3 and include reports by Jean Périllié, the French consul, and much interesting information about the negotiations that followed the capture of the presidio. See also *Voyage en Espagne d'un Ambassadeur Marocain, 1690–1691*, H. Sauvaire (trans.), Paris, 1884.

The poem by the mufti of Fez is quoted in ez-Zayyani, *Le Maroc*. There are many surviving documents about the siege of Ceuta, which continued on and off for many years. The most interesting are in de Castries, *Les Sources Inédites*, series 2, vols. 4 and 5.

For background material, and an analysis of the Spanish presidios in Morocco, see Friedman, *Spanish Captives*, and Blunt, *Black Sunrise*.

5: Into the Slave Pen, pp. 91–109

pp. 91–100: The accounts of the Meknes slave pens are many and varied. One of the most interesting is Nolasque Neant, *Relation des Voyages au Maroc des Redempteurs de la Merci en 1704, 1708 et 1712*, published in de Castries, *Les Sources Inédites*. There are hundreds of other references to the slave pens scattered throughout de Castries' work. Brooks, Busnot and St Olon also provide much additional information about the conditions in which slaves were held.

Accounts of the sufferings of the English slaves are to be found in the PRO. John Willdon's letter to his wife is in SP71/16, f. 503. John Stocker's letter is in SP71/16, f. 465. The inadequate food and inedible bread were the subject of numerous complaints. See especially

Busnot, *History*, pp. 157ff.; and Ockley, *South-West Barbary*. Whitehead, 'His Relation of Barbary', is particularly interesting on the inedible food.

Pellow's account of the terrible conditions in Meknes is amply corroborated by the letters written by his comrades.

pp. 100–9: For a general account of Meknes palace, see Blunt, *Black Sunrise*, chapter 6. There is an excellent account of Moulay Ismail's role in the palace's construction in ez-Zayyani, *Le Maroc*, pp. 25ff. See also al-Nasari, *Chronique*.

There are good descriptions of Meknes palace, *circa* 1690, in the *Mémoire de Jean-Baptiste Estelle*, dated 19 July 1690, in de Castries, *Les Sources Inédites*, series 2, vol. 3, pp. 312ff. See also Estelle's description in vol. 4, pp. 389ff., and a further description in the same volume, pp. 689ff.

Other interesting eyewitness accounts include Busnot, *History*, pp. 13ff.; and St Olon, *The Present State*, pp. 71ff. For more on the exquisite gardens of Meknes, see Mouette, *Histoire des Conquestes*, in de Castries, *Les Sources Inédites* series 2, vol. 2, pp. 141f.

Descriptions of the terrible daily routine of enforced labour are to be found in almost every surviving slave account. Mouette, *The Travels of Sieur Mouette*, is particularly perceptive, while Whitehead, 'His Relation of Barbary', recounts the physical hardships endured by the captives. Mouette outlines the hazards of the plague in his *Description du Maroc*. This forms the third book of his *Histoire des Conquestes* and is also in de Castries, *Les Sources Inédites*, series 2, vol. 2, p. 174.

Thomas Goodman's letter is in the PRO at SP71/16, f. 506, while Thomas Meggison's is SP71/16, f. 505. John Willdon's complaint about having been forgotten in his native England is a common one; most slaves feared that they would never again see their friends and families.

6: Guarding the Concubines, pp. 110–30

pp. 110–18: King George I was as unpopular with his subjects as he is with royal biographers. The most comprehensive is Ragnhild Hatton, *George I: Elector and King*, 1978. See also Sir H. M. Imbert-Terry, *A Constitutional King: George the First*, 1927. There are some fascinating details about the king in Bruce Graeme, *The Story of St James's Palace*, 1929. For more on life at court, see J. M. Beattie, *The English Court in the Reign of George I*, Cambridge, 1967, pp. 279ff. A general picture of the political manoeuvrings during the years 1715–18 can be found in W. A. Speck, *Stability and Strife*, 1977.

The petition of the wives and widows of English slaves is in the PRO; SP71/16, f. 497. Jezreel Jones's tireless devotion to the plight of the slaves is outlined in Rogers, *Anglo-Moroccan Relations*.

For more information about the political career of Joseph Addison, see Peter Smithers, *The Life of Joseph Addison*, 1968. Admiral Cornwall's mission to Gibraltar and Morocco is outlined on pp. 405f. of Smithers' book. See also Rogers, *Anglo-Moroccan Relations*; and Stetson Conn, *Gibraltar in British Diplomacy in the Eighteenth Century*, New Haven, 1942.

Lancelot Addison's colourful tales were published in 1671 under the title *An Account of West Barbary*. Joseph Addison's essay on Moulay Ismail is in Addison, *Works*, 6 vols., 1901, edited by Richard Hurd and Henry Bohn, see vol. 4, pp. 436ff. The document that he took to the cabinet meeting on 31 May 1717 is in the PRO; SP71/16, f. 507. Moulay Ismail's letter to Admiral Cornwall is in J. F. P. Hopkins, *Letters from Barbary, 1576–1774*, Oxford, 1982.

The account of Coninsby Norbury's mission to the Moroccan court, including the various reports by Kaid Ahmed ben Ali ben Abdala and others, is in the PRO; SP71/16. There is much about Consul Hatfeild in Rogers, *Anglo-Moroccan Relations*. A great deal of Hatfeild's correspondence is contained in SP71/16. See also Dominique Meunier, *Le Consulat anglais à Tétouan sous Anthony Hatfeild*, Tunis, 1980.

pp. 118–24: Much of this section was taken from Pellow's *Adventures*. Maria Ter Meetelen's fascinating account of life in the harem was first published in The Netherlands in 1748. This is no longer extant. I used the 1956 French edition, published under the title *L'Annotation Ponctualle de la description de voyage étonnante et de la captivité remarquable et triste durant douze ans de moi*, translated by G.-H. Bousquet and G. W. Bousquet-Mirandolle, Paris.

pp. 124–30: This section is also largely derived from Pellow's own account. His description of the brutality of Moulay Ismail is amply supported by dozens of other eyewitness accounts. The sultan's habit of breeding slaves also receives considerable notice. The story of Chastelet des Boyes was published in the *Revue Africaine*, vol. 12, no. 67, pp. 28ff., under the title 'L'Odyssée, ou diversité d'aventures, rencontres et voyages en Europe, Asie et Afrique, par le sieur Du Chastelet des Boyes,' L. Piesse (ed.), Paris, 1869.

7: Rebels in the High Atlas, pp. 131–56

pp. 131–5: The anonymous letter, which appears to have been written in the first week of March 1717, is in the PRO; SP71/16, f. 499. For more on the ongoing palace building works, see ez-Zayyani, *Le Maroc*, and al-Nasari, *Chronique*. There is an interesting description of the stables in St Olon, *The Present State*, pp. 75f. See also Busnot, *History*, p. 54. Busnot noted wryly that 'the king of Morocco's women and children would be happier if he loved them as he does his horses.' The size and scale of the stables, which now lie in ruins, remain extraordinarily impressive.

The sultan's obsession with cats is noted by several observers. Busnot, *History*, p. 59, provides detail.

The slaves who made it home to England wrote little about religious practices inside the Meknes slave pen. Cotton Mather's sermon, which includes details about the sufferings of the American captives, was first published in Boston in 1703 under the title, 'The Glory of

Goodness'. It was republished in 1999 in Paul Baepler (ed.), *White Slaves, African Masters: An Anthology of Barbary Captivity Narratives*, Chicago. Joshua Gee's poignant narrative was first published in Hartford in 1943 under the title *Narrative of Joshua Gee, of Boston, Mass., while he was a captive in Algeria of the Barbary pirates, 1680–1687*, Charles A. Goodwin (ed.). According to Sumner, *White Slavery*, Mather was a friend of the Gee family. In January 1715, 'he dined with Mr Gee, to celebrate the anniversary of the return of his son from Algiers.'

Ellen Friedman, *Spanish Captives*, includes some information about religious practices inside the slave pen and is particularly interesting on the Catholic services that were occasionally tolerated by Moulay Ismail. See pp. 85ff. for more information about Father Francisco Silvestre. She also writes in some detail about the Spaniard, Father Francisco Jiminez, who was working contemporaneously in the *bagnios*, or slave prisons, of Algiers. For further information, see her 'The Exercise of Religion by Spanish Captives in North Africa', published in *The Sixteenth Century Journal*, vol. 6, no. 1, 1975. See also her 'Christian Captives at Hard Labour in Algiers', published in *The International Journal of African Historical Studies*, vol. 13, 1980.

Brooks, *Barbarian Cruelty*, gives an eyewitness account of the practices of the English slaves in Meknes (p. 71). Busnot, *History*, provides similar information for the Catholics (pp. 156f.). One of the most interesting accounts of Christian religious life among the slaves of Algiers was written by the captured pastor, Devereux Spratt. His account is published in T. A. B. Spratt, *Travels and Researches in Crete*, 2 vols., 1865; see vol. 1, appendix II, p. 384. Spratt was eventually freed from slavery, but elected to remain with his erstwhile captives, 'considering that I might be more servisable to my country by my continuing in enduring afflictions with the people of God than to enjoy liberty at home'.

pp. 135–45: Most of this section is from Pellow's own account. Morsy, *La Relation de Thomas Pellow*, provides many interesting footnotes about the places to which Pellow travels and the various characters he meets.

St Olon was right to note the important role of European renegades in Moulay Ismail's army. In common with his late brother, Moulay al-Rachid, Moulay Ismail was dependent upon military expertise to overcome his many enemies.

pp. 145–56: Most narratives by former slaves include details about the thousands of renegades serving under Moulay Ismail. For more about Carr, see Braithwaite, *History*, pp. 185ff. The story of Laureano is in Busnot, *History*, p. 19. Joseph Morgan's comments are to be found in his *A Voyage to Barbary*, 1736. The second edition of this book was published as *Several Voyages to Barbary*, by which title it is more commonly known. See also Clissold, *The Barbary Slaves*, for much information about renegades throughout Barbary.

The infamous black guard was much feared by the European slaves. See Brooks, *Barbarian Cruelty*, pp. 60ff.; St Olon, *The Present State*, pp. 113f. and 127f. There is a most interesting account in ez-Zayyani, *Le Maroc*, of the manner in which the black guard were reared from childhood. See also Blunt, *Black Sunrise*, pp. 45ff.; and Budget Meakin, *Land of the Moors*, 1901, pp. 155f.

This account of the Jews in Morocco is drawn from Busnot, *History*, pp. 17ff. and 42ff.; Ockley, *South-West Barbary*, p. 99; St Olon, *The Present State*, pp. 79f. See also Blunt, *Black Sunrise*, pp. 43f.

It is unfortunate that there is so little information about the monstrous Lala Zidana. This portrait is drawn from the accounts of Busnot and Ockley. Her huge size was, perhaps, what made her so attractive to Moulay Ismail. St Olon noted that 'the fattest and biggest women are the most admir'd in those parts, for which reason that sex never put on any stiff-bodyd gowns.'

The Moroccan poem extolling Moulay Ismail's virtues is quoted in ez-Zayyani, *Le Maroc*, p. 141. The sultan's religious fervour was genuine. He observed all the fasts and feasts of Islam, prayed frequently in public and was constantly consulting the Koran.

8: Turning Turk, pp. 157–71

pp. 157–61: For more about the history of Penryn, see Palmer, *Penryn*. This also contains invaluable information about Valentine Enys. For further information about Enys, see June Palmer (ed.), *Cornwall, the Canaries and the Atlantic: The Letter Book of Valentine Enys, 1704–1719*, Institute of Cornish Studies, 1997.

Hatfeild's list of slaves is in the PRO, SP71/16, ff. 584–7, and is entitled 'List of English Captives in Mequinez'.

John Pitts' letter to his son was published in Pitts, *A True and Faithful Account*. Services of repentance and thanksgiving were often held for slaves that successfully made it home. The Laudian rite for returned renegades, first published in 1637, is reprinted in Vitkus (ed.), *Piracy, Slavery and Redemption*.

pp. 161–7: *The Renegado* was most recently published in Daniel J. Vitkus (ed.), *Three Turk Plays from Early Modern England*, New York, 2000. This book also contains *Selimus* and *A Christian Turned Turk*. The various petitions of the English wives of slaves are in the PRO; SP71/16.

For more information on Alexander Ross, see Nabil Matar's excellent book, *Islam in Britain*, Cambridge, 1998, pp. 73ff. See also Bernard Lewis, *Islam and the West*, New York, 1993. The British Library holds a 1688 copy of *The Alcoran of Mahomet*, Alexander Ross (trans.). Humphrey Prideaux's book, *The True Nature of Imposture, Fully Displayed in the Life of Mahomet*, was published in numerous editions. I referred to the one published in 1697.

Criticism of the Islamic world was not the exclusive preserve of theological and pseudo-historical works. Penelope Aubin, *The Noble Slaves*, 1722, recounts the fictional tale of four nobles captured by the Barbary corsairs. In the preface to her book, Aubin reminds her readers that white slavery has continued unabated for many decades in North Africa. In the epilogue, she notes that 'a large number of Christian slaves are, at this time, expected to return to Europe, redeemed from the hands of those cruel infidels, amongst whom our noble slaves suffer'd so much, and lived so long.' See also G. A. Starr, 'Escape from Barbary: A 17th Century Genre', in the *Huntingdon Library Quarterly*, 29, 1965.

Cotton Mather's 1698 sermon was first published in Boston under the title, 'A Pastoral Letter to the English Captives in Africa'. A microfilm copy of this rare pamphlet is in the British Library.

Simon Ockley is a fascinating individual and worthy of further study; see his entry in the *Dictionary of National Biography*, vol. 41. There is further information about his life in the 1847 edition of his *History of the Saracens*, 2 vols., 1708–18.

pp. 169–71: This account of the campaign outside the walls of Guzlan is taken from Pellow's *Adventures*.

9: At the Court of Moulay Ismail, pp. 172–95

pp. 172–95: For more about Hatfeild's years in Morocco, see his correspondence in PRO; SP71/16. His letter concerning torture in Tetouan was published in Windus, *Journey to Mequinez*, p. 199. See also Rogers, *Anglo-Moroccan Relations*. For the complaints of the London merchants, see Leo Stock (ed.), *Proceedings and Debates of British Parliament, respecting North America*, Washington, 1924; see vol. 3, pp. 432ff.

Little has been written about Commodore Charles Stewart. There is a brief biography in Edith Johnston-Liik (ed.), *History of the Irish Parliament, 1662–1800*, 6 vols., Belfast, 2002; see vol. 6. Stewart is also mentioned in Romney Sedgwick (ed.), *History of Parliament: The House of Commons, 1715–1754, Members*, 2 vols., 1970; see vol. 2, pp. 447f. See also John Charnock, *Biographia Navalis*, 6 vols., 1794–8; see vol. 3, pp. 304ff.

The list of presents that Stewart took to the Moroccan court is in SP71/16, f. 613. Much of the rest of this chapter, dealing with Stewart's time in Meknes, is taken from Windus, *Journey to Mequinez*.

Windus had an eye for detail and wrote one of the finest descriptions of Meknes palace. For a modern study of the palace's construction, and a complete survey of the ruins, see Marianne Barreaud, *L'Architecture de la Qasba de Moulay Ismail à Meknes*, Casablanca, 1976.

10: Escape or Death, pp. 196–216

pp. 196–202: The return to England of Commodore Charles Stewart received widespread coverage in the press. The report in the *Daily Post*, dated Tuesday, 5 December 1721, is the most comprehensive. But see also the items in the *London Journal*, 16, 23 and 30 December 1721. Daniel Defoe, *A Tour*, provides a colourful description of London as it was at the time of Stewart's return. Most other details have been drawn from London newspapers. William Berryman's sermon was published in London in 1722 under the title 'A Sermon Preached at the Cathedral Church of St Paul, December 4, 1721, before the Captives Redeem'd by the late treaty with the Emperor of Morocco'.

pp. 202–16: The accounts of Pellow's two escape attempts have been drawn from his *Adventures*. Other captives left detailed descriptions of the hazards encountered by slaves escaping from Moulay Ismail's Morocco. See Mouette, *The Travels of the Sieur Mouette*, pp. 38–62; Phelps, *A True Account*, pp. 504f.; Brooks, *Barbarian Cruelty*, pp. 86ff.; Busnot, *History*, pp. 165–71 and 231ff.

Busnot also gives details of the dramatic escape of two French slaves, John Ladire and William Croissant. The most extraordinary flight from North African slavery was undertaken by William Okeley and a small group of friends. They built a collapsible boat, smuggled it to the seashore and managed to sail it to Majorca. See Vitkus (ed.), *Piracy, Slavery and Redemption*, pp. 124–92.

11: Blood Rivals, pp. 217–41

pp. 217–22: The account of Jean de la Faye's mission is to be found in a very rare volume entitled *Relation en forme de journal, du voiage pour la redemption des captifs aux Roiaumes de Maroc & D'Alger pendent les Années 1723, 1724 & 1725, par les Pères Jean de la Faye, Denis Mackar, Augustin d'Arcisas, Henry le Roy*, Paris, 1726. A copy is held by the Middle East Library, St Anthony's College, Oxford. For more on Father Garcia Navarra's missions to North Africa, see M. Garcia Navarra, *Redenciones de cautivos en Africa, 1723–5*, Madrid, 1946.

pp. 222–7: For more on John Russell, see Rogers, *Anglo-Moroccan Relations*. There is a wealth of fascinating detail about Russell's mission to Meknes, much of it in Braithwaite, *History*. For more on Moulay Ismail's death, see Adrian de Manault, *Relation de ci qui s'est passé dans le royaume de Maroc depuis l'année 1727 jusqu'an 1737*, Paris, 1742; see especially pp. 42ff. See also Blunt, *Black Sunrise*.

Pellow provides much detail about the rivalry – and battles – between Abdelmalek and Ahmed ed-Dehebi. His version of events is largely corroborated by Muhammad al-Qadiri, Norman Cigar (ed.), *Nashr al-Mathani: The Chronicles*, 1981. This gives a year-by-year account of the turmoil that followed Moulay Ismail's death, and his tight chronology enables key events to be given precise dates. For more on Ahmed ed-Dehebi's character, see de Manault, *Relation*, pp. 56–7. See also al-Nasari, *Chronique*. There is additional information in Louis de Chenier, *The Present State of the Empire of Morocco*, 2 vols., 1788.

pp. 228–34: The account of Russell's progress towards Meknes is taken from Braithwaite, *History*. This book contains a wealth of information about European renegades living in Morocco. It also provides additional evidence about Pellow and the way in which he had been changed by his years in Morocco. See especially pp. 192ff. There is much of interest about Russell's mission in the PRO. See especially SP17/17, part 1.

pp. 234–40: The events that led to civil war are recounted in Pellow's *Adventures*; Braithwaite, *History*; de Chenier, *The Present State*; and al-Qadiri, *The Chronicles*.

pp. 240–1: Moulay Abdallah was to prove as unpredictable and violent as his father. See de Chenier, *The Present State*; and al-Qadiri, *The Chronicles*.

12: Long Route Home, pp. 242–68

pp. 242–51: Much of this is drawn from Pellow's own account. See the notes in Morsy, *La Relation*, especially pp. 161ff. For more information about French exploitation of Guinea, see P. E. H. Hair, Adam Jones and Robin Law (eds.), *Barbot on Guinea: The Writings of Jean Barbot on West Africa, 1678–1712*, 1992. See also William Smith, *A New Voyage to Guinea*, 1744.

pp. 251–3: For more on John Leonard Sollicoffre's mission to Morocco, see PRO; SP17/18. The mission is also discussed in Rogers, *Anglo-Moroccan Relations*. The Duke of Newcastle's letter to Sollicoffre is in SP17/18, f. 97.

pp. 253–68: This account is taken from Pellow's *Adventures*. See also Colley, *Captives*, pp. 95–6. I tried, without success, to locate the newspaper article written about Pellow's arrival in London.

Epilogue, pp. 269–80

pp. 269–71: The capture and enslavement of the *Inspector*'s crew is told in Thomas Troughton, *Barbarian Cruelty*, 1751. For general background to Sidi Mohammed's reign, see Meakin, *The Moorish Empire*, pp. 262ff. For a much more detailed assessment of his character and foreign policy, see de Chenier, *The Present State*, pp. 279–364. De Chenier includes a list of all the treaties that Sultan Mohammed signed with European powers. See also Clissold, *The Barbary Slaves*, pp. 152ff.; Lloyd, *English Corsairs*, pp. 157ff.; John B. Wolf, *The Barbary Coast: Algiers under the Turks, 1500–1830*, 1979; and Lane-Poole, *The Barbary Corsairs*, pp. 273ff. Within a few years of American independence, American shipping was being hit hard by the Barbary corsairs. Sumner, *White Slavery*, offers an excellent overview of the various attacks on American vessels and the response they produced; see especially pp. 30–42. For a more detailed analysis, see James A. Field, *America and the Mediterranean World, 1776–1882*, Princeton, 1969; and R. W. Irwin, *The Diplomatic Relations of the United States with the Barbary Powers*, Chapel Hill, 1931.

pp. 271–8: There were many in the early nineteenth century who believed it was time for a grand military offensive against Barbary. See Filippo Pananti, *Narrative of Residence in Algiers*, 1818. For more about Sir Sidney Smith, see Clissold, *The Barbary Slaves*. See also E. Howard (ed.), *Memoirs of Admiral Sir Sidney Smith*, 1839, 2 vols; see especially vol. 2, p. 194.

The exact number of slaves being held in North Africa at any given time is extremely hard to calculate. Father Pierre Dan claimed in 1637 that the slave population had already topped one million – an assertion for which he provides little evidence. His claim that Algiers had a constant slave population of about 25,000 is almost certainly more accurate, for it is corroborated by many other reports. Diego de Haedo, writing in the last quarter of the sixteenth century, estimated that there were 25,000 Christian slaves in Algiers; see his *Topografia*, Valladolid, 1612. Father Emanuel d'Aranda provides similar figures (25,000) for Algiers in the 1650s; see his *Relation de la Captivité à Alger*, Leyden, 1671. Felipe Palermo, a captive, wrote in September 1656 that there were 35,000 Christian slaves in Algiers; see Friedman, *Spanish Captives*. Chevalier Laurent d'Arvieux claims in his *Mémoires du Chevalier d'Arvieux*, Paris, 1735, that there were almost 40,000. The diplomats Laugier de Tassy and Joseph Morgan, writing in the eighteenth century, paint a similar picture. See Laugier de Tassy, *Histoire d'Alger*, Amsterdam, 1725; and Morgan, *A Voyage to Barbary*.

The subject of the white slave population of North Africa has been addressed most recently and comprehensively in *Christian Slaves, Muslim Masters: White Slavery in the Mediterranean, the Barbary Coast and Italy, 1500–1800* by Robert C. Davis, 2003. Davis has made a detailed study of corsair activity between the 16th and 18th centuries and has also compiled a list of all the available slave counts for this period. Furthermore, he has looked at the death rate of captives – whether through torture or sickness – and the numbers redeemed by padres and ambassadors. He concludes that between 1530 and 1780, 'there were certainly a million, and quite possibly as many as a million and a quarter white, European Christians enslaved by the Muslims of the Barbary coast.' See part one, chapters one and two.

For more information about Sir Edward Pellew, see Cyril Northcote Parkinson, *Edward Pellew, Viscount Exmouth*, 1934. The best single-volume account of Pellew's campaign against Algiers is Roger Perkins, *Gunfire in Barbary*, Havant, 1982. Playfair, *The Scourge of Christendom*, contains lengthy quotations from Pellew's despatches, as well as the eyewitness account written by William Shaler; see pp. 258–80.

Index

Index

Picture Acknowledgements

© British Library, London: *The Cryes of the City of London* c1688, 9 below left. Pierre Dan *Histoire van Barbaryen* 1684 Amsterdam, endpapers, 1, 3, 4, 7 below left, 8, 10 above, 12 below, 13 below. Pierre Dan *Histoire de Barbarie et de ses Corsaires* 1637 Paris, 10 below. Joseph Morgan *Several Voyages to Barbary* 1736, 5 above, 9 above. Monsieur de St Olon *The Present State of the Empire of Morocco* 1695, 7 below right. Thomas Troughton *Barbarian Cruelty* 1751, 2 below, 7 above. F. Brooks *Barbarian Cruelty* 1698: 13 above. J. Davis *History of the Second Queen's Royal Regiment* 1887: 2 above left. J. De la Faye *Relation - du Voiage pour la Redemption des Captifs* 1726: 12 above. © National Maritime Museum London: 11 above and below, 14. The National Archives: 5 below (TNA ref SP71/16), 9 below right (TNA ref SP17/16). © Giles Milton: 15, 16. G. Mouette *Histoire des Conquests* 1682: 6 below right. Private Collections: 6 above right and below left, 11 centre. The Royal Collection © 2004 Her Majesty Queen Elizabeth II: 2 above right. Thomas Troughton *Barbarian Cruelty* 1751: 2 below, 7 above. John Windus *A Journey to Mequinez* 1725: 6 above left